G·R·E·A·T
EXPECTATIONS

The Toddler Years

Everything You Need to
Know About Your
1- to 3-Year-Old

Sandy Jones

STERLING

New York / London
www.sterlingpublishing.com

STERLING
New York

An Imprint of Sterling Publishing
387 Park Avenue South
New York, NY 10016

STERLING and the distinctive Sterling logo are registered trademarks of
Sterling Publishing Co., Inc.

ISBN 978-1-4027-5816-4 (trade paperback)
ISBN 978-1-4027-8932-8 (ebook)

Library of Congress Cataloging-in-Publication Data Available

Distributed in Canada by Sterling Publishing
c/o Canadian Manda Group, 165 Dufferin Street
Toronto, Ontario, Canada M6K 3H6
Distributed in the United Kingdom by GMC Distribution Services
Castle Place, 166 High Street, Lewes, East Sussex, England BN7 1XU
Distributed in Australia by Capricorn Link (Australia) Pty. Ltd.
P.O. Box 704, Windsor, NSW 2756, Australia

For information about custom editions, special sales, and premium and
corporate purchases, please contact Sterling Special Sales at 800-805-5489 or
specialsales@sterlingpublishing.com.

Manufactured in the United States of America

2 4 6 8 10 9 7 5 3 1

www.sterlingpublishing.com

This book and the information contained in this book are for general educational and informational
uses only. Nothing contained in this book should be construed as or intended to be used for
medical diagnosis or treatment. Users are encouraged to confirm the information contained herein
with other sources and review the information carefully with their physicians or qualified health-
care providers. The information is not intended to replace medical advice offered by physicians
or health-care providers. Should you have any health-care-related questions related to yourself or
your child, please call or see your physician or other qualified health-care provider. The author
and publisher will not be liable for any direct, indirect, consequential, special, exemplary, or other
damages arising therefrom.

Acknowledgments

I would like to express my deepest appreciation to my daughter, Marcie Jones Brennan, for her contributions to this book and her unflagging support of the *Great Expectations* series. I would also like to acknowledge the warm and always helpful input of the series editor, Jennifer Williams, at Sterling Publishing, and Melanie Gold, whose exquisite editing not only corrected the manuscript but made it stronger and better. In addition, I would like to recognize the efforts of designer Rachel Maloney for laying out the book so beautifully, and Elizabeth Mihaltse for the terrific cover. Last, but not least, a big thank you goes to Editorial Director Michael Fragnito, for keeping the faith; to Publisher Jason Prince; Leigh Ann Ambrosi, VP of Marketing and Publicity; and Marcus Leaver, President and CEO of Sterling, for their continuing support of the *Great Expectations* series.

Contents

Introduction

WELCOME TO THE ADVENTURE OF A LIFETIME!

A toddler, by definition, is somebody who gets up on his feet and walks. The word *toddler* is a combination of the Scottish words *todder* and *waddle*, and it refers to the awkward way that babies get up and walk like drunken sailors, with their legs spread apart, arms held up in the air, and with lots of lurching around.

As you'll soon discover, there are many wonderful aspects of life with a toddler, including his boundless energy, passion for exploring the world, spontaneous expressions of affection and clever shenanigans, and leaving babyhood behind as he continues on toward becoming an independent child.

As his sense of self and boundaries begin to take shape, there will be times when your toddler is likely to throw tantrums, to refuse to eat what you put before him, to stiffen and adamantly resist being strapped into his stroller or car seat, to be extremely upset because you can't read his mind, and to refuse to share his toys with his playmates. These are all typical behaviors for this incredible and very unique stage in the human life span.

Your toddler's language skills will leap from only one or two words at 12 months to a huge vocabulary of 900 to 1,000 words (or more) by the end of these momentous two years, and he will ultimately be able to speak short, intelligible sentences that are completely understandable.

Physical skills will evolve from barely being able to stand up and take a few wobbly first steps to running, jumping, climbing, and kicking. Skills in every other area of his life will also be making quantum leaps forward.

Not only are you going to have the opportunity to introduce your toddler to a lot of wonderful new experiences, but he'll be teaching you lessons, too—the luxury of slowing down to watch a caterpillar cross the sidewalk, the fun of splashing in mud puddles with abandon, the art of creating shapes from damp sand, and then smashing them—all primal joys of childhood.

Hopefully, parenting your toddler will also be teaching you indelible lessons about loving and being human. You'll learn about showing affection and giving spontaneous hugs, thinking really fast on your feet and paying attention to two things at once, cultivating more patience, laying out plans and then letting them go, and communicating clearly in the simplest words possible. Best of all, you'll learn that you're stronger than you think you are, that you should trust your gut instincts, and that you have the power to "keep on keeping on" even when you're so tired that you're nearly cross-eyed, because you care so much about your little one.

About This Book

Great Expectations: The Toddler Years: Everything You Need to Know About Your 1- to 3-Year-Old is designed to serve as an informative parents' handbook. It offers research-based insights into toddler temperament and learning styles as well as practical advice about getting through the hard parts. Plus, it offers hundreds of developmentally based activities for sharing enjoyable moments together.

Here you'll find tips to help optimize your child's mental, physical, and emotional growth, and options for dealing with the important issues you're likely to encounter over the next two years, including discipline, toddler nutrition, toilet training, and sleep problems. There's also a chapter on ways to encourage independence in your toddler. For ease of reading, we have elected to alternate chapters between "he" and "she" pronouns.

We often refer to "young toddlers" and "older toddlers." The book classifies young toddlers as 12- to 18-month-olds whose bodies are still developing along with their communication and eating skills. "Older toddlers" are 19- to 36-month-olds who are more skilled, are able to move around, and have better communication skills.

We welcome your feedback on this book. You can write to us in care of Sterling, the publisher of the Great Expectations series, or connect with us online at www. GreatExpectationsPregnancy.com.

Warmest regards,
Sandy Jones

1

Your Unique Toddler

Every Child Is Different

As parents can attest, every child is unique, and there is simply no such thing as "typical" when it comes to describing children and their differences.

Just as each child has a unique fingerprint, every child comes with unique gifts and vulnerabilities. There's no one-size-fits-all solution for how to manage a toddler, which is why parents are so important. They are the best judges of what is best for their child using all that they know about his personality, his maturity, and ways of responding that they are always in the process of learning.

As your dynamic child grows, you will be figuring out answers to some important questions about him: What does he like to do the most? What are his strengths and vulnerabilities? What's he most curious about? What does he dislike? What's his favorite way of communicating? What are the ways

he likes to learn? What is changing about him? What is staying the same?

This chapter explores how toddlers' personalities are shaped, and it gives you some rough guidelines to help you in dealing with some of the unique characteristics of your child.

YOUR TODDLER'S EMERGING PERSONALITY

A toddler's temperament has a powerful effect on how he learns and reacts. Temperament can be difficult to pinpoint, since toddlers can be so unpredictable, but the term refers to those personality traits that tend to remain the same from one day to the next.

How might you characterize your toddler to someone else? Do

you consider him a live wire? Is he shy? Is he clingy? Is he easy-going? Is he an avid explorer? Or is he someone who prefers to pause and look around before he leaps?

Competent parents sometimes have very challenging children, and not-so-good parents sometimes have very easy-going, well-balanced children. And, as many families can attest, there are frequently wide personality differences among children in the same family.

A sensitive, cautious toddler is more likely to back off and withdraw while a volatile child is more likely to have irregular sleep/wake patterns. And, as you've probably already discovered, toddlers are often mellow at one moment and acting out at the next.

The important thing to discover as a parent of a toddler is that you don't always have to bear such a strong burden of responsibility for something over which you really have little control.

Some toddler traits are more likely to stick around through childhood and into adulthood, such as being slow to warm up, or mostly being positive or negative in mood; others are likely to change over time.

Here are some examples of typical toddler traits, with suggestions for handling them:

EASY-GOING AND RELAXED

First let's look at the characteristics of an "easy-going and relaxed" toddler. People might describe this child as a "good boy (or girl)." Toddlers are good in their own special way, of course,

but these super-amenable children seem mostly to have a sunshiny, positive outlook on life. Neither sluggish nor hyper, when they're awake and alert, they're generally calm, seem to enjoy themselves, and have moderate rather than extreme activity levels.

Whether stacking blocks, putting toys into a box and taking them back out again, rolling on the floor, or trying to scribble with a fat crayon, this toddler's attention span helps him to stick to what he's doing without getting overly distracted by other things, at least for a while, without interruption.

An easy-going, relaxed toddler seems willing to adapt readily to new situations without a lot of fuss, and usually is able to strike a balance between caution and curiosity. This, of course, is a best-case scenario when you're dealing with toddlers who are, by nature, somewhat unpredictable.

HIGHLY ACTIVE

Highly active toddlers thrive on the deep-muscle sensations they get from climbing, whirling, and jumping onto and off of things. They are drawn to wild, impulsive activities and go out of their way to find new physical feats to master. Sometimes strong exploratory urges make them vulnerable to injuries and falls, and they may seem restless, difficult to control, and easily upset.

Generally these are not the children to patiently wait in a line or sit in the doctor's office while calmly entertaining themselves with a picture book. Toys are interesting for only half a minute, then the urge to move strikes again and they restlessly move on to something else.

Being confined or bored can sometimes lead to tantrums, aggression, or destructiveness, and trying to strap these little wigglers into a high chair or car seat could be a struggle complete with back-arching protests and more. Grocery shopping with super-energized toddlers can quickly turn into a nightmare, especially when they protest loudly, escape the shopping cart and disappear down another grocery aisle, or pull cans and boxes off the shelves.

Some parents worry that their super-active toddlers have attention-deficit hyperactivity disorder (ADHD), but at this age it's simply too early to know for sure, and many toddlers who are highly active may naturally calm down as they age. Once they have better physical control, they learn how to channel their energy in more constructive outlets.

Parenting Tips for Highly Active Toddlers

Parents of highly active toddlers are often especially vigilant, since their little ones are more apt to take risks than other children of the same age. It's typical to worry about your child's physical safety (as well as your own sanity), so give him plenty of opportunity for physical exertion and build in some respite for yourself whenever possible.

If you have a highly active toddler, here are some things to try:
• **Wear him out.** This child needs a lot of vigorous exercise every day, preferably outdoors, to help him let off steam. Toddler-safe playgrounds can be a great help since they allow him to have outdoor adventures, hopefully without hurting himself. He'll also gain physical coordination by splashing around in water, working out in a toddler gym class, or running around in an uncrowded mall to supply him with the physical stimulation he hungers for.
• **Keep his hands busy.** If he has to be still for a while, give him something to do with his hands, such as squishing a small ball of play dough, peeling stickers off his arms or shirt, rolling a push toy in his lap, tossing foam balls that won't knock anything over, or turning pages in a board book or magazine.
• **Create a "no accident" zone.** In addition to childproofing your home, set aside a special zone where your toddler can move around freely with your supervision, such as in a designated area in the den or the basement. If he likes to jump and spin, give him safe places to do just that. Set up a portable toddler-sized sliding board, a crawl-through tunnel, or other items that encourage activity.
• **Build in R & R for you.** It's unrealistic to expect yourself to be able to cope with your highly active toddler 24/7. You've got to have time off to restore. It's as simple as that. Find others to relieve you at least once or twice a week for as many hours as you can wrangle to give yourself the self-nurturing you need for the next round of toddler chasing.

It helps to find other parents with similar toddlers to share shoptalk.

HIGHLY SENSITIVE

Highly sensitive toddlers feel sensations more acutely than most toddlers and have a hard time getting used to or making sense of them. Sounds, sights, lights, music, and temperature changes—any of these sensations can evoke distress.

Not all toddlers are sensitive in the same ways. Children with a highly reactive sense of touch may find soft caresses unnerving. A soft pat on the head could evoke a strong response akin to experiencing pain. Clothes may feel too scratchy or too tight, and even the smallest clothing tag or seam in a sock could be annoying to the point of distraction.

Even a routine well-baby examination could terrify this child and evoke a strong pain reaction, potentially leading to either clinging to a parent in stark terror, or causing an intense meltdown followed by a glazed-eyed withdrawal, as if your child has undergone a profound emotional shock or is "zoned out."

A toddler with auditory sensitivity may be acutely aware of sounds, such as a humming refrigerator, that seem to be unbearable. What is a background noise to you will be maddeningly distracting to him. He may never acclimate to certain everyday sounds, such as children screaming, doors slamming, dogs barking, a vacuum or a television running, or even a clock ticking, never mind smoke alarms, loud vehicle mufflers, or music played over public-address systems.

Children with a highly sensitive sense of taste are often described as "picky eaters." Temperature, texture, and flavor—food qualities that barely faze other children or adults—may cause a very strong negative reaction in this toddler. This isn't just a matter of a child turning up his nose. Instead, it's consistently too smooth or too crunchy, too hot or too cold, but, unlike Goldilocks, he may have to try more than three options to find something he'll accept as "just right."

Your toddler may recoil and try to tuck his head into your shoulder or hide behind your leg as a way of protecting himself from feeling too overwhelmed. It's the directness of others' approaches, their loud voices, and their scents that he's reacting to, the fear of a touch, grasp, or hug.

Some highly sensitive toddlers become hyper, distressed, or inconsolable as bedtime rolls around because their acute sensibilities make it hard for them to shut their systems down for sleep. This child may require a very snug wrapping in a blanket, ritual vibration, or being rhythmically being rocked into slumber. If he has a "lovey," a well-worn (and smelly) blanket or bear, it may help him relax and finally drift off to sleep.

A highly sensitive child may not adapt well to group child-care settings. He may find being confined in quarters filled with lots of objects and noisy, demanding children to be overwhelming. A "skin sensitive" child may recoil at having his hands wet or dirty, which will cause him to withdraw from sandbox play, wearing sandals or walking barefoot on grass, or having tactile experiences that typically evoke pleasure in other children.

If you observe any of the previously described scenarios coupled with your tot tending to isolate himself and withdraw into a corner, it could be his way of trying to protect himself from the onslaught of stimulation that makes him feel threatened and distressed inside.

Parenting Tips for Highly Sensitive Toddlers

Here are some practical suggestions for parenting a highly sensitive toddler:

- **Don't force it.** It doesn't help your child to try to coerce him into being less sensitive or reactive. Not only can he not be anything other than his authentic, difficult-to-figure self, forcing the issue either will make him even more withdrawn and self-protective or may lead to other behaviors, such as physical aggression. Instead, pay attention to what attracts him, and engage him with activities that help him relax and feel calm.
- **Build in security.** Tightly wrapping him in blankets and familiar objects can be useful to your highly sensitive child. They may feel like a shield when everything else seems to be bombarding him. Some children are calmed by vibration, and retailers offer both handheld or

battery-operated devices that fasten to cribs.
- **Make a "nest."** Create a safe haven for your highly sensitive child that he can retreat to, such as a small tent or an appliance box, with a small crawl-through entrance. Decorate the inside with stuffed animals and soft textures to give him a place to retreat, play quietly, and regather himself if he's feeling stressed by other children, pets, or noise. When possible, err on the side of a quieter home environment, where he can concentrate on listening to you and not be overtaxed by too many auditory stimuli at once, such as a constantly blaring television.
- **Explore touching options.** Some skin-sensitive toddlers prefer deep, massagelike touches to light, feathery ones. Others like being gently brushed from head to toe with a soft-bristled brush. Gently offering chances to play with clay, sand, and water may help your toddler become more accustomed to having gooey or messy hands, an experience likely to come up frequently later in playgroups and classrooms.
- **Be creative with food.** If your toddler is a picky eater, or put off by food textures, consider pureeing foods or invite him to use his hands for eating food pieces so that he can get tactile input before placing food in his mouth. Use a soft, coated spoon so that he doesn't associate eating with mouth and gum discomfort. Consider letting him have a small, pure-fruit pop before meals to see if numbing

his highly sensitive taste buds makes foods more palatable.

- **Try soothers.** Visual soothers, such as a lava lamp, a fish tank, or a nightlight that projects images on the ceiling, could be ways to help your toddler relax and feel more secure when it's time for sleep. Auditory soothers may help him to relax, too, such as gentle "New Age" sounds, orchestral music, white noise, or ocean sounds from a sleep machine.

TIP

For more information on sensory processing disorders, try Lucy Jane Miller's *Sensational Kids: Hope* and *Help for Children with Sensory Processing Disorders and Raising a Sensory Smart Child* by Lindsey Biel and Nancy Peske.

CAUTIOUS AND SLOW TO WARM UP

A slow-to-warm-up or "behaviorally inhibited" child is uncharacteristically quiet and shy, and may seem clingy most or all of the time.[1] He may often wear a worried, serious, sad, or pouty expression on his face. When he feels pushed into meeting any new people or when he's confronted with any unfamiliar situation, he's likely to recoil even more than seems typical, and he may become desperately clingy, needing to stay close to you.

You'll soon discover that it doesn't help to try to force him to be warm, friendly, or sociable. While a more typical toddler will accept being left at child care after a few protests, a cautious child is more apt to stay upset longer, even if the person he is being left with is a familiar and gentle caregiver, a neighbor, or a relative. Since he reacts consistently even with familiar people, you can tell it's not the garden variety of stranger anxiety. (For more on stranger anxiety, see page 46).

Rather than loudly acting out, as a highly active toddler might when he's uncomfortable or stressed, a cautious child is more likely to suffer in silence, becoming even more fearful and withdrawn. On the outside, he may not appear to be reacting to stress, but research shows that some cautious children's heart rates are elevated and their blood pressure goes up when they're feeling anxious or their ability to cope is overtaxed.[2]

Your cautious child may initially thrive better in a calmer, in-home child-care setting with fewer kids to interact with, or in a center that has teachers with the special training needed to understand and relate to young ones with difficulty transitioning and/or feeling secure.

Parenting Tips for Slow-to-Warm-Up Toddlers

Here are some practical ideas for helping your shy, cautious, or slow-to-warm-up toddler:

- **Build in warm-up time.** Give your child some time to adapt to new situations before you pull away. As you leave, explain that you will be coming back, but don't belabor your departure.

- **Try not to hover.** It's tempting to try to shield your child from the distress of unfamiliar situations, but it works better to give him more space and allow him to come to you, rather than always leaping to his side to protect him. When responding, start with the most low-key reaction you have in your repertoire to see if that satisfies his need for reassurance.
- **Teach social skills slowly.** Step by step, try teaching your child simple social skills one at a time while rewarding each time he gets closer to the mark. Coach him about reaching out to others at his current comfort level. For example, rather than forcing your child to say "hello" and "good-bye," encourage him to wave instead. (He might wave but keep his head averted, avoiding eye contact.) After he waves, praise him for being polite, and make mental notes for how you can add to that for next time.
- **Offer experiences.** To help him with social confidence, consider low-key one-on-one experiences, such as with an older (or, in some cases, a younger) child or with another non-aggressive toddler. If he's playing alongside other children, stay near so he can use you as his home base until he is ready to join in. Or simply accept that, for now, he's happiest with his own solitary play style.
- **Watch for subtle signs of stress.** An exceedingly shy child with excessive fears may, in fact, feel anger or other strong emotions keenly but suffer them silently because of the trouble he

has letting them out. Try to be aware of the subtle signals that show you he may be stressed. Offer physical reassurance with hugs and verbal feedback ("Does this feel scary to you?") and reassurance ("I'm here, and you're safe").

HIGHLY INTENSE AND INFLEXIBLE

While strong independence, clearly formed opinions, and determination are extolled as good qualities in adults and often considered virtuous in leaders, toddlers who are strongly independent, intense, and inflexible can be very challenging for their parents. "Strong-willed" is one descriptor sometimes given a child with this nature. He may be perceived by others as stubborn, spoiled, or ill-tempered when his reactions are negative or moody, as they often are.

Lots of toddlers show these characteristics between their second and third birthdays! So how do you know the difference between garden-variety stubbornness and a highly intense toddler? It has to do with the frequency and intensity of your toddler's behavior. Most toddlers can rebalance rather quickly and go on about their play and exploration after an upset or a change, but some toddlers appear to go from one upset to another. Having tantrums every few days is one thing, but having five or more daily is another.

While a less-intense toddler will eventually come to accept

time-outs and will ultimately comply with rules so long as you're rigidly consistent, you may find that a toddler with this temperament aggressively fights against any correction from others. If he perceives something as someone else's idea or he feels that he's being forced into something, he's likely to dig in his heels and turn balky or defiant.[3]

Eating and sleeping patterns tend to be especially quirky and downright irregular. Whether it's getting ready for child care in the morning, or having to come indoors after playing outside, transitions are a huge challenge for this toddler.

Behavior and emotions are beyond unpredictable, and he can sometimes react in a physically aggressive manner. He may be vehemently unwilling to wear certain clothes or might react to touching as if he's been hurt, or he might adamantly insist on only a narrow range of foods that he's willing to eat, gagging on other foods with certain qualities or textures, such as "wet" green beans or "gooey" cereals.

In time, parents of an intense child often realize that all the explaining, reasoning, reassuring, nurturing, redirecting, ignoring, rewarding, and punishing are not only exhausting, but they simply don't work.

New situations can cause a child with this temperament to become anxious. Anger storms arrive quickly—sometimes they seem downright spontaneous and unprovoked—and emotions escalate rapidly to a very intense level. Temper tantrums tend to be frequent, repeated, and lengthy (15 to 30 minutes or longer), and may include screaming and thrashing. They also may continue into his school years, beyond the age when his peers seem to have outgrown them. When the tantrums happen in public, onlookers may be quick to judge you as either too wimpy and "not setting boundaries" or at fault for having reared a "spoiled" child. (For more on temper tantrums, see page 66).

Parenting Hints for Highly Intense, Inflexible Toddlers

Here are some practical parenting suggestions for dealing with a highly intense, inflexible child:
- **Stay cool.** If you respond in an inflexible, angry manner, then you increase the likelihood of a meltdown, and you may be fueling an adversarial relationship. If the meltdown has already occurred, that's an even more compelling reason for you to be calm.
- **Troubleshoot.** Identify what is most likely to set your child off— those situations that routinely lead to explosions—and what triggers them. Keep an eye open to warning signals for an approaching storm, and take action immediately when you spot them. (Keeping a journal may help.)
- **Don't punish for noise.** Don't punish your intense child for being loud when he is upset or unhappy, just as you wouldn't punish him for screaming with glee when he is happy. It's his nature, and at this age, he can't help it.
- **Avoid the blame game.** Resist taking your child's behavior

personally. Recognize how hard you are trying, and regardless of what others say, don't accept the explanation that you're a poor parent or poorly motivated or that your child is spoiled.

- **Hold steady at the helm.** Try to keep daily routines predictable. Keep a little booklet of drawings that depict each element of your daily schedule in the order in which they happen. Keep the drawings in a small photo album so that you and your toddler can flip the pages. Refer to the drawings throughout the day and before transitioning to each task.

COMPLEMENTARY THERAPIES

If you have a child who frequently moves in and out of stress and experiences almost daily meltdowns, you may want to explore alternative destressing modalities from practitioners experienced in working with babies and children. Keep your mind open to the restorative techniques used in aromatherapy, massage therapy, chiropractic care, and acupuncture. Administered by trained professionals, these therapies are known to benefit toddlers and even babies.

Genes and Personality

Since a toddler shares half of his genes with you and half from his other parent, the question is: What specific personality traits has he inherited from each of you? One way scientists approach this is by studying how twins are alike or different from each other.

Fraternal twins, or dizygotic (DZ) twins, share only 50 percent of their genes, which is the same percentage of genes shared by siblings who aren't twins. Identical, or monozygotic (MZ) twins, share 100 percent of their genes. If genes affect children's personalities, then identical twins could be expected to act more like each other than fraternal twins or their other brothers and sisters do. On the other hand, if children's environments exert the most influence on children's personalities, then DZ twins who

have been reared together will turn out to be more alike than twins who have been reared separately from each other.

Researchers have discovered that genes are very influential in determining children's personalities, temperaments, and the way they act, but each individual's unique life experiences have profound effects, too. Even when identical twins are reared in the same environment, they don't become clones of each other.

In scientific circles, the old idea that somehow parents are solely responsible for how their children behave or eventually turn out later—either from the passage of genes or the environment in which they're raised—simply doesn't hold much water.[4]

Inheritance and environment both seem to play a part in

children's behaviors.[5] For instance, scientists have discovered that the tendency toward shyness that first appears in babies and young children is a trait that tends to remain constant throughout life. Do shy parents pass down genes that determine shyness, or is a shy child that way because his shy mother or father taught him by example?

Studies of shy children have yielded some interesting findings. Parents were rated on their sociability and other scales designed to identify shyness, such as introversion (being inward focused) versus extroversion (being outward focused). One study suggested that when biological mothers were rated high in shyness, their adopted babies (who didn't live with them) were also shy, adding weight to the possibility that the genetic personality link for shyness could overshadow family influences.[6]

In another study, twins who were adopted into separate families were studied along with twins who remained with their biological parents. The results showed that shy parents raising their own twins together were more likely to have shy twins, too. Similarly, shy parents who adopted twins were more likely to produce shy children as well. These findings appear to underscore that personality traits such as shyness are the combined result of inheritance and home environment.

Between 20 percent and 60 percent of temperamental traits in toddlers and children are influenced by family genes, according to the current scientific thinking. Identical (MZ) twins tend to be more alike temperamentally than fraternal (DZ) twins or other siblings in a wide variety of ways, including how emotional they are, how active they are, their "stick-to-itiveness" (ability to pay attention and persist with tasks), how adaptable they are, and how positive or negative their moods tend to be.[7]

Your Temperament Counts, Too

As shown by the shyness studies, your relationship with your toddler will be affected not only by his personality traits and the way he reacts to things, but also by your, your partner's, and your child's siblings' temperaments, too. The mix of all of the personality qualities in your family will affect how you interact with one another and contributes to your child's overall environment.

Child development experts talk about the "goodness of fit" between a parent and child, that is, how well a parent's personality meshes with the child's. Sometimes the personality fit between parent and child is smooth and well balanced, but sometimes differing personalities result in friction and make getting along together more difficult. (No surprise there. *All* toddlers—and their parents—can be easy-going or difficult at times!)

Whether the members of your family are shy or outgoing, rigid or flexible, emotional or logical, these dimensions exert an effect on your family's overall balance and well-being.

A mellow mom or dad and a mellow toddler can move together smoothly without a lot of ruffled feathers. But if your temperament is intense and your toddler's is, too, or if your parenting philosophy seems to clash with your child's personality, there may be sparks flying in your household! It's par for the course when you're parenting a toddler.

TIP
There's no "one-size-fits-all" way to parent a toddler.

TIP
This important time of learning and adapting benefits everyone.

Physical Skills

Move, move, move. Oh, how a toddler loves to move!

Not so long ago, your baby strained to climb upward and balance herself into a standing position. She used every ounce of strength she could muster to get upright and take her first steps. She pulled on couch pillows, the coffee table, her brother's hair, your clothes or earrings. She used *anything*.

Once she is able to walk on two feet, it will become abundantly clear that your child is leaving babyhood behind and is now compelled to control her body. It's called "mastery motivation."

Even though she probably still can't pronounce the word *gravity*, over the next two years your little Newton will be intensely researching how the forces of gravity work and its effects on her body or anything she can grasp, pick up, or throw. Her mastery motivation will move on to running, jumping, hopping, twisting,

turning, and hoisting. She'll also handle and mouth hundreds, if not thousands, of objects.

No matter the bruises, bumps, and swollen welts on her face and body. Like an obsessed rock climber or Olympic snowboarder, your toddler will be waging her fight to overcome gravity, again and again. Once she succeeds in becoming a biped, you will get (or have already gotten) to experience her swelling with pride, her eyes shining with delight at having *finally* achieved what was just beyond her reach for so long!

This chapter sheds light on your toddler's quest for body mastery. You'll find lots of ways to channel your child's natural exuberance into positive outlets while she transforms herself from a dependent baby into a 3-year-old who can talk in sentences, run, dance, jump, feed herself, and even dabble in art.

Your Toddler's Changing Body

Looking back over her baby pictures, you can definitely see how your little one's appearance has undergone a gradual transformation. Although her body is still fleshy and soft, now it is less babyish and more childlike. Between 18 and 36 months, her "baby fat" or body padding will start to diminish. Overall, she will begin to look more lean and muscular. (Boys will be generally slightly larger and heavier than girls.)

When your toddler's first-year growth spurt tapers off, she will continue to grow at a slow and steady pace, mixed in with occasional growth spurts, until she's well into her teens. During the first year of her life, she tripled her weight, but during toddlerhood, she will grow an average of two and a half inches per year and will gain about five pounds of body weight. Every child follows her own growth curve, but when it comes to acquiring and perfecting physical skills, the old saying "practice makes perfect" definitely applies.

Cultures that encourage unrestricted movement for their children and offer early skills practice tend to produce children with more advanced body skills than those that don't. Research shows that children who have daily chances to exercise and play freely develop skills faster than those who lead passive, sedentary lives or who don't get many opportunities for active movement.

While she's learning to move her body through three-dimensional space, she will be constantly practicing and repeating actions. She will wonder, "What happens when I throw this? Can I climb up on that? Can I balance on this? How can I get down? Can I pull this down?"

Your toddler will also be trying to make sense of what her eyes and her visual feedback systems are telling her as she mentally calculates the dimensions and characteristics of objects and their position in space: What's longer and what's shorter? What's heavier and what's lighter? What's in back and what's in front? What's on top and what's underneath?

Your toddler's physical accomplishments in this short two-year span will be simply amazing!

HOW BODY SKILLS CHANGE

When child-development experts look at children's body abilities they refer to *gross motor skills*, or the way children coordinate large muscles such as those used for walking, reaching, sitting, walking, running, keeping balance, and changing positions. Sometimes the term refers to a child's awareness of her posture and control, the parts and sides of her body, and how everything moves in space.

Fine motor skills refers to the delicate movements of smaller, more refined muscles, such as those in a child's wrists, hands, and fingers. These affect her ability to manipulate objects, feed herself, handle toys, put on and take off clothes and shoes, draw, hold onto a crayon, squeeze and shape clay, or fit together blocks and puzzle pieces.

Skills Development Overview

Body skills don't develop uniformly like trains arrive at the station, so this chart shows broad-brush guidelines. Each child's physical skills will unfold uniquely to her and her body's readiness.

12–17 MONTHS GROSS MOTOR SKILLS	FINE MOTOR SKILLS
Cruises along standing upright while holding onto furniture.	Uses pincer grasp (thumb and index finger) to pick up tiny things.
Stands alone without support for at least a few seconds.	Finger-feeds herself small, soft food pieces.
Bends to pick up objects from the floor while holding onto something else.	Grasps 2 small toys in one hand.
Takes 2 to 3 unsteady steps unsupported.	Places tiny objects in and out of containers.
Sits down backward from a standing position.	Uses hands to poke, bang, pull, turn, and twist toys and objects.
Tries to crawl up stairs.	Gives and takes toys.
Sits and pushes a ball back and forth with another person.	Drops things to see and listen to what happens.
	Balances 1 block on top of another.
	Pulls lids off boxes and containers.
	Pushes wheeled toys and may make vroom-vroom sounds.
	Tries to turn doorknobs and open drawers.
	Fits large pegs into a pegboard.
	Tries throwing a ball, but without much aim or direction.
	Attempts to pick up balls as they roll.
	Holds crayons with whole fist, thumb up, while scribbling on paper.
	Drinks (and dribbles) holding cup with 2 hands.

12–17 MONTHS (CONTINUED) GROSS MOTOR SKILLS	FINE MOTOR SKILLS
	Makes noise by pounding on table, toy drum, or with spoons on pots.
	Enjoys using a finger to poke play-dough balls placed in an egg carton or ice cube tray.
	Tries to wash hands and toys with soap.
	Tries to squeeze water out of a sponge or washcloth while bathing.
	Activates toy sound makers with push buttons and twisting knobs.

18–20 MONTHS GROSS MOTOR SKILLS	FINE MOTOR SKILLS
Enjoys climbing.	Opens and closes things: doors, drawers, books.
Runs stiffly.	Turns book pages, 2 or 3 together at a time.
Tries walking backward.	Uses index finger to point to something she wants.
Backs into a small chair to sit down.	Inserts large, simple shapes into a puzzle.
Crawls up stairs and creeps down backward.	Dumps objects out of a container.
Tries to climb stairs holding the handrail.	Likes carrying things around in both hands.
Rides on a foot-propelled, wheeled toy.	Builds tower of 3 or 4 blocks.
Scrambles into an adult chair and turns around to be seated.	Uses spoon or fork well.
Walks into a ball but can't kick it yet.	Throws ball overhand or tosses it backward over her shoulder.
Quickly wanders away from caregivers.	Scribbles with a crayon and tries to imitate the way others make strokes.
Likes to explore and move containers: laundry baskets, drawers, wastebaskets.	Pulls off hats, mittens, socks, and shoes.
Helps with undressing and tries to remove clothes herself.	Enjoys taking things apart.
Likes moving to music.	
Might fall out of the crib trying to climb over the rails.	

21–24 MONTHS GROSS MOTOR SKILLS	FINE MOTOR SKILLS
Moves constantly, then tires easily.	Takes apart and puts together simple puzzles.
Walks with fewer falls.	Holds crayon with thumb and all fingers, forearm turned to point thumb down.
Walks up and down stairs putting 2 feet on each step.	
Attempts awkward jumps with both feet.	Imitates lines or circles with a crayon or marker.
Likes climbing on furniture.	Uses whole hand to smear paint or pudding on paper.
Tries walking backward and on tiptoes.	Builds a tower of 3 to 4 blocks.
Kicks a ball forward.	Makes a "train" of 4 to 5 blocks.
Catches a slightly deflated ball (8 to 10 inches in diameter) tossed at chest level when arms are out and ready.	Imitates paper folding.
	Opens boxes, drawers, and lids.
	Totes things around in a basket or purse.
Puts on pieces of large clothing.	Makes shapes or molds things in wet sand.
Balances in a bottom-down squatting position.	Rolls play dough into a snake shape.
Dumps things into trash cans.	Pounds toy "nails" with a hammer on a play carpenter's bench.
Imitates sweeping and cleaning.	Turns 1 page of a picture book at a time.
	Tries to put on socks and shoes (sometimes on the wrong foot).
	Drinks from a glass using 2 hands.

25–30 MONTHS GROSS MOTOR SKILLS	FINE MOTOR SKILLS
Walks with a smooth heel-to-toe motion.	Picks up cup, drinks from it, and places it back on a table.
Briefly stands on 1 foot.	Unfastens large buttons.
Jumps up and down with both feet.	Recaps markers when asked.
Opens doors.	Attempts to use a napkin or tissue.
Makes a tower of 6 blocks.	Names what she's drawing (even if it's unrecognizable to others).
Catches and throws a ball.	Turns pages in a book at the right time in a story.
Rides a tricycle with supervision.	Holds spoon with a palm-up grasp.

30–36 MONTHS GROSS MOTOR SKILLS	FINE MOTOR SKILLS
Has a steady, foot-forward gait with arms at her side.	Builds a tower of 9 or 10 blocks.
Alternates feet while walking up and down stairs.	Holds crayons with fingers like an adult.
Can stand briefly on 1 foot.	Imitates drawing a cross and circle with a crayon or marker.
Makes sharp turns without falling.	Cuts fringe with scissors.
Makes broad jumps with both feet.	Likes to pound on boards.
Tries running on tiptoes.	Pulls apart and puts together puzzles with knobbed pieces.
Dresses and undresses with marginal success.	Rarely spills when feeding herself with a spoon or fork.
	Zips and unzips a coat once it's fastened together.
	Unscrews caps.
	Washes and dries hands.
	Puts on shoes, but sometimes on the wrong foot.
	Turns spigot on and off.
	Imitates hand movements for songs such as "If You're Happy and You Know It."

BE CONCERNED IF:

Your 12-to-17-month-old:
- Can't stand unsupported or hasn't attempted to pull up to stand.
- Crawls favoring one side.
- Doesn't point to show you things, doesn't use her thumb and forefinger to pick up things, or is unable to transfer objects from hand to hand.
- Doesn't try to search for something you've just hidden.

Your 18-to-20-month-old:
- Hasn't started walking by 18 months.
- Isn't interested in playing simple games with others.
- Doesn't attempt to put objects in containers or take them out.

Your 21-to-24-month-old:
- Can't point to body parts on request.
- Doesn't play simple pretend games with herself or toys.
- Can't grasp how simple objects are used, such as a spoon, a toothbrush, or a telephone.

Your 25-to-30-month-old:
- Isn't interested in trying to climb up and down stairs.
- Doesn't try to imitate others' actions.
- Is unable to stack blocks one on top of the other.

Your 30-to-36-month-old:
- Can't stand on one foot momentarily.
- Is still using a fisted grasp or grip rather than her finger and thumb or can't draw a straight line or imitate a circle with a marker or crayon.
- Can't sit still for a few minutes to look at a high-interest picture book.
- Is unable to follow simple, 2-step commands, such as: "Pick up the ball and put it in the basket."

Learning to Walk and Climb

Starting to walk is a major human achievement, but not even the nation's top locomotion experts can predict precisely when that happens. Those first, shaky steps are typically taken sometime between 8 and 17 months, but even children in the same family may walk at entirely different ages. As a general rule, girls tend to walk sooner than boys.

Some children attempt a few lurching steps only to decide that trying to walk is just too awkward and slow for getting somewhere. Or they may fall, become scared of the feat, and decide it's easier (or safer) to scramble around on all fours, at least for a while. (Husky or loose-jointed babies generally tend take longer to walk.)

Since your toddler's legs don't

have strong muscles, her early steps will be fairly wobbly and tentative, resulting in a quick collapse onto her bottom. She will rapidly shift weight from one foot to the other, lurching and almost losing balance while trying to lift the opposite leg off the ground. In between each step, she will frequently pause to attempt to regain balance.

When she starts walking, you will notice that she appears sway-backed and her stomach will stick out in front. Her belly and back muscles simply aren't strong enough to support her in a rigidly upright position. As she grows stronger, she will become more erect. Over time, her chubby, ankleless legs will gradually become more defined and muscular.

A new walker's arms are held high, almost at shoulder level, which helps her maintain her balance like a tightrope walker. Within the next 4 to 6 months, walking will become steadier as she gains more confidence and her leg and back muscles have gotten stronger from practice. Around 24 months of age, the stiff, wide-legged gait will turn into a flexible, steady walking pattern with adultlike leg swinging and heel-to-toe movements.

Practice is one of the most important parts of learning to walk, and your toddler will be driven to engage in endless hours of doing it every day while she's mastering the intricacies of balancing and getting her stepping skills smoothed out. One study found that if toddlers weren't held back by their parents or restricted in space, they would walk as much as 6 hours a day and take between 500 and 1,500 steps per hour, comparable to traveling the length of twenty-nine football fields![1]

Once she masters the basics, your toddler will then negotiate new or different surfaces, such as grass, sidewalks, and slick floors. And she will try making more sophisticated movements, such as turning corners, speeding up and slowing down, or stopping and reversing her body. By 36 months your toddler will be walking more steadily, will be much more graceful, and might even be able to run. (Brace yourself!)

TRIPS, FALLS, AND BLUNDERS

Between 12 and 16 months of age, your toddler's understanding of spatial relations will be limited at best. Until her body and the neural pathways from her brain and spinal cord become more mature, you can expect a lot of spills, tripping over her own feet, and lurching around.

Between 18 to 24 months, it will be literally a case of your toddler's head not knowing what her feet are doing. Her walking will be smoother, and her hands and arms will be in a lower position, and her coordination and timing will rapidly improve. During this transition, how graceful your toddler is may change from one day to the next. She could perfectly execute a maneuver one day, only to seem clumsy and fall more the next.

Sometimes your toddler's trips and falls will simply be a case of poor judgment. When descending the stairs, your toddler might carefully watch where she's going, slowly putting one foot down at a time. But then another time she could misjudge and stumble, especially if she gets distracted, such as by focusing on a toy she wants at the bottom of the stairs or when she tries to speed up to follow you.

Later, a 24-month-old may cruise around the house without any problems, only to crash into the wall because she's looking over her shoulder while propelling herself forward at the same time. She will still be refining her ability to stop once she gets started, and she may lose balance when one foot doesn't hit in the right place, or if she leans too far forward or lists too far to one side.

It may be reassuring to know that all these clumsy twists, waddles, sways, and tumbles have little bearing on how graceful an athlete she might turn out to be later.

UNUSUAL WALKING PATTERNS

Toes and feet are complex organs. There are more than a dozen major joints used for standing, keeping balance, and walking. Unusual walking patterns can develop, but typically, what seems to be unusual works itself out by the time your child is in preschool.

Flat feet are normal for toddlers, and true flat-footedness that lasts beyond toddlerhood is usually an inherited trait. (About 15 percent of adults have flat feet.) Often toddlers look positively pigeon-toed when they walk. Toes-in gives

more stability than when feet point straight ahead. But neither outward- nor inward-toeing feet are problematic and are usually outgrown within a few years.

Some toddlers appear bowlegged, seem knock-kneed, or walk on their tiptoes. Almost all babies are bowlegged at birth but usually outgrow it before they reach 24 months.[2] As they near the 36-month mark many toddlers appear to be knock-kneed, but this problem, too, usually corrects itself by the time a child reaches age 4. Toe walking usually corrects itself, too. These and most other gait problems completely resolve by age 8, including clumsiness and frequent falls.

You can keep an eye out for the following conditions: If your toddler starts out as a heel walker and later becomes a toe walker, or if she walks on tiptoes solely on one foot but not the other, she might have tight tendons or other leg problems that orthopedic specialist should see and treat. Rigid and inflexible feet, tight heel cords or stiff muscles in the calves, feet that won't easily flex upward or don't immediately bend at the ankle, and feet that draw up into an awkward position need to be checked out, too, first by your child's health-care provider, and possibly by an orthopedist.

CHOOSING SHOES

Even though your toddler has started walking, there's no need to race out to buy a pair of miniature track shoes, or those with thick, crepe soles or artificial arches.

Nonslip soles can lead to stumbling, especially when they snag on carpet fibers. Fake arches in shoes make balancing more difficult and can lead to impediments, since your toddler relies on feedback from the bottom of her feet and her toes pressing into the floor to help her adjust for her swaying body and develop her arch naturally.

Shoes are primarily for protecting feet at this stage (and keeping socks clean). The best option is to allow your toddler to roam around barefooted indoors or use soft, flexible moccasins. Though toddlers go through shoes really quickly because their feet are growing fast, the good news is that children this age really need only a few pairs at a time: an everyday pair, possibly a spare pair, and specialized or seasonal shoes, such as snow boots or water shoes for the pool.

Too-small shoes will hurt and too-big shoes will be hard to walk in, so you should have your child's feet measured at a shoe store every couple of months. You can also buy handy home shoe sizers for $20 or less (search "children's shoe sizer" on the Web). Having your own home sizer comes in handy if you plan to buy shoes online or through mail-order catalogs.

When venturing outdoors, your toddler will need sturdier shoes with flexible but protective soles. One good option is thick, leather booties with easy-on Velcro or elastic closures that are easy to put on and take off. Old-fashioned, ankle-high, baby lace-up shoes with stiff soles are simply too clunky and impede walking instead of helping it.

Inspect your toddler's shoes frequently to make sure her big toe isn't getting squeezed in the front (called the "box") of the shoe, and take a moment to examine your child's feet each time you remove her shoes and socks to make sure there's no redness from chafing or pressure points. If your toddler insists on taking her shoes off all the time, consider that they may be too small or uncomfortable, or perhaps she's afraid that if you know it, you'll require her to "retire" her favorite shoes.

Cotton-knit socks are a better choice than those made with tightly knit manmade fibers since cotton absorbs moisture. Socks should be a little longer than your toddler's foot to allow some wiggle room. If they're too tight, they could cause her toes to curl, affecting the use of her foot muscles and her gait. Seams should be smooth with no stitched edges that could chafe or loose threads that could wrap around small toes and cut off circulation.

Inevitably, socks disappear, but no one has proven that washing machines really do eat them. To prevent mismatched pairs, consider buying multiple pairs in the same color or all in basic white.

To keep pairs together while laundering them, tie them together with one sock knotted over the other or fold one cuff over the other, or wash them all in a mesh laundry bag so they're easier to sort when they're done.

CLIMBING

Some toddlers will climb every chance they get. You may not

know that your toddler has the mountaineer drive in her until you encounter her perched on the bathroom sink, trying to get into the medicine cabinet, or up on top of the refrigerator, peering down at you, like a cat waiting to pounce on its prey.

Being an avid climber just means that your toddler is an ambitious and curious kid. As you'll quickly discover if you have a climber in your house, you won't be able to turn your back on her, even for a few minutes! Most parents who are gifted with these highly active explorers develop a second sense, like finely honed radar, that sets off an alarm in their heads when there's too much silence and they don't know where their toddler is.

Never leave a climber in a room by herself. If there's a way to scale to the top of something, she will quickly find it. In rare cases, curious climbers have fallen out of windows, crashed television sets on top of themselves, tugged chests and bookshelves over on themselves, gotten into locked gun cabinets, or sustained head injuries from falling off of tabletops.

Here are some tips for keeping your little climber out of trouble:

- **Batten down the hatches.** Secure freestanding shelves and chests to the wall with L-shaped brackets (available at hardware stores). Appliance cords should be covered or unplugged and removed from reach. Floor lamps should be placed so that they're not used for pulling up or climbing. Put the television up high or mount it on the wall so your tot won't be tempted to pull on it for balancing or climbing.

The room housing your computer, keyboard, small flash drives, and all those tempting wires should be completely off-limits.

- **Give her safe places to climb.** Just like supplying your cat with a climbing tower, a toddler-sized indoor climber with a slide may be just the thing for your child. If you don't want to buy a new one, consider shopping online or in thrift stores for one, or stack up a couple sofa cushions or pillows for her to wrestle with.

- **Lock her out.** Install unreachable latches high up on the outside of the bathroom door, basement door, and any door that you don't want your little explorer to open. Make sure medications, razors, cleaning products, and so on are not stored in any cabinet she can access. Make it a habit to move chairs away from the dining room table so she can't use them as ladders for climbing up.

- **Use safety gates, but don't completely trust them.** Climbers find children's safety gates a wonderful challenge and will quickly learn to scale them using their arms and toes to vault themselves over and tumble down the stairs on the other side.

PUSHING AND PULLING

Once your child is a confident walker, she'll discover the joy of dragging or pushing toys along. She'll love wheeled noisemakers with pull strings, toy vacuums and lawnmowers, doll strollers, and wheeled, wooden-handled corn popper push toys.

You also can tie a twelve-inch string (no longer than that, to avoid strangulation) onto a toy car for pulling, or invite her to propel an overturned plastic laundry basket. Pushing and pulling while standing helps to improve coordination and balance and encourages her not only to move forward, but also to attempt walking backward.

SQUATTING

It takes time for toddlers to learn how to squat down, balance, and rise, instead of bending down at the waist to pick things up off the ground. But once they master how to do it, they're much better at doing the butt-down position than adults, who have trouble balancing once they're down.

Next time your toddler starts to bend at the waist for an object, try showing her how to bend at the knees to squat and invite her to practice. Unlike many adults, she'll be able to lower her butt with her knees and ankles aligned while keeping her feet flat on the ground. Line up a few small handheld toys on the floor and get her to squat to pick them up and drop them in a basket for you.

Stair-Climbing Basics

Around the end of their first year, most babies are eager to master stair climbing and are fearless about them. They don't grasp that a fall down a flight of stairs could cause bruises or a serious head injury. You might discover your toddler teetering on the top step as she peers down, nearly losing her balance trying to decide whether to scramble down after a toy she's thrown below.

Staircases loom for your toddler like Mt. Everest, and conquering them will be an important learning process that could help protect her from falls and injuries later. Basic stair negotiation skills could be useful if someone forgets to close a door or latch a safety gate.

It will take about six months from starting to learn how to crawl up the stairs until your toddler will be able to climb up or down in an upright position while holding your hand. By 36 months, she will likely be able to negotiate the stairs by herself.

The safest way to start stair-climbing practice is to teach your toddler to crawl from the bottom of the stairs upward, one step at a time. It's important to stay right beside your aspiring little climber, since she may assume that she can crawl *down* the same way she crawled *up*, or she may try to stand and take giant steps facing forward as she's watched adults and children do, not realizing she doesn't have the strength or stability to do so without losing her balance.

The safest way for your little novice to go from top to bottom is to back down, diaper leading the way. But she will need to be taught how to do that one step at a time. You may need to take her body and put her in the "go-down-backward" position, over and over, until she gets the idea that she has to blindly feel her way down.

FALL-PROOFING STAIRS

Stair falls are major hazards for people of all ages. Not all stairs are the same: Some are wide and covered with soft carpet, which can help soften falls. Others are narrow, steep, or made with slats that are open in the back, which could allow your toddler to slide through or capture her head while her body dangles below.

Stair railings are typically placed about 32 inches above the stair tread, which works for adults, but aren't the right height for toddlers and young children. Too-high railings force children to adopt an awkward posture that throws them off balance. A second, lower set of railings installed at child height, about 24 inches above the tread, will help to make stairs safer for your child over the next few years. A smaller railing—less than 2 inches in diameter—will work best for small hands.

Fortunately, the most stair falls don't result in serious injury. If a fall happens, as it inevitably does, it's not necessarily a huge calamity. However, watch her closely for a few hours after a fall, especially if her head hit a hard surface at the bottom of the stairs or you detect any swelling, redness, or bruising of the head.

Seek help immediately if she becomes unusually sluggish, vomits, has breathing problems, or acts oddly. In those cases, she may have an internal head injury that needs emergency intervention.

Additional tips for maximizing stair safety:

- **Stay close.** Stay within grabbing distance when your toddler is practicing her climbing skills so you can jump to the rescue if she decides to do a U-turn midway. The safest place is to sit next to her on each step with your hand on her back, especially when she's still a beginner.

- **No play zone.** Don't let your toddler use the stairs for playing—it's simply too risky. Teach her that she has to either be moving up or down the stairs, but she can't stop in the middle to sit and play.

- **Keep stairs clear.** Don't let toys, shoes, books or other clutter pile up on the stairs, which could pose a tripping danger for everyone. The stairwell should also be well lit, and non-carpeted steps may need stick-on, slip-resistant treads available at hardware stores. If you are carrying a toddler up or down in your arms, move slowly, watching every step, since a fall could injure both of you.

- **Close off dangerous staircases.** Stairs to the outdoors, basement, or garage, especially if there's a concrete floor at the bottom, could cause serious head injuries if there is a fall. Keep access doors shut, install latches on both sides of these doors beyond your toddler's reach, and, just in case, cushion the flooring at the landing with a padded rug or mat.

40 FUN BODY BUILDERS

There's no need to try to buff up your toddler's abs and pecs at this stage. Simply offer her lots of encouragement and challenge her with feats to stimulate her physical awareness.

Here are forty fun things to do with your toddler to build on her physical skills. Use these ideas based on your toddler's current skill level:

1. Go for a walk! Try exploring different textures and angles: on gravel, sand, and grass; up and down hills.
2. Blow up an inflatable mattress and gently jump up and down on it. (Keep your toddler's fingers away from the pump fan.)
3. Dance, bounce, and wiggle to upbeat music.
4. Try crossing a path of stacked books without letting pretend alligators (dolls and stuffed animals) "eat" you.
5. Together, squat down low, then raise your arms and jump straight up.
6. Play in front of a mirror and mimic what she does.
7. Slither together on the floor like snakes.
8. Act like a monkeys and make silly monkey noises.
9. Clap cheeks, hands, hips, or bottoms.
10. Quack and waddle like ducks. Jump and croak like frogs. Gallop like horses.
11. Play a gentle game of tag: Chase and get chased on sand or grass so a fall-down won't hurt.
12. Holding hands, hop down from the first step to the landing of the stairs; then, try hopping down from the second.
13. Give your toddler a "bucking bronco" ride on your leg while you're in a seated position.
14. Sing and do the Hokey Pokey.
15. Give your toddler a "horsey ride" while you're down on all fours.
16. Throw and catch a large air-filled balloon.
17. Do clean-up together, picking up small things and putting them in a box or trash can.
18. With your arms close to your side, try rolling down a short hill.
19. With another adult's help, hold a blanket or sheet as a big sling, with your toddler nestled inside.
20. Ask your toddler to help with lightweight, unbreakable grocery items using a satchel or sturdy grocery sack.
21. Roll cans and try stacking them one on top of one another.
22. Jump on bubble wrap to make the bubbles pop.
23. Try to catch soap bubbles or stomp them on the ground.
24. Make an obstacle course for your toddler to ride through on a wheeled, foot-powered toy vehicle.

25. Stack plastic storage containers with their lids on.
26. Toss paper balls into a trash can, cardboard milk carton, or a hoop made from an old lamp shade.
27. Slide down a low toddler slide.
28. Demonstrate, then ask for help in sweeping, mopping, sponging, and scrubbing.
29. Push dolls and stuffed animals around in a play stroller.
30. With your toddler or the whole family, play crawl-around and peek-a-boo.
31. Put blocks on the floor, then build a tower by bending down to pick up each block.
32. Step in and out of a Hula-Hoop, or chase it down a short hill.
33. Dump toys out of a carton or laundry basket, then put them back in again.
34. Move around to music with scarves attached to your wrists.
35. Toss around a sealed paper bag filled with packing peanuts.
36. Stomp in mud puddles with your boots on.
37. In warm weather, run through a sprinkler.
38. Using a watering hose, fill up some containers with water.
39. Scramble in and out of a play tunnel.
40. Play Ring around the Rosey. (Don't forget the "All fall down!" part.)

Hand and Arm Skills

Buttoning a shirt, tying a shoelace, and writing with a pen are a few of the daily fine-motor skills that older children and grown-ups have learned to do with ease. Mastering them takes years and lots of practice. As with walking, hand skills follow a predictable progression.

The part of your toddler's brain that controls hand movements is separate from the areas that control standing, balance, and walking. Although her vision and her sense of touch affect the accuracy and dexterity of her hand movements, mental maturity plays a strong role, too, since spatial awareness is important, too.

Eye movements still aren't very well coordinated or precise since the vision center in your toddler's brain is still learning how to process incoming visual signals. This brain immaturity could make your toddler appear clumsy and unteachable when it comes to fine-motor skills, such as cutting with children's scissors, tying shoes, or throwing a ball toward a target. It's not because she's not trying or is destined to be uncoordinated, it's just that her body isn't ready yet.

Between 8 and 12 months, your child's magnificent pincer grasp is likely to emerge. This is a uniquely human skill. From a neurological point of view, the pincer grasp marks a huge milestone in the synchronization of the brain, the nervous system, and the large and small muscles that control arm, hand, and finger movements.

Once your toddler masters the finger-thumb position, everything within grasp is fair game, from peas to strings on the floor. Each small item is eagerly plucked up, examined, then mouthed for further scrutiny. Caution is advised! Once your former fumbler masters the pincer trick, Aunt Edna could be in for a retaliatory cheek pinch as a greeting.

Around 18 months of age, your toddler is apt to become very interested in stacking, emptying, gathering, and nesting objects. She'll be able to hold writing instruments and attempt to draw lines and scribbles. Hands and arms will move separately and cooperatively: one hand will stabilize an object while the other hand manipulates it.

More complex hand skills include pushing, pulling, twisting, pounding things, and stringing a few fat, wooden beads onto a shoelace tied at one end. Even more refined are turning the individual pages of a book, putting a key in a lock, closing snaps, turning doorknobs, buttoning and unbuttoning, and forming shapes with clay. Even more difficult coordinated movements such as being able to fully dress herself or use scissors won't be mastered until about age 4, when her brain wiring is more complete.

Studies have shown that children's hand skills typically improve through show-and-tell. They learn quicker when they are shown and told what comes next. As with other body skills, coordination improves slowly with guidance and lots of trial and error.

LEFT-HANDED OR RIGHT-HANDED?

Deciding whether your toddler is destined to be right-handed or left-handed isn't as simple as it might appear. When it comes to how hands are used, babies, toddlers, and, in fact, people of any age don't always fall into neat categories. Some will use one hand for throwing and another for writing or doing other tasks. Typically, most toddlers change back and forth between hands, or they use both hands equally well, depending upon what they're trying to do.

By 36 months, three out of five toddlers show a hand preference, and those that don't may not show a clear preference until they are nearly school age. This is particularly true when children perform two-handed tasks, and they use their hands interchangeably with one hand serving as the leader and the other as the supporter.

Once handedness becomes clearer, about 60 percent of children are clearly right-handed, 36 percent use different hands depending upon the task, and 4 percent are primarily left-handed. Less than 1 percent of people are truly ambidextrous throughout life with no marked preference for either hand and equally skilled in using both for all tasks.[3]

Meanwhile there's no reason to push your toddler to use one hand instead of the other. Handedness appears to mostly be built into the brain and is an outward sign of which side of the brain dominates—the left side for right-handed people, the right side for lefties.

Be aware, though, if your 30- to 36-month-old constantly switches back and forth between hands without being able to coordinate either hand very well. That could be a sign that she's having coordination problems and needs an assessment of her fine-motor skills. Early intervention could help to improve dexterity.

THROWING

Between 18 and 36 months, toddlers love dropping and throwing things. Unfortunately, they have trouble telling the difference between what's "throwable" and what isn't. So not only will balls become airborne, but so will books, toys, and anything else that can be picked up and sent flying.

If you haven't already done so, now is the time to toddlerproof your home. At the same time, you might consider establishing a "no throwing" rule in your household or a toddler "safe zone" where there are no breakables and where it would be okay (at your discretion) for your child to burn off some energy by tossing soft, light items.

Even though your toddler's mischief may not seem very educational, in fact, she will be teaching herself important spatial skills, about the weight and heft of things, how gravity works, and the way objects move through space and water. She's also learning how her body works.

Your toddler will almost instantly forget your instructions not to throw. Model what you're asking her to do, give just a couple steps, and be consistent in enforcing the "house rules."

Here are some tips if throwing is a problem in your house:

- **Offer alternatives.** It's hard to control a toddler's urge to throw things, but you can help to teach her *what* she's allowed to throw and *where* she can throw it. Having lots of harmless things she can throw can help to decrease the temptation to throw things you don't want her to.
- **Redirect.** If your toddler throws something indoors she shouldn't, such as a shoe or book, calmly remove it, saying, "Shoes are for wearing, *balls* are for throwing."
- **Make it easier for yourself.** Fasten items such as pacifiers, teething rings, and small toys to your toddler's high chair, car seat, and stroller, so they're more easily retrieved.
- **Play the "Pick-up Game."** Try making a game of clean-up time. Get down on your hands and knees together to see how fast the two of you can pick things up and throw them into a box or basket. Playfully demonstrate how you toss socks in the hamper, throw junk mail in the wastebasket, and toss toys into the tub when it's bath time.
- **Halt aggressive throwing.** If she comes close to hurting someone else or a pet by throwing

things, be consistent. Declare a firm "No throwing," and warn her of the consequence of doing it again. If she does it again, follow through on the consequence . . . every time.

- **Promote other physical activities.** Let her sometimes be in situations where hitting and throwing are okay, typically outdoors. A toddlers' toy golf set of an oversized golf ball and fat clubs, or a toddler-height ball stand with a fat bat may work.

PLAY BALL! BALL HANDLING BASICS

Most toddlers follow a similar progression as they learn how to kick, throw, catch, or hit balls, but children differ in how skilled they are at it at any given time, or how deftly they perform these skills. Young toddlers nearly always appear quite awkward, and it will take repeated attempts to learn how to capture a slow or partially deflated ball with both hands, more practice learning how to let go at the right time when throwing, and even more to catch and throw with just one hand rather than using both.

In addition to lacking the motor skills and arm strength for graceful ball handling, children at this stage also have trouble tracking moving objects because of the imprecise movement of their eyes and poor eye-hand coordination.

Minor farsightedness makes it easier for most toddlers to focus on nearby objects rather than those at a distance; plus, the immature vision centers in their brains simply are not

very efficient at processing incoming visual information. In addition, your toddler's visual tracking skills, a brain function, are still immature. She will have problems zeroing in on a ball (or other object moving toward her) or judging how fast or slow it is going. Even though your ball toss may be dead center, her arms and hands will be too slow to close around and capture it.

Most toddlers love to throw and catch, but even the most eager ball player has a limited attention span. For that reason, you might consider keeping ball games short, working on rolling the ball before throwing it, and celebrating every throw and catch.

Here's how ball-handling skills typically progress:

At 12 months, your toddler might sit on the floor and roll a ball back and forth with an adult or another child. She might try to throw the ball but with poor aim and direction. At 18 months, she can throw the ball overhand and enjoys flinging it to someone else. At 24 months, she kicks and dribbles the ball with her feet like a small soccer player. At 36 months, she is able to catch a large ball, and perhaps kick the ball in a defined direction.

Ball handling is a learned skill, and it works best to introduce it to your toddler in gradual stages. The larger the ball, the slower it will roll and the easier it will be to capture and throw. Softballs and baseballs are too hard and could hurt if your toddler gets struck by one. Later on, you can gradually reduce the ball size and make it go faster once her eye-hand coordination improves.

Good beginner toss-'ems include beach balls, air-filled bouncing balls, soft foam balls, small cloth beanbags, socks stuffed with tissue paper, and air-filled Mylar balloons. (Latex can cause allergic reactions, and latex balloons are a suffocating hazard if they are chewed or popped.)

One way to begin ball practice is to sit on the floor facing your toddler with both her and your legs stretched into a "V" shape. Gently roll the ball to her, and have her push the ball to you, moving your bodies farther apart each time. Next, try rolling a ball to your toddler while she is standing across the room and invite her to retrieve it and bring it back to you.

Here are catching and throwing ideas for sharing playtime with your toddler:

- **Appeal to touch.** Introduce your toddler to balls with different surface textures—bumpy, shiny, squeezable—and different sizes and weights so that she has to adjust her hand and arm muscles to use them.
- **Practice with targets.** Build a small block or empty soda can tower and invite your toddler to knock it down using two hands or by rolling a ball across the floor.
- **Try an over-the-shoulder throw.** Your toddler may be able to toss a ball backward over her shoulder more easily than a forward throw. That's because most toddlers have trouble letting go in front, while her fingers naturally unfold when she raises her arm and tosses backward.
- **Model simple catching.** Move in close and have her try throwing the ball into your cupped arms.

Teach her to hold her arms in the same position, and direct the ball to her chest using use a slightly deflated ball 8 to 10 inches in diameter.

Workouts with Toddler

To help develop strength and balance—for grown-ups and toddlers—you or your partner could try these great ideas that both adults and little ones enjoy:

- **Modified sit-ups.** Lie down on your back with your knees bent, shoulder width apart. With your toddler sitting between your knees, facing you, make her your tickle target while you do crunches.
- **Nosy push-ups.** With your toddler lying with her back on the floor, do nose-to-nose push-ups with her underneath, being sure you have the strength for them. As an alternative, have your toddler sit on your back while you do the push-ups.
- **Dead lifts.** With your toddler standing in front of you, facing outward, grasp her around the chest beneath her armpits, bend your knees, and lift her up and down.

Early Sports Activities

Team sports are virtually impossible for toddlers. Like little bees, they will all swarm around a ball to kick it or pick it up and be totally oblivious to their "coach" (or parents) yelling what to do. That's because toddlers are very concrete thinkers and don't yet have the ability to process instructions or think abstractly: "Here's what I need to do now (or next)."

You might be surprised if you could hear what's going in your toddler's brain. While others are yelling, "Get the ball! Get the ball!" she's probably thinking, "Don't fall down! Don't fall down!"

Overloading your toddler with too many signals while she's concentrating on walking, running, or pursuing a ball just makes it harder for her to do it. Later on, when she no longer has to try so hard just to keep her balance and not trip or crash, running, jumping, batting, and throwing will come much easier and she'll be able to process multiple directions.

By the time your child reaches age 5, practicing pre-sports skills will be more of a possibility and coaching will be more likely to pay off. Before then, there's really no need to try to press her into skills her body and brain aren't ready to achieve yet.

Meanwhile, your primary goal should be to provide her with lots of fun and playtime. (See more about toddler play in Chapter 6.)

Swimming

Toddlers should never be unsupervised around water, and keep in mind that "swimming" for them has more to do with play than with trying to learn formal swim strokes. Your toddler won't be able to accomplish that until around 4 years old or older, and only after she's gotten the basics down, such as bubble blowing and breath holding under water.

Most toddlers enjoy splashing around in water, but it may take a while for your child to try putting her head under the water. Before she can hit the swimming pool, lake, or ocean, she'll need to get used to having water on her face, something that can be practiced as a game during your toddler's bathtime play.

She can learn to flutter-kick while you tow her around in the water, but don't expect your toddler to be able to operate her arms and legs very gracefully. Kicking can be practiced in a bathtub or a shallow wading pool, but in a regular pool, she will need you to support her at all times.

Once she's had water on her face and she's a confident kicker—that progression will be different for every child—then you can gradually teach her how to hold her breath, but head submersion should not be rushed. That's something she needs to master herself, and possibly much later, perhaps with a certified American Red Cross swimming instructor.

Trying to float on her back can initially be scary to your toddler, just as she might dislike lying back to have her hair washed. Short, frequent swim lessons over an uninterrupted period seem to be more productive than longer but short-term or sporadic sessions.

If you'd like more information, numerous books and videos can be found online that teach techniques to help babies and toddlers how to swim. Local YMCA and recreation centers also offer swim lessons for tots.

Unfortunately, swimming isn't always about happy playtime. If you swim around others, particularly at a public pool, you'll need to be aware of swimming-related illnesses, as they are becoming more widespread.

Germs can be spread by breathing or swallowing contaminated water in swimming pools, hot tubs, water parks, water play areas, interactive fountains, lakes, rivers, or oceans. Illnesses caused by contaminated water, called Recreational Water Illnesses (RWIs), include a wide variety infections, such as those that affect the intestinal tract, and can lead to vomiting, severe diarrhea, skin rashes and infections, and ear and eye infections.

The most common waterborne illness is diarrhea caused by a virus or bacteria. Examples include Crypto (short for Cryptosporidium), Giardia, Shigella, norovirus, and a specific type of *E. coli*. Illnesses are spread by swallowing water that carries germs, usually from other people's feces. Sunlight, dirt and debris, and material from swimmers' bodies

can reduce chlorine levels in pool water, which is why chlorine levels have to be repeatedly measured. Sometimes germs can survive for days, even in a well-maintained, chlorinated pool.

A pool's pH level is also important. If pool water isn't kept at the proper levels, then chlorine's ability to kill germs decreases and swimmers will have skin and eye irritations.

Use some of your senses to determine whether a swimming pool, hot tub, or water park is being properly maintained:

- **Smell.** When chemicals are well balanced, there should be no strong chemical smell, including a chlorine odor, which indicates a maintenance problem.
- **Hear.** Pumps and filtration systems make a noise, and you should be able to hear them running.
- **Touch.** The sides of the pool or hot tub should be smooth, not sticky or slippery. You should also feel water coming out of water vents.
- **Look.** You can test the pool's water yourself. Test strips are available at local home improvement stores, discount retailers, and pool supply shops. Chlorine or bromine levels should be 2 to 5 parts per million and the pH level between 7.2 and 7.8. (Follow the product's directions.)
- **Ask.** Don't hesitate to ask what the health inspector's grade was for the pool at its last inspection, and inquire how often pH levels are checked (should be twice per day, including weekends when the pool is likely to be used the most).

Beaches can become contaminated with waterborne illnesses, too. The Centers for Disease Control and Prevention (CDC) recommend that families avoid swimming after a heavy rain, when storm drains are more likely to be carrying microorganisms into the ocean. Trash or other signs of pollution, such as oil slicks in the water, are also signs that conditions are unhealthy for swimming. Local health and environmental agencies often monitor beaches for water quality, and the Environmental Protection Agency maintains a Web site to notify swimmers about beach quality. Visit *http://iaspub.epa.gov/ waters10/beacon_national_page. main.*

TIP

Babies and toddlers need supervision at all times around water. Don't allow for any distractions!

WATER SAFETY

Here are ways to help ensure pool sanitation:

- **Stay home.** Don't take your child swimming if she has diarrhea or other illnesses, or if you see any fecal matter in the pool.
- **Be a good citizen.** Teach your child about showering before entering the pool and after leaving it.
- **Don't swallow water.** Caution your toddler about swallowing water and keeping her mouth

closed when she swims or plays in a public pool, at a water park, or at the beach.
- **Protect others.** Check swimming diapers often or give your toddler frequent potty breaks. If you hear "I have to go potty," it's probably too late. Change diapers in a bathroom or diaper-changing area, not poolside. Germs can spread to surfaces and objects in and around the pool and spread illness. Wash your child thoroughly, especially her diaper area, with soap and water before re-entering the pool.
- **Take other precautions.** Use eye goggles to protect your toddler's eyes from irritations. Use sunscreen, and don't swim in the middle of the day, when sunburn is more likely. Shower thoroughly with soap and water after swimming. Dry ears thoroughly and use vinegar or alcohol drops to prevent "swimmer's ear," a bacterial or fungal infection from moisture trapped in the ear canal.

Q & A

Q: I wonder if our 18-month-old daughter is hyperactive. She walked early, and now from the minute she wakes up she's running around grabbling everything, fiddling with the DVD, or pestering the dog. She gets into trouble over and over, falling into things and breaking stuff. I'm exhausted from just having to watch her all the time. What can I do to make life livable again?

A: Most likely, your daughter isn't hyperactive; she's simply very energetic. Perhaps she feels confined, bored, or even trapped indoors. Consider getting her outside at least once or twice a day to a safe area where she can explore to her heart's content. Props can help, such as a big ball, a play lawnmower, or a wagon that'll encourage her to get moving. Childproofing your house is essential.

If you can, turn a bedroom or another area in your home into a safe play place. Equip it with a tot-sized gym and slide for rainy days when she can't get outside. (Big cardboard boxes make great playthings, too.) When you want to help her calm down, put on soothing music, spread a "quiet"

quilt and pillows on the floor, and give her your full attention while pulling out a basket of interesting toys, such as a plastic bottle with blocks to drop in or a stack of magazines or thrift-store books that she can pretend to read. Sharing gentle time with her, if only for 5 to 10 minutes at a time, may give you a moment's rest while teaching her self-calming skills.

TIP

Offer your toddler vigorous exercise. It will help build physical strength and coordination, and it may even make her sleep better.

3

Emotions

Have you wondered why your toddler's emotions can be so up and down? That seemingly easy-going baby is now calm and positive one minute, then quickly upset and throwing a fit the next. Huge surges of affection can be quickly followed by sudden fits of rage. There seems to be little or no predictability in your child's emotions.

During this stage, your toddler will be actively figuring out how to put words to his feelings and he'll be starting to realize that other people have feelings, too. It will take a long time, though, until you can expect your little one to be completely aware of his emotions or to be able to express how he's feeling inside.

During toddlerhood, developing empathy for others begins gradually. With a lot of practice, he'll start learning how to manage and channel his strong emotions in constructive, rather than destructive, ways. (Some people never seem to master this, even after they're "all grown up"!)

So we're going to peer into toddlers' emotional world, which often dictates how they operate. Learn about what makes your toddler tick, and find lots of ideas for how to foster his awareness, communication, and ability to bounce back from life's inevitable stresses.

How Your Toddler's Brain Works

To understand why emotions are so important during toddlerhood, we'll begin by looking at the basic engine that runs your toddler's central processing unit—his brain. The powerful forces at work inside your child's brain help to explain why a toddler can be so perplexing, excitable, changeable, and sometimes downright resistant and moody.

Chemicals help to convey messages across nerve connections, called synapses. Your child's "switchboard" is so complex that a single brain cell may connect with as many as fifteen thousand other cells.

By the time your toddler reaches his third birthday, his amazingly dense brain will have formed about *1,000 trillion connections*, about twice as many as an adult's. When he is a teenager his brain will start to seriously pare back on unneeded connections and start imposing order out of the thick entanglement of neurons and mental pathways. By adulthood, all the small side paths, the potential directions his brain could have taken but didn't, will have completely disappeared.[1]

BRAIN WIRING AND TODDLER EMOTIONS

Like a living, electrical loom, a young child's brain is constantly in motion, weaving new patterns day and night to create a dynamic map of who he is, what he is going to become, and how he will fit into the world in which he was born.

Here's what happens to our brains over time. At about the eighth week of gestation, the brain orchestrates all the key processes that are key to survival—heartbeat, breathing, reflexes, and so on—and then connects together the many other parts that run the body, such as the emotion centers. Then your baby's brain generates about 250,000 new brain cells per *minute*. During his first year following birth, his brain nearly doubles its weight and turns into a kind of complex, organic electrical switchboard.

At around the midteens, the brain links together the layers of the executive cortex, in the front of the brain, in preparation for adulthood. The executive cortex oversees higher thinking processes, such as the ability to concentrate, think abstractly, hold back emotional impulses, make wise decisions, and solve complex problems.

During the toddler stage, such higher mental processes simply haven't developed yet, but the areas that control emotion are very much up and running. This helps explain why your toddler is uninhibited, impulsive, and repetitive. His limited memory and awareness of others' feelings, meltdowns and frustrations, and inability to put words to feelings are all a result of normal brain development. (Interestingly, as the brain begins to shut down at the end of life, elders may exhibit similar, toddler-like behaviors.)

Your toddler isn't purposely being willful or spoiled with his testy behaviors, but his active brain still has a lot of growing to do. As different areas of your toddler's brain connect while others don't, your toddler may seem to behave in "fits and starts" and be unpredictable. Sometimes, when the brain is being challenged or becomes overstimulated, a full-scale (but brief) meltdown will occur. But take heart, because this, too, shall pass. At about 36 months, a calmer and more amenable child will appear.

Thinking and Feeling

During the toddler stage, experiencing feelings and learning how to connect feelings to actions and words are two of your child's most important developmental tasks. Research has shown that toddlers' understanding of emotions and feelings grows right alongside their understanding of language. And, like learning to climb up and down stairs or being able to communicate well, emotional facility takes time and lots of practice.

A few toddlers might begin to use words to describe their feelings as early as 20 months, such as "happy," or, more rarely, "sad." By about 24 months, at least half of all toddlers in one study were able to express at least one word for how they were feeling, such as "sad" or "mad,"[2] but they couldn't always read the difference in those two expressions on people's faces. Later two-word sentences, such as "I 'fraid," or "Mommy happy" emerge.[3] This research has been corroborated by many similar studies.

While your toddler's brain is busily wiring up its higher mental processes, there comes a period of time when his comprehension far exceeds his ability to express himself. That's when squealing, biting, tantrums, and other expressions of extreme frustration peak. Around 20 months to 30 months of age, your toddler's verbal abilities will start improving at a rapid pace, and simultaneously emotional storms will start to calm and lose their intensity. (There are always exceptions, of course, such as toddlers with slowed language development.)

By the time your toddler reaches his third birthday, he will seem positively calm in comparison to the tumultuous year and a half that preceded it. He will be able to express his feelings in more detail, talk about feelings remembered from the recent past, and apply "feeling words" to how he perceives other people's emotions, such as happy or sad. Some parts of the emotional world will remain out of his grasp, such as the fact that someone could feel two different things at the same time.

By the end of toddlerhood, some children will be able to combine their newly acquired feeling words into simple sentences, showing that they are aware of someone else's feelings, or they will invent other feeling-word combinations.[4] But until your toddler acquires more skill in communicating what he's feeling, he will sometimes become supremely frustrated, especially since most toddlers implicitly expect their grown-ups to understand what they're feeling, even though they can't express it. (For more on tantrums, see Chapter 4, and for more on how toddler language develops, see Chapter 5.)

As his ability to form thoughts and elaborate what's going on inside him evolve, your toddler will resort to facial expressions, gestures, body language, and sometimes screams and wails in his attempt to convey his exasperation.

How Emotions Grow

At the beginning of toddlerhood, your child will likely be practicing how to connect feelings with words, weather "feeling storms," comfort himself, and overcome fears. During his preschool years, he'll make huge leaps in his ability to express and control his emotions and understand the feelings of others.

When and how emotional abilities mature is unique to each child, but here are some general guidelines for when things happen, beginning at birth, through toddlerhood:

AGE	ABILITY
Beginning at birth	From the beginning, your child's body shows feelings. His lips, chin, forehead, eyes, and eyebrows all express interest, pleasure, joy, disgust, fear, and surprise. He tries to self-soothe by sucking his fists or fingers. If too overwhelmed, he may withdraw, turn away, or become sluggish and hard to awaken.
3 months to 6 months	He reads facial expressions and can discriminate between happiness, anger, surprise, and other emotions in others. He shows anger when he's restrained, such as by being restrained or blocked.
9 months to 12 months	He expresses positive and negative emotions, including stranger anxiety. He's possessive of caregivers and mistrusting or fearful of others. He might cry when viewing someone else in distress.
12 months to 18 months (and older)	He freely expresses a full range of emotions. Self-awareness grows alongside his understanding of language. He gains a clearer sense of the person he is, what he wants, and where he wants to go.
18 months to 24 months (and older)	He imagines doing things before enacting them. He shows frustration when others don't seem to understand his thoughts or feelings. He may offer a toy or other comfort item to someone who seems upset or sad. Due to separation anxiety, he vacillates between wanting to be independent and feeling vulnerable and needy.

AGE	ABILITY
24 months to 36 months	Emerging feelings of embarrassment, guilt, and pride are signs your toddler is more aware of himself as a separate person. His sense of self and heightening awareness of his powers (or lack thereof) continues to expand. He may use single words that express feelings, such as "happy," "sad," "mad," "tired," or "scared," most often used to convey distress and ask for help. Affectionate gestures emerge, and he may express "I love you" or a variation of these important "connection words."
36 months (and older)	He may pretend to cry or be angry, or imitate others' distress.

EMOTIONS IN CHILDREN

Raising a child with warmth, acceptance, and affection has a lot to do with how well he will be able to cope with his own emotions. Being emotionally supported by you can have a profound effect on his self-esteem, how connected he feels with you, and how he relates to others throughout his lifetime, including his life partner.[5]

During this emotional time in your toddler's life, most of his lessons about feelings will come from you, his parents. As your toddler's primary coach, you will be teaching him about feelings by what you say and the way you model emotion toward the significant others in your life. Some parents are gifted emotional teachers; others are not so good—perhaps because they're still in the process of learning how to deal with feelings themselves and how to express them.

At the same time, you will be demonstrating which of your toddler's emotions are acceptable, and which, if expressed, could get a child in trouble. If you tend to yell and shout when you get angry or upset, or to strike out physically, your toddler will be likely to model those behaviors in his interactions with others.

Your toddler is working on higher-level skills that include how to control impulses and delay gratification, how to read other people's body language and other cues to figure out what they're feeling inside, how to feel empathy for others, and ultimately how to use his inner thoughts for managing life's inevitable ups and downs, and build resilience.

BOYS, GIRLS, AND EMOTIONS

When it comes to expressing emotions, most parents are more

influenced by gender than they realize. Research shows that parents show their own emotions differently depending upon whether they are communicating with a boy or a girl. They model a greater range of emotions for their girls than for their boys, which gives girls an advantage when it comes to expressing themselves.[6]

One study found that when viewers were told they were observing a baby girl's expression of emotion (whether the baby was actually a girl or not), parents interpreted the baby's emotion as "fear." On the other hand, if they thought the baby was a boy, they labeled the boy's emotion as "anger."[7] Another study found that parents tended to smile at a boy if he was angry, but they frowned at an angry girl.[8]

Parents, especially fathers, have also been found to respond more positively to boys' irritability and negative emotions than to the same emotions in girls.[9] That may have to do with parents' beliefs about how acceptable certain temperamental attributes are for boys versus girls which leads them to react differently depending upon a child's gender.

Observational studies show that as children, boys come to expect their parents will respond negatively to their expressions of sadness, and they therefore express less sadness. Girls expect their mothers to react negatively if they express anger and to react positively if they express sadness, and so they express less anger and more sadness than boys do.[10]

On the other hand, parents may discourage boys from expressing certain other emotions. An upset little boy might not want to be held and stroked as a young toddler or, as he ages, might be strongly instructed (directly or indirectly) that "big boys don't cry" or that he should "calm down," and so on.

For a toddler, learning how to regulate emotions doesn't mean making them disappear or changing them from one feeling to another. Instead—like learning to operate the volume control on an iPod—your toddler will need to learn how to modulate his feelings so they're either less intense or more intense and how to slow down strong emotions that make him "get carried away."

Not all toddlers are equally gifted when it comes to emotional control. A shy child may feel anger or sadness equally as strong as an outgoing and very expressive child, but not have the tools (or confidence) to express what he's feeling outwardly. Instead, he may withdraw, or suddenly and unexpectedly strike out at others in his desperate attempt to manage strong feelings that threaten to overwhelm him.[11]

Children have the ability to alter how long they feel something and to manage emotional changes, such as by muting their excitement when they enter a birthday party, appropriately expressing their sadness when they need to be cuddled and nurtured, and using emotional displays to get something they want, as in the candy bar at the grocery store checkout.

Learning How to Express Feelings

It will take years and lots of practice for your child to learn how to balance himself and his feelings and how to express them. Again, some toddlers will do it better or sooner than others, but it is no reflection on the child's character or his future personality.

As you've probably already discovered, one emotionally charged word that takes on special significance during the toddler stage is the word *no*. For a toddler, *no* can mean more than one thing. It could be his way of reminding himself "don't do that," or he could use the word to tell you something's missing that he needs: "No milk!" Then again, it could also be an attempt to command someone else to leave him alone or not take away something he is clinging to, as if he was saying, "No! That's mine!"

There are ways to help your toddler understand and express his feelings. Let's discuss five possibilities.

Signing

While your toddler's word skills are still in formation, you may be able to teach him sign language for feelings, which may help him express himself and diminish his sense of frustration at not being able to communicate.

For instance, there are signs to express sadness (sad face and rubbing tear from eye), anger (scowling face and fist), and happiness (fingers on either side of a big grin) that you and your toddler practice using with one another. There are a number of resources (including free online information and videos) for teaching your toddler to sign, such as the Signing Time! Web site. Or you can invent your own.

Reading

Some picture books may help to show an older toddler what feelings are all about. Saxton Freymann's *How Are You Peeling?* features large photographs of fruits and vegetables portraying different emotions. Todd Parr's *The Feelings Book* uses large stick figures of people and animals to demonstrate different feelings with a touch of silliness, and Anthony Lewis's *Carrots or Peas?* is a board book that invites toddlers to determine whether the child is happy or sad on each page. Dr. Seuss's *My Many Colored Days* is a nonrhyming, simple book about day-to-day feelings.

Looking at Images

Clip images from magazines, online sources, and elsewhere of babies, children, and adults showing feelings. Place the images into a small photo album that your older toddler can thumb through. Talk about what the faces must be feeling. A mirror can help you and him to play a mimicking game for expressions. Looking into the mirror, use great emotion when you say, "I am feeling s-o-o-o happy!" Repeat using the words *sad* or *mad*.

Putting Words to Feelings

As long as he doesn't damage property or hurt someone, your toddler should be allowed to express feelings, even angry ones. If he is unable to put feelings into words, you can help by expressing them for him: "You're really *mad* about that." "You are *sad* that I am going." You can ask him, "How does that make you feel?" "Can you say the word *mad*?" to encourage him to put words to his feeling states.

Toddler Emotions

Here's a quick reference to help you read your toddler's emotions.

- **Pause.** Slow down; take a minute to read your toddler's cues to see if you can discern what he may be feeling.
- **Decide.** Figure out if this is a good moment for teaching about emotions.
- **Validate.** Go eye to eye and emphatically (and simply) express what you sense your child is feeling. Keep trying until you find the brief statement that brings a look of recognition from your toddler. *(That makes you feel sad. Or: You want to go home NOW!)*
- **Control.** Take action or set limits if necessary while exploring with your child alternatives for how the problem could be solved. *(We have to stay here now, but you can hold my keys for me. Or: Do you want us to go home now? We can go home now.)*

Taking Cues from Others

Your toddler will be encouraged to communicate his feelings by mimicking others and learning new words, such as *bored, confused, comfortable, excited, fed up, impatient, nervous, proud, relieved, scared, tense,* and *tired.* Hearing these words can lay the groundwork for your toddler's emerging awareness of the complexities of human emotions.

HELP FOR SEPARATIONS

Before age 8 months or so, your child didn't have a concept of what is called "object permanence." That is, if he couldn't see it, it didn't exist—whether "it" was a toy or a parent.

During toddlerhood, your child realizes that if he drops his cup from his high chair, it still exists (albeit on the floor), and, in fact, the cup often reappears (when you pick it up) for him to drop again, and again. He also understands that you still exist even after you drop him off at, say, day care. But he doesn't know when you're coming back, which can lead to tears, because he prefers to be with you.

Walking away from your toddler's pitiful, teary face can be downright heart-wrenching for you. Separation anxiety may make you worry or evoke pangs of guilt for leaving him, but his reaction is a sign of the healthy attachment the two of you have built together.

Fortunately, most separation-anxiety dramas are short-lived.

Although it may be tempting to try to protect your toddler out of empathy for his distress, such as when you leave him in child care, you may discover, however, that your pulling back to let him solve the problem, rather than rushing in to rescue him, could help to lessen teary episodes. You're nudging him toward managing strange situations and building his confidence based on experience.

If your toddler is in child care and cries, clings, or reacts strongly to your departures, it helps to plan in advance how you will react so you can act consistently each time the issue comes up. Here are some suggestions for easing separation woes:

- **Ask for the caregiver's help and advice.** Most children's separation dramas are momentary and quickly over. Let your toddler's teacher help you come up with strategies (and distractions) to make separations less challenging, such as presenting an enticing new toy or a mirror to look at.
- **Prepare ahead of time.** Images may help an older toddler who has separation issues. Ask the children's librarian at your local library to recommend simple children's books about separations and going to child care. Consider creating your own picture album of the center, its children, and teachers to help build positive anticipation for going to the center. Francesca Rusackas's *I Love You All Day Long* is a sweet story about separations and love. Elizabeth Verdick's *Bye-Bye Time* is a simple dad-and-child separation story.

- **Get acquainted with the new place.** If you will be starting your toddler off with a new caregiver or at a new child-care center, try a "test drive" for a few days when you drop by and sit and watch your child play and adjust. Hanging around as a "teacher's aide" will help you to get to know the other children there, too, so that you feel better and less torn about leaving your child behind.
- **Start gradually.** If you have some flexibility in your schedule, try starting your child in a new care setting for just two hours a day so he can become secure in the concept that if you go away, you will come back.
- **Stay positive.** Try not to convey your fears and worries to your child. Always talk about child care as an upbeat experience. At the end of the day, talk with teachers so you know the highlights of your toddler's day, learn the names of other children there, and even consider scheduling a playdate with one of his preferred playmates to build familiarity.
- **Use in-car preparation.** While driving to child care in the morning, talk about where you're going and name the teacher and some of the children who will be waiting there to see your toddler. Reinforce how you're going to return, put him in his car seat, and drive him home "after lunch."

Or you could explain it this way: "You're going to play with your friends now, and I am going to see my friends at work. After you have lunch and a nap, I'll come back in the car to drive us both home."

- **Mirror his feelings.** Let your toddler know that you are aware of his distress. "I'm sorry you're sad, but I have to leave in three minutes." Then spend a few minutes with a ritual of cuddling or reading a book before bidding a quick adieu.
- **Relax and be affectionate.** Good-byes need to be brief, affectionate, and end with a clear statement that you'll be coming back and when: "I'll be back after lunch." Leave without hesitation and resist the urge to peek back in on him.
- **Share the job.** Let your partner or a grandparent take your child to school on designated days. He'll build familiarity and trust with other trusted adults, you won't have to manage the whole responsibility every day, and your child will learn that he can manage this.
- **Avoid long absences.** Because separation is a big issue for your child, try to avoid overnight absences, which can heighten his fear of being abandoned. When there's just no avoiding a separation, use the same methods of reassuring that you will be back, when you'll be back, and what you can look forward to when you return.

Fears, Obsessions, and Anger

TODDLER FEAR

Fear is a normal emotion for humans of all ages. It is nature's way of alerting us to react to danger, and it helps protect us from threatening situations. But because toddlers are more sensitive emotionally than older children and adults, they are still learning how to cope with changes and the unfamiliar.

Studies show that toddler fears appear and disappear in an ordered, patterned way that is similar from one child to another. Each new developmental stage brings its own characteristic fears, and as your toddler matures, what he fears will change. Some toddlers, though, are more cautious and fearful by nature, while others appear so fearless that they often endanger their own safety.

Although it's impossible to take away all of your toddler's fears, some can serve a useful purpose, such as the fear of cars on a busy street or the fear of unfamiliar dogs. And sometimes toddlers can be strongly affected by their parents' fears, such as the fear of spiders, air travel, or night sounds.

Over time, as your toddler gradually begins to become familiar with the unknown, his experiences in mastering unfamiliar things and situations will give him confidence rather than causing him to draw back or shrink away. Wherever your toddler is on the fear continuum, it's important to help him learn to deal with fear in a way that preserves his dignity and self-worth.

Here are some ways to help your toddler become better at managing his fears.

- **Acknowledge and accept the fear.** Don't make fun of your toddler's fears. Talking about fears helps children to work them out and helps to make events less frightening. Ask your child how he is feeling: *I wonder if you are feeling afraid? Does this make you afraid? Yes, being in the dark can feel scary.*
- **Deal with the monster.** If the monster in the closet is real to your child, then deal directly with the monster. Kick him out of the house. Admonish him loudly to leave and never come back. If fear of the dark is the problem, leave a dim light on, or hand over a childproof and easy-to-turn-on flashlight for shedding light on the situation.
- **Tell the truth.** Telling your child that shots or other medical procedures won't hurt may make him feel that he is alone in his fear and must deal with it all by himself. Instead, describe in as much detail as you can what's coming up, with the reassurance that he will only feel it for a moment (snap your fingers), but only if that's truly the case.
- **Rehearse and reassure.** To help your toddler feel less threatened, rehearse exactly what is going to happen, then give your child honest reassurance.
- **Distract.** Rather than trying to dissuade your toddler from feeling fear, consider an enticing alternative that takes his mind off of his fear. He may warm up if his focus is taken off of the fearful.

TODDLER OBSESSIONS

As you will quickly learn, toddlers cling to all things familiar, whether it's a favorite blanket, a stuffed bear, a beloved pacifier, a favored cup, or a certain kind of cracker. These obsessions can be tiresome to adults, but predictability can be very reassuring to a toddler who is discovering so many new things.

Starting around 2 ½ and peaking between ages 3 and 4, repetitive behavior often morphs into a single-minded interest in a character, animal, or favorite color. You can watch your toddler change from passively seeing imaginary figures on television or in books to actually being able to pretend that he is the character that has captured his interest.

As toddlers' capacity to imagine soars, they often become obsessed with certain colors, such as the color blue for boys, with fictional characters such as a cartoon superhero, or favorite videos and books that they insist on watching over and over. Or the obsession may be with a specific toy that seems to offer comfort and security, and may even seem like a real being to your child whose head is rapidly becoming filled with fantasies and ideas.

During this phase, you will discover your child slipping out of "reality" and into his own pretend world where he gets to try on different personas. Sometimes pretending can help your child feel more powerful and better able to cope with things that are scary, such as going to the dentist's office, or pretending to be strong and invincible might help him find a way to overcome a fear of being injured or victimized.

An outgoing child is likely to be very creative and dramatic and to get very deeply involved in his imaginary scenarios. On the other hand, a quiet, introverted child is more likely to do quiet, private things, such as collecting toys or cars and lining them up in a certain order that can't be disturbed without some protest.

Besides helping your child cope with his fears, pretend play also helps your toddler relate to other children, even nonverbally, especially when the pretending is shared, maybe because both are wearing similar clothing and props, such capes, cowboy boots, or ballet tutus, or they are playing with blocks or trucks on the floor together.

Enduring your child's obsession can get tiring after a while, especially when he constantly corrects you and insists that you call him by his pretend name, rather than his real one, or you're forced to return home to retrieve his favored object, accidentally left behind.

It makes sense to simply yield to your child's obsession, as long as it's reasonable, rather than trying to make him buck up and "face reality." Still, there may be times when you have to put your foot down, such as if his obsession interferes with accepted behavior in public. At those times, one way to negotiate with your tot is to set limits about where costumes and other security props can be used and where they are considered off-limits.

The obsessions—some parents and early childhood professionals prefer to call them "passions"—will usually fade away on their own before your child reaches kindergarten. If not, or if your child is doing strange repetitive behaviors and not relating to others well, then it may be time to discuss your concerns with your toddler's pediatrician or a child development specialist.

TODDLER ANGER

When you think about it, toddlers have a lot to be angry about. They're little. They can't have most of the things they want. They fail at many things they attempt. Bigger people are always telling them what to do, and those people sometimes have loud, scary voices and strong, large bodies.

It takes time for toddlers to learn to modulate their anger. Sometimes even the most quiet and reserved child can lash out in anger because he still doesn't know how to respond to others, especially to other children who feel threatening to him. His first impulse may be to withdraw, but if he feels cornered, he may hit or bite.

Your toddler's aggression could be triggered by another child who grabbed his toy or hurt him. It could be a reaction toward an unfamiliar grown-up who prevented him from doing something, or someone who confined him when he wanted to roam. Or perhaps there was a significant family change, such as the arrival of a new baby, a move, an impending separation or divorce, or a change in caregivers. Toddler aggression is often expressed by screaming, hitting, or kicking.

Angry lashing out happens because toddlers don't have any other channel for handling strong feelings of frustration. Nor do they possess the ability to negotiate their way out of situations. By the time your toddler reaches kindergarten, anger won't usually explode in him like it does during the toddler years. By then most children will have learned how to better manage those impulsive urges—such as by pouting, sulking, and whining. (You can find more tips on managing toddler aggression in Chapter 4.)

Here are some tips for teaching your toddler about anger and how to manage it:

- **Watch for anger cues.** Most toddlers will give physical signals that they're getting frustrated and are about to act out. Look for clamped jaws, a furrowed brow, tightened facial muscles, or grimacing. It makes sense to intervene. Express words for what you're seeing while you plan your next move: "I can tell that you are starting to get mad," then act as quickly as you can to either talk your child through the trouble (using empathy and age-appropriate vocabulary), distract him from what is annoying him, or remove him from the situation.
- **Don't take it personally.** Toddler anger should not be perceived as a personal insult. Just because he's supremely upset doesn't mean that your child is bad or that you have failed as a parent. If you are who is he angry

at, chalk it up to the burden of parenting. As tiring and trying as this period of development may be, it actually is a sign that your child is right on schedule, moving toward becoming a strong, independent person who can cope with the emotional distresses of life.

- **Be realistic.** Simply telling your toddler to calm down is unlikely to change his behavior . . . the first or maybe even the tenth time. It will take lots of repetitions to finally sink in. Remember, his brain isn't wired yet to rationalize.
- **Draw the line.** Your toddler's anger doesn't give him free rein to hit, push, pull hair, or hurt anyone. Issue a short, strong "NO hitting!" followed by the consequence for doing it again. When he hits again—and he will—be consistent, no matter how tiring it is, and follow through on the consequence each and every time.
- **Teach alternatives.** Offer lots of chances for your toddler to express his feelings, including anger, in acceptable ways. Venting strong feelings and excess energy in safe play areas can help, as can pretend play with toys and dolls when your toddler develops the mental capacity to do that. Make it okay for him to pound a pillow or to have one doll hit another doll, since it is "just pretend." Offer physical alternatives to striking, such as suggesting, "When you are angry you can stomp up and down."
- **Help with transitions.** Some toddlers are better at transitions from one activity to another. A

3-year-old who loses control when he is tired or abruptly separated from something he enjoys doing needs several advance alerts for upcoming change. Some children like the neutrality of a timer bell to signal the end of an activity. Again, consistency and predictability are key.

• **Practice self-calming strategies together.** Try playing games with your older toddler to teach him calming skills, such as lying on his back and making a book on his belly go up and down with deep breaths. Or make up an "angry song" that the two of you can share, or a quick story about an angry lion or other animal that can help put his anger in perspective. And sometimes, just offering a drink of water or a quiet moment may help to slow down the physical escalation of anger.

Encouraging Empathy

Empathy is the ability to put oneself in someone else's place and imagine how that feels. A younger toddler might not be able to empathize until later, when he understands emotions better. Having empathy means that your toddler is aware that someone else's distress is separate from his own, but it is a distress that he can relate to.

Some scientists now believe that empathy is hard-wired into babies' brains. A newborn next to another crying baby will start crying, too, and even the youngest babies will cry when they hear the recorded voice of another baby crying, but not the recorded sound of their own voices, which shows that some very basic empathic connections are already there. By 6 months of age sympathy crying has mostly diminished, but babies will grimace at the sight or sound of others' discomfort.

"Social referencing," waiting to react until they glimpse the faces, voices, or gestures of adults, is something that babies and toddlers often do. In one experiment, babies as young as 4 months of age reacted differently to a peek-a-boo game when they were presented with someone who didn't show a happy, smiling face during the "boo" part. When they were presented with a sad face, the babies looked away and didn't want to look back. Called "gaze aversion," it's considered a sign of baby distress. An angry face got their attention again, but their expressions changed from pleasure to alertness and vigilance.[12]

Toddlers' circle of empathy begins to widen sometime between 12 and 18 months of age, when it begins to dawn on them that they are separate from others—others who could feel differently.[13] Your child, for instance, may stop playing and look up with a concerned expression when another child gets upset in a group setting.

A 13- to 15-month-old may become upset himself when another child throws a tantrum. If a child is crying, he may offer his special security blanket or toy for comfort, or lead his mother by the hand to the child. Sometimes toddlers will show sympathetic distress if an older brother or sister is upset.[14]

A 16-month-old may imitate a calming strategy he has just seen his teacher or mother use, such as by gently patting another person on the back.[15] Reactions are dicey at this stage: Toddlers may stand near a crying child and quietly watch him, or they might move away from him, or they might try to hit him to shut him up. At this stage, empathy can't really be experienced in the same way that you, as an adult, might feel it.

Around 2 years of age, toddlers in groups stop crying contagiously when another child does. At this stage, instead of "catching" the crying, toddlers are more able to detach themselves and sometimes try to respond according to what they observe is happening with the distressed child by soothing gestures or trying to help him out.[16]

Around 30 months, toddlers can be seen "trying on" emotional expressions of others to see how they "fit." As he nears age 3, your toddler may begin to play out scenarios that help him understand others, their actions, and their feelings. He may be able to communicate empathic feelings, such as by saying, "Joshua is sad because Jenny took his cup," or by patting a distressed child on the back and offering to give him a snack.[17]

As your toddler's emotion coach, you can help nurture his growing sense of empathy by modeling what caring behavior looks like. By being empathic and kind to others

and expressing your understanding of what they feeling, you are setting up behavioral patterns that he can learn to emulate over time.

- **Vocalize others' feelings.** Help your child learn about others' feelings by talking about them. By saying, "You made me feel very happy," or by simply saying, "Ouch!" and pointing to an injured place, you're helping describe what another child could be feeling. You can engage older toddlers even more by interacting and saying something like, "Look at Jacob's face. What is he feeling? Does he feel sad because his daddy just said good-bye?" or "When you pushed Sarah, she started to cry. That hurt and made her feel sad and mad."

- **Practice good, old-fashioned manners.** Although reinforcing "please," "thank you," and "you're welcome" may seem like somewhat shallow social conventions, those basic words are part of helping your child to understand the connection between himself and others. Having a grasp of social niceties is still usually rewarded, especially at this age.

- **Set some basic be-kind-to-others rules.** Even though your toddler is too young to remember and follow rules very well, having some basic guidelines in place will be useful for the years ahead. Even if you're using basic one- or two-word commands to correct behavior, done consistently they establish fundamental rules for behavior toward all others.

- **Read and interact.** When you're reading bedtime stories, invite your toddler to imagine things about the characters as a way of expanding his awareness of others. You can help him imagine himself in the story even if he still has limited verbal skills. Examples: "What did the bunny say when the thorn got stuck in his foot?" "Do you think big bear is having fun at his birthday party?" or "Is Olivia's mama happy or sad?"

• **Invite imaginary play.** As your toddler ages he will begin to enjoy simple imaginary scenarios. Playing "mommy" or "daddy" and bringing toy animals and dolls to life is another way of learning about others' worlds. Puppets, too, can be used to express feelings by crying, smiling, laughing, and coaching your child about how other people's feelings can be different than his own.

Guiding Your Stressed Toddler

Although all parents want to protect their children from stress, sometimes things happen that are not under parents' control. Mild, short-lived stresses may simply cause a brief change in a child's heart rate or brief surges in the levels of stress hormones, for example, when your toddler is faced with new situations, or he has to deal with frustration and limits. These stresses are an important part of learning.

Your toddler doesn't have a lot of words to express his anxiety or stress. He'll likely show it by being agitated and hyperactive, extra irritable and fussy. His body may be tense and his movements jerkier than usual. He may have sleep problems or regress to more babylike behavior. Or he may turn sluggish and less responsive, and his eyes might glaze over when he feels especially threatened or overwhelmed.

Moderate stress symptoms include his becoming easily upset by small things, regressing and acting more like a baby, wanting to return to the bottle, reverting to baby talk, or forgetting toilet

training. Some stressed children become hyperalert and watchful, refusing to eat, acting sick or in pain even though they are apparently well.

Severe stress could be caused by the serious illness or death of a loved one, frightening injury, hospitalization, divorce, physical or emotional abuse or neglect, poverty and malnutrition, or severe parental depression, substance abuse, or violence.

The way a child responds to severe stress depends upon his age and his ability to understand what has happened to him. Toddlers tend to first look to their parents or other adults to observe their reactions. Small children don't appear to have flashbacks, as adults do, but reminders of their trauma, such as something seen, heard, or smelled, may arouse upset feelings all over again. While some young children have immediate and strong reactions when something extreme happens; others may take longer to react.

Toddlers undergoing severe stress might react in one of two

ways: Either they will become overly aroused and alert, or, they may withdraw and appear glazed and distant. Some children show both signs at different times.

During extreme stress, familiar calming and soothing strategies may no longer be very effective. Some toddlers will cling more desperately to their caregivers, and separation anxiety may intensify and be more prolonged. But the single most common reaction of older toddlers to trauma is some form of reexperiencing the event.

When children are exposed to severe, prolonged stress, hormone levels change and cortisol levels rise, which trigger the fight-or-flight response and physically hinder brain cell growth. Long-term effects include impairment of a child's social functioning, weakened nervous and immune systems, and negative effects on learning, behavior, and mental and physical health. Extreme stress also makes children more sensitive to stress later on, so that they're more prone to stress-related physical and mental illness.

He may relive the experience through nightmares or fears of monsters, or he may simply replay the experience over and over in his head like a horror movie. His responses will be affected by emotional or developmental problems he's currently experiencing, his past exposure to other stressful or traumatic events, and any difficult family circumstances.

Having caring parents and other supportive adults in his life who are nurturing and responsive is the best protection a child can have when it comes to recovering from stress and trauma.[18] Here are suggestions for helping the two of you weather the storm:

- **Help your child feel more secure.** Let your child know that you are present and available to comfort him.
- **Increase his sense of control.** Trauma of any kind, including medical interventions, makes a person feel as if he has no control. Give your child options to help him feel he has some control, even if it is only two small options: Would he like a drink of water now, or later? Does he want the bedroom door open or closed? Which toys would he like to play with right now?
- **Help prepare for changes.** Your child is apt to be frightened of sudden and unexpected changes, which can make things feel out of control again. Gently prepare him in very concrete ways for what's coming in the next hour or two, since neurologically he can't handle much beyond that.
- **Encourage self-expression.** Being able to communicate about what he's feeling and to re-create painful experiences from the past are ways that older toddlers try to cope with bad memories. Encourage your toddler to put into words or to play out what he remembers.
- **Lighten the mood.** It may be a challenge, but help your child take his mind off of what's distressing by introducing positive, playful moments. Find laughter wherever it can be found.
- **Get your own needs met.** Trauma for your child is also trauma for you. Take care of

yourself so that you can begin the process of healing for yourself, which will enable you to continue to focus on providing a caring, supportive relationship with your child.

• **Get help.** You can help to reduce your child's stress load by finding help and support for your child and your whole family. Use resources from the phone book, community support organizations, child-advocacy groups, and so on.

Strengthening Resilience

Putting on the brakes is very hard for motion-driven toddlers, but it is possible to help them learn self-control. The now famous Marshmallow Test conducted by Walter Mischel that began in the 1960s showed that while some preschoolers had trouble holding back, others didn't.

The children were taken into a lab and observed through a one-way mirror. They were presented a plate with one marshmallow on one side and two marshmallows on the other and a "bring-me-back" bell. The experimenter asked the children, "If you have to choose, would you like to have one marshmallow now or would you like to have two?" Most children would say, "Two!"

The experimenter then explained the "game": "I am going to leave the room. While I'm gone, if you can stay here and wait for me to come back, then you get two marshmallows. If you don't want to wait, you can make me come back right away, but then you get one marshmallow, not two."

The experimenter would be gone up to 15 minutes. Some children knew how to delay gratification, and others didn't. The children who were the most adept at delaying distracted themselves by paying attention to something else or pretending the marshmallow was a cotton ball or a cloud floating in the sky. If, instead, a child zeroed in on the marshmallow and began to think about how yummy it was, then he was more likely to give in to temptation.

The longer the preschoolers were able to wait and resist the marshmallow temptation, the better their SAT scores were as young adults, and the better they were able to pursue their academic and other goals successfully decades later. They were less likely to use drugs, obtained a higher educational level, and had a higher sense of self-esteem.

Coaching children to refocus their attention enabled them to extend their waiting from only 60 seconds up to 15 minutes or longer. For toddlers, this kind of coaching might include the following: "You can think about fun things while you are waiting, like Mommy swinging you, or sing happy songs to yourself."

EXECUTIVE FUNCTION, SELF-CONTROL, AND BUILDING RESILIENCE

Executive function is the term child development experts use for a child's growing ability to pull together feelings and think in a way that helps him to exert self-control. It is thought to be connected to the maturation of a specific part of the brain, the prefrontal cortex, which allows a person to think things through, to set goals, to control impulses, and to entertain multiple things at the same time.

Toddlers' brains simply don't have operational executive function yet and won't for years to come, so waiting, patience, and self-control simply aren't in the toddler's book of virtues. But you can help to encourage your toddler's waiting skills in small increments by using the word *wait* and using it frequently in your vocabulary and by gesturing using a raised palm (in a "stop" gesture) at the same time to signal what you expect.

Start by saying the word *wait* while simultaneously giving him the hand signal. Then you can promptly serve him his snack or deliver whatever he demanded, followed by praise: "Thank you for waiting."

A digital oven timer can help your child learn that there is a reward at the end for being patient. The familiar "ding" will signal that what he wants will be promptly delivered, first after a minute's delay, and then after 2 and 3 minutes.[19]

Like the Marshmallow Test, you can help your toddler exercise his "waiting muscles" by teaching him ways to distract himself with counting games (counting slowly to 5, and then to 10), word games, or a repertoire of songs, such as the "Alphabet Song", before presenting him with what he wants.

When you're talking on the phone or in person with someone, and your toddler demands your attention, you can help him learn waiting and patience by teaching him to place his hand on your arm, shoulder, or leg to signal his need for attention.

Researchers over the past 30 years have been trying to discover how some children are able to bounce back from adversity, while others facing similar challenges seem to sustain deeper and more lasting damage.

It's not that resilient children don't feel the effects of stressful events. They still get sad, angry, or scared under difficult circumstances, but they are better at soothing themselves, brushing themselves off, and carrying on with productive activities afterward.

At first it was thought that resilience is an inherited trait or directly related to temperament.

TIP

Toddlers should not be put on hold for very long, but the Marshmallow Test showed that delaying gratification reaps numerous rewards besides marshmallows.

More recent studies suggest that resilience hinges on a child's having support around him—specifically a responsive, protective parent or other adult in his life to support him, such as a loving grandparent or other caregiver.[20] Researchers found that the families that produced resilient children were often very involved with relatives and neighbors. Often they had strong religious ties in their communities and drew upon health and social services and other forms of community support. Positive-thinking parents also helped instill in their children a belief that they could overcome adversity, too.

In some cases, a child's temperament made a difference. Sociable toddlers and those who were alert, independent, and interested in seeking out novel experiences were more likely to show resilience in overcoming adversity, as did those who had the ability to elicit positive attention from their parents and other adults.

First and foremost, though, for a child to be resilient, he needed to feel connected to parents or other caring adults and able to feel secure that these buffering elders were there for him, allowing him to be free to explore and turn to them when he needed support and reassurance.

He also needed simple problem-solving skills, so if he hit roadblocks he knew how to devise ways to get around them. Finally, it helped if a child had regular patterns of living—eating, sleeping, and so on.

But even without all the benefits of intellect, problem-solving, and so on, those children who had supportive parents and lived in environments that fostered their strengths and coping skills were more likely to develop resilience.[21]

Positive strategies help build the foundation for resilience and competence later.

- **Be supportive.** Having you as an affectionate and responsive parent can strengthen your child in untold ways. This kind of parenting helps to shelter a child from storms. A positive parent conveys that even though her child may act badly, that doesn't mean that *he* is bad. Use words such as: *Do you need a hug? Your hugs make me smile.*

- **Respond to cues.** Taking time to respond to your child's communications—including preverbal ones—help him to feel understood and could even help ward off explosive behavior when frustrations mount. Use words such as: *Are you feeling scared that I have to leave? I will come back today and every day after lunch. Should we read a short book together before I go?*

- **Offer decision power.** Giving your toddler options whenever possible—even if both options lead to the same outcome—helps him feel strong and capable and in control of something. Most toddlers can only handle two options at a time, so use words such as: *Do you want to take your bath now? Or kiss everyone good night and then take your bath?*

- **Teach logical consequences.** Although toddlers may have a limited ability to entertain "this-leads-to-that" thinking, you can start now to reinforce that your child's actions affect others and have natural outcomes. Use words such as: *As soon as you put on your coat, we can play outside. You threw the truck, so now we have to put it away for a while.*

• **Nudge toward problem solving.** Rather than immediately stepping in to help your older toddler with dressing himself or completing other tasks, it's useful to slow down and take time to work with him on figuring out solutions, so that later on he will gain more confidence in generating his own alternatives. You can help him to think about alternative ways of dealing with upsetting situations, such as preparing him in advance for them. Use words such as: *I can see you are working hard to hold all these toys at once, but they keep dropping. What would make carrying them easier? You really tried hard to figure this out, and now you found an answer!*

• **Provide opportunities to succeed.** Start teaching your child early on to believe in his own abilities by providing him with small tasks that he can succeed in and then relating his success to his ability to do them. Use words such as: *Look how you washed your hands—you made your hands very clean. You sat very still—you waited and waited.*

• **Stay neutral about gender.** Invite your daughter to climb, play with trucks and blocks, lift heavy objects, and be assertive, and encourage your son to play in the kitchen, to feed baby dolls, pretend to cook, and openly express his feelings and tender emotions, not just his anger. Try reading typical "boy" books on trucks and dinosaurs and gender-neutral stories of firefighters and police officers to your daughter, and ballerina and princess stories to your son. The object is to help your child to become more gender open and flexible, and thus more resilient.

Q & A

Q: I have a 2-month-old and a 2-year-old. My 2-year-old, who is usually friendly and smart, became defiant when we brought home her baby brother. She won't listen to me, and if I ask her to do something, she adamantly refuses. She has become very headstrong, and when I try to discipline her, she throws a tantrum. Time-outs just don't work! She laughs at me, and I find myself getting louder and louder and sounding like a broken record. What can we do to get her to listen to us?

A: First, your daughter may be showing the temperamental characteristics of a "strong-willed child." (See our tips for handling a strong-willed child in Chapter 1). Second, her behavior suggests that she is worried and sad that you're replacing her with someone else to love. That's only heightened by your own exhaustion as you adjust to your new baby and your frustration with her. Try to have empathy for her situation. Think how you might feel if your husband brought home an adorable younger woman to live closely beside you in your house. It simply will take time for your toddler to adjust to this bewildering and worrisome new situation. Hopefully in time she will learn to enjoy her little brother and be proud being the "big girl" in the family. Meanwhile, a lot of reassurance and hugs are called for. This would be a good time for her dad (or another relative) to pitch in with one-on-one time away from home (such as walks in the park or game time at Grandma's house), and gentle, predictable bath and bedtime rituals.

TIP

Communicate with your toddler to help him feel understood. It can help teach him powerful early lessons about patience and resilience.

Behavior

There's a sweet and adorable side to toddlers, and then there's the beastie side. Oh, we know intellectually that toddlers can't help that their brains aren't mature yet, that they're emotional, boundary-setting, puzzling little people, yet somehow that knowledge doesn't help us or them when behavior is an issue.

What do we mean by behavior being "an issue"? If you're the parent of a toddler, it means when you come out of the bathroom to find your child hugging a bottle of laundry bleach—even though the laundry cabinet was supposed to be "toddlerproofed." It means when she is red-faced and screaming, "I don't want you!" in a crowded store.

If you're like most parents of toddlers, you're probably eager like to find something—*anything*—to help deal with your toddler's misdeeds. And, unfortunately, toddlers don't come with owner's manuals. But we can help.

For your toddler, life is a just series of experiments: What happens when I pull Kitty's tail? Poke this? Eat that? Climb the bookshelves in the living room? If only she could picture that the bookshelves could fall on her head and hurt her! If she could, then just maybe she would stop climbing them like you've told her for the third time in a row. But her drive to conquer is so strong that it's overriding the sound of your voice.

This chapter is designed to help you in getting around typical toddler antics in ways that are helpful, rather than harmful. It will show you how to build a communication style that's easy for your toddler to grasp so she'll be more cooperative.

Toddler Behavior

Is your toddler able to stop what she's doing to listen to you? Can she understand what you're trying to tell her to do? Is she able to follow your simple directions? Can she remember any family rules for more than a few minutes at a time?

If your answer is *no* to any of these questions, you may be carrying higher expectations for your toddler than she is able to deliver. Her mind is only able to make the simplest of connections. "If Daddy laughed at my cat trick, maybe pulling the dog's tail will be funny too!" "If Mommy spanked me, then I can spank other people, too." Nor can she reason to herself: "If I do this, Mommy might get mad and put me in time out!"

Your younger toddler won't "get" that it's wrong to poke others with sticks because it hurts, or not to bite somebody when her space is invaded. Instead, her complete focus is all about getting what she wants and needs *right now*. But you can guide her and work on empathy building.

Civilization is built on self-discipline and respect for others. You may never be able to get a 12-month-old to say *please* or chew with her mouth closed, but it's never too early to teach your child that some things are dangerous, and that it's not okay to hurt people, animals, or property.

The path to civilization can seem long and frustrating, but take heart. During your child's toddler years, you can establish some basic ground rules that will help your child toward keeping herself safe, being considerate of others, and maybe even using words instead of pointing and screeching to get what she wants.

This chapter tackles the many common behavioral issues that parents of 12- to 18-month-olds face, and evidence-based tips on managing them.

First, here's a quick overview of what most toddlers can and can't do by age:

TIP

If you're concerned about a child, the Childhelp National Child Abuse Hotline (800-4-A-CHILD, *www.childhelp.org*) offers 24-hour support and local referrals by trained professional counselors.

AGE	ABILITIES AND LIMITATIONS
12 months	Tries to cooperate for getting dressed by holding out her arms or legs.
	May try to follow simple one-step commands, such as "Bring the ball," but could forget midway.
	Mimics the word *no* or shakes head for no, but continues unwanted behavior anyway.
	Driven to touch, pick up, and mouth things, even if told *no* a dozen times in the past minute.
	Drops objects over and over just to watch them fall.
18 months	Has strong exploratory drive and can't sit still.
	Wants to play with adult objects—remote control, keys, cell phones—and resists letting go of them.
	Tries to climb shelves and furniture. Pulls off clothes and socks. Tries to take things apart.
	Refuses certain foods.
	Wanders away from caregivers.
24 months	Can follow two-step directions—"Come here and sit down"—but frequently forgets what she was about to do.
	More responsive to humor and distraction than to logic and reason.
	Low frustration threshold, often negative and short-tempered. May show aggression (hitting, pinching, biting, kicking) and little or no impulse control.
	Has trouble making choices (e.g., wants to be inside and outside at the same time).
	Wants to give orders.
36 months	Can follow multiple-step directions.
	Is more compliant and less demanding, yet is assertive.
	Better able to communicate needs and wishes.
	Enjoys having familiar routines all the time (e.g., peanut butter for lunch every single day).
	Occasionally reverts back to being babyish and clinging to Mommy or Daddy.

AGGRESSION

Being aggressive is a part of normal toddler development, especially between the ages of 18 months and 36 months. The roots of aggression can be traced back to babyhood. A 4-month-old will scratch, a 6-month-old will pull hair, and a 12-month-old will bite others on purpose. Around 15 to 18 months, acts of outright aggression become more commonplace, such as kicking, hair pulling, and striking others with a hand or an object.

One of parents' biggest challenges is how to deal with a child who is physically aggressive, especially if she strikes or bites other children. Even though the aggression may simply be a phase your toddler is passing through, it affects others, and it also can evoke a strong response from other parents if their child is bitten by yours in a playgroup or at day care. In fact, biting is one of the main reasons toddlers are "expelled" from day care or preschools.

Biting and being bitten are much more common in the toddler world than most parents realize. One study found that half of children in day care are bitten at one time or another, and the average is three bites per year. Biting is worse in groups of children who are stressed, overcrowded, or just learning how to manage social relations with their peers.

TIP

According to a 1997 journal article, no other childhood factor predicts adult aggression as well as childhood aggression.[1]

WHY TODDLERS BITE

When it comes to trying to figure out why toddlers use their mouths and end up inflicting discomfort on somebody else, it helps to take a look at other primates, our nearest kin, among whom biting is a very common form of self-protection and warning.

Toddlers, who are still operating out of their lower brain processes, simply don't have the sophisticated wiring as yet to rein in their feelings of anger or frustration. And, like chimps, they are also very territorial about possessions.

Almost all kids try out their teeth on somebody else at some point. Being little and relatively weak, they're not coordinated enough to hit or kick very effectively (unless they're picked up off of their feet), but they do have sharp teeth, and biting is one thing they can do easily and well.

And it *is* very effective! It fends off unwanted intruders by delivering a strong message, protects a treasured object, and stirs up a lot of excitement and attention. Sometimes it's a way to vent pent-up anger or frustration, or just to experiment to see what makes sparks fly.

While most bites can be easily

The Lift and Turn Maneuver

If your child is clearly upset and acting extremely aggressively, you may need to use a stronger physical tactic to intervene. The maneuver will also clearly demonstrate to other parents that you won't tolerate aggression.

Here's how to perform the L&T:

- **Do a quick lift.** While your toddler is facing you, raise her into the air by holding onto her chest under her arms. While still maintaining complete self-control, put on your meanest frowny face while calmly announcing once: "No hitting" (or "No biting" or "No kicking").
- **Turn her away from you.** This demonstrates clearly to your toddler that you can and will physically control her if her actions merit it. Either turn her so her back is to you as you're lowering her from this raised position, or, if that's too much weight to manage, silently march her from behind by her shoulder to the corner of the room or face her into an empty wall.
- **Hold her forward-facing.** Without speaking, hold her, back still toward you, for 20 seconds for a child younger than 2 years, and no longer than 1 to 2 minutes for an older toddler.
- **Turn her to face you.** Repeat the words "No hitting" (or "no biting" or "no kicking"), but this time use a kind and loving facial expression and voice when you say the words.
- **Let go.** Lower her or move away from her without saying more about the behavior or indicating in any way with your facial expressions or body language that you're still upset, disappointed, or angry.
- **No warning.** If you want the L&T maneuver to work, never verbally warn your toddler that you are going to use it as a way of getting her to stop doing something. And never just do a partial version of the maneuver because your hands are full or you're not in a good setting to do the whole maneuver.

handled with some warm water and soap and an antigerm ointment if the skin is broken, the emotional issues that biting can arouse aren't as easily treated.

Although toddlers will typically take it in stride and quickly forget about it, having *your* child bitten by another child can be upsetting and enraging. Not only do you get angry at the child who hurt yours, but you also feel betrayed by caregivers who failed to protect your child. And some parents bear grudges against both the parent and a biting child, or, might even try to get a child kicked out of a playgroup or child-care setting, especially if the same child bites more than once.

Biting behavior may persist longer among toddlers who are lagging behind in development, such as those who have trouble speaking or have poor visual, perceptual, or motor skills.

If your child is doing the biting, there are a couple of things you need to take a look at: Are aggressive behaviors going on at home? Your toddler may be getting mixed messages that hitting and other forms of aggressive behavior are okay if aggressive acts are being used for punishment at home or modeled as a form of play.

Whether it's spanking, pinching, kicking, slapping, tickling, wrestling, nibbling, or mock boxing, your toddler may decide that being aggressive is normal and therefore acceptable behavior. It may be time to address this issue with other family members.

Now let's address some of those classic toddler situations that make any parent want to slither down a drainpipe. That's right, we're talking about breath holding, head banging, and tantrum.

Breath Holding

Between 6 months and 18 months of age, some children begin to have breath-holding spells, which usually peak between 24 months and 36 months. Witnessing one, especially the first time, can be scary for a parent!

There are two types of breath holding: blue (cyanotic) and white (pallid). Three-quarters of breath holding is the blue kind, and it seems to be brought on by a change in breathing patterns. Your child may screech a couple of times as if she's going into a tantrum only to stop in the middle of a cry, fall silent, turn blue, and pass out. Her breathing will switch over to autorun and will keep on going. She'll return to consciousness within about 20 seconds with a sudden intake of air.

During a white attack, your toddler will go limp and pale and fall to the ground as if she's fainted. It happens soundlessly without a screech, signs of rage, or breath holding. Usually the fainting is a strong response to fear or injury, not unlike adults fainting at seeing blood, getting shots, or having minor surgeries. In this type of episode, your child's heartbeat patterns may briefly change.

You panic and wonder whether you should splash your child's face with cold water, start mouth-to-mouth resuscitation, or dial 9-1-1.

Actually, breath-holding spells aren't all that rare for toddlers, and they're not harmful unless your toddler strikes something as she falls during an episode. Spells occur in approximately one out of twenty otherwise healthy children, and usually begin in the first year of life and peak at age 2. They usually disappear by age 4 in 50 percent of children and by age 8 in about 83 percent of children. Typically, breath holding is set off by some kind of emotional trigger, such as anger, agitation, pain, or frustration.

It's important to bring up your toddler's breath-holding spells with your health-care provider and ask for a thorough physical exam for her, if for no other reason than to reassure yourself that she is completely healthy.

In some cases, a sudden spike in a fever may be the reason for the seizure. Passing out may indicate that your child has anemia, or much more rarely, a seizure disorder or heart rhythm problems. A very small number of toddlers have a genetic disorder called familial dysautonomia, but if that were the problem, your child would already have shown other signs of being seriously ill.

The main thing to do during one of these episodes is to keep your toddler safe, especially if she faints.

Head Banging

As a baby, your toddler likely thrived on the rhythmical motion of rocking. The back-and-forth motion had a soothing, lulling effect, perhaps because it mimics the vigorous motions they experienced during pregnancy when you went on walks.

Lots of toddlers still crave the sensation they get from repetitive motion. Between 5 percent and 15 percent of young children bang or rub their heads or rock themselves back and forth. Usually these behaviors set in before 2 years of age, and more than two-thirds of head bangers are boys.

Fortunately, these self-stimulating behaviors are considered "self-limiting," meaning that although there may be mild bruising from the same place being hit over and over, toddlers seldom hurt themselves doing it.

Why does your child do it? It's a way to comfort himself by stimulating the part of the inner ear called the vestibular system. If your toddler is a deliberate head banger, especially at bedtime, she may be using the motion and physical sensation to comfort herself or let off steam.

In most cases, toddlers who bang their heads or do other repetitive, self-stimulating activities are perfectly normal and don't have developmental problems. If your toddler seems otherwise healthy and happy, then it's likely to be a passing phase.

If the head banging has a sudden onset or seems to be getting more intense, have your toddler examined by her pediatrician. Some studies have linked head banging in some children with ear infections or teething pain, and the doctor may recommend medication or a mild painkiller to see if that helps. If your child habitually self-stimulates and also seems withdrawn or lacking in social relatedness, she could be showing early signs of developmental problems or autism, and your health-care provider can help rule out these causes, or suggest ways to get your child formally assessed.

If you're open to alternative treatments, a massage therapist or chiropractor experienced in treating children may also be able to pinpoint contracted muscles or jaw or spine misalignment, which could be the underlying cause for the head banging.

If the head banging is purely behavioral, address it as you would any other behavioral issue (you'll find tips a little bit later in the chapter). But if it's a mask for some other medical issue, (1) consider giving your toddler lots of vigorous physical exercise so she is tired at bedtime and has less energy to invest in head banging. (2) Invest some time in the rhythmic stimulation that seems to make her feel better, such as swinging back and forth, to supplement your child's strong drive for vestibular stimulation. A child-sized rocker or a small round trampoline that's near to the floor may do the trick as well. (3) Make head banging harder to achieve by padding your toddler's bed or crib.

Temper Tantrums

Temper tantrums, that dreaded crying, screaming, and flailing on the floor, are frequent events for toddlers, and they happen equally among boys and girls. Typically, these sudden meltdowns appear at around 18 months and gradually phase out as children near the 3-year mark. This happens to be the same time that their expressive skills improve.

Tantrums aren't necessarily misbehavior, but a healthy release of stress and frustration that toddlers feel during the stage before they master self-control and language skills. They are part of the stage of learning self-expression and trying to figure out alternative ways to let off steam.

Some researchers believe that tantrums could help to lower toddlers' blood pressure, and to excrete stress-related chemicals from the body through tears to restore the body's chemical balance. (Who knew?)

Sometimes parents inadvertently reinforce temper tantrums by rewarding their tantruming tots with lots of attention or by giving in to a child's demands.

Some children's tantrums worsen when they start giving up their naps. Others act out more when they are stressed, whether from changes in child care, the eruption of family crises, or the arrival of a new sibling—all of which may stress a toddler and encourage him to think his parents are withdrawing their attention and affection.

Oncoming illness or other physical problems, such as poor nutrition, lack of sufficient sleep, and allergies or anemia, can also cause a child to tantrum. Finally, some toddlers simply don't manage stress very well and are more vulnerable to emotional meltdowns than others. Some children may be very mild protestors and seldom have meltdowns while others may pull out all the stops, more than once a day.

A TYPICAL TANTRUM CYCLE

Like other forms of toddler behavior, tantrums have predictable cycles if you look closely.

Your child may start out normal and balanced. Life is relatively calm, your child is reasonably cooperative, and you both can go about your usual business. But then the rising tension becomes obvious, and indicates that a meltdown could be coming. Some children erupt in a nanosecond, while others build up more slowly. A full-blown tantrum ensues. Your child cries or screams, is loud and dramatic, and may flail or fall onto the floor. Trying to intervene, soothe, or threaten punishment only intensifies and prolongs the tantrum.

Finally, there is a recovery phase. The storm has passed and now your child may be whimpering, breathing irregularly, or hiccupping, and she may have swollen, red eyes and may not want to talk.

Handling Toddler Behaviors

Most parents of toddlers agree that having some very basic rules in place are helpful in preventing chaos and making life easier on everyone. Rather than being a negative experience for your toddler, setting rules and limits can help her to feel secure, noticed, and protected. Consistently enforced, rules can give your toddler predictable boundaries and send her clear signals about what is permissible and what is unacceptable, even if she forgets them at times or repeats the same errors over and over. When your child can predict how you're going to respond to a certain behavior, she eventually can self-assess behavior and decide whether she wants to act on an idea. Bingo—you've accomplished a primary goal of parenting.

But let's not get ahead of ourselves. Let's take a closer look at rules and boundaries. For our purposes, there are two kinds.

LEVEL 1: THE ABSOLUTES

It helps to have different levels of rules. The Absolutes are the hard-and-fast rules that you plan to strongly enforce each and every time your child breaks them, even if she protests or cries. One of the reasons may be because there are serious safety issues involved.

Here are some examples of Absolutes:

- No standing on tables, chairs, and in grocery carts.
- Always hold my hand when we cross a parking lot or the street.
- Always ride in your car seat.
- No playing around the dishwasher.

LEVEL 2: THE NOT-SO-ABSOLUTES

These rules are more flexible, and you and the family can decide when to apply them. Sometimes whether to let certain behaviors slide is a judgment call, though be aware the more inconsistent you are about a rule, the more likely your toddler will test it. The acronym NTI can help you come up with a solution. Is this **N**egotiable? Is this a **T**eachable moment? Or is it **I**gnorable?

Your toddler balks at eating anything but certain cereals or pizza. You want her to have a balanced diet. Is this Negotiable, Teachable, or Ignorable? Chances are, you'll choose the third option. And chances are, your pediatrician will agree with you. Your toddler won't starve. As long as she's not losing weight, there is probably no cause for concern.

Here are some examples of Not-So-Absolutes:
- Balls are for throwing outside.
- No throwing books.
- No pulling the pet's tail or getting near its face.
- Bedtime is at 7:30 p.m.

Corrective Guidelines

There is a lot of advice out there on how to effectively parent. There are vibrant debates on all manner of parenting subjects. Is it discipline, punishment, correction, behavior modification, or some other euphemism? The bottom line is: You want your toddler to continue to grow and become a productive participant in society. Let's look at a couple common schools of thought before we give you our opinion on effective correction.

SPANKING

Spanking and other forms of physical punishment are hotly debated subjects among parents, child development experts, and even casual observers. Everyone has an opinion, and perhaps you already do, too.

Spanking advocates believe that an occasional spanking isn't likely to inflict any permanent damage on a toddler's psyche, and they feel that the sting of a quick swat to the bottom often works when words don't seem to.[2] Parents who were themselves spanked (not to be confused with beaten) in childhood sometimes gravitate toward using it with their children, because they feel they were actually kept in line with an occasional spanking.

Those opposed to spanking argue that corporal punishment may make children resentful or distressed, that it fails to model correct behavior, and that it teaches a child that physical aggression is an acceptable double standard that benefits grown-ups.

Current child development research is inconclusive. There are so many interpretations of what spanking is—whether it's done with a flat palm on a diapered bottom, striking a child on the wrist or other places on his body, or hitting her in the face. (For what it's worth, Merriam-Webster's dictionary defines a spank as a strike on the buttocks with an open hand.)

Studies tend to be vague, failing to determine how mild or harsh children's spankings were or the emotional context in which the spanking occurred. How often was a child spanked—several times a day, a couple of times a week, or rarely? And finally, the studies overlook the differing temperaments of children, which could affect children's reactions to spanking. For instance, an aggressive, highly active child is likely to respond to physical punishment differently than a sensitive and easily controlled one.[3]

If you're still weighing the odds, consider some of the arguments below and decide whether spanking is something you would consider in correcting your child's behavior.

ARGUMENTS FOR SPANKING	ARGUMENTS AGAINST SPANKING
It's fast. Usually, even a sound spanking takes only a few seconds of time.	**It's a short-term answer.** Toddlers are bound to repeat behaviors, whether they've been spanked or not.
It's easy to understand. A toddler who has limited verbal skills will understand the meaning of a spanking.	**It engenders mistrust.** When a parent handles a child physically, the child may become frightened and mistrusting rather than respectful.
It's effective. A spanking will quickly stop your toddler from doing something, at least for the moment.	**It doesn't teach positive behavior.** Spanking doesn't show a child how she is expected to behave. The focus is on punishing instead of guiding by example.
It's memorable. A child is more likely to remember a spanking incident than things you say to her.	**It is easy to overuse.** Routine spanking eventually loses its shock value, and sometimes that causes parents to do it longer and stronger, which could be physically and emotionally harmful to a child.
It's not abuse. A spanking to correct behavior is not the same as child abuse.	**It emphasizes unfairness.** The rule "I can hit you, but you can't hit me" could lead to confusion, anger, or aggression in a child.

TIME-OUTS

The time-out, also called the "time in" or "the naughty seat," is a popular discipline strategy was once reserved for use by British nannies. But now it's being applied to toddlers by parents, sometimes with mixed results. The definition of *time-out* is giving a child time away from reinforcement and attention. It basically imposes losses of freedom and interesting things to do, and it's usually accompanied by a strong message of disapproval for unwanted behavior.

Here are the basics:

• **Warning with statement of rule.** You issue a brief warning to stop what he's doing (unless your toddler is doing something hurtful and aggressive, then there's no warning). When a showdown is unavoidable, you express yourself clearly and firmly in as few words as possible what he's doing that needs to stop.

• **Go to time-out place.** Using the same, uninteresting place each time for time-outs, you physically escort your child there and sit her down: "Now you are going into time-out." The location could be a small cushion or chair in the corner of a room or a mat on the floor, always near where you are (but never behind a closed door or in her room). If she refuses, continue to physically guide her into the time-out place until she complies. Be firm.

- **Time the time-out.** Using an oven timer or other device, the time-out lasts about a minute per year of your child's age (so, 3 minutes for a 3-year-old), or sooner if your child calms down and apologizes.

- **Accept an apology.** Once the bell has rung and the time-out has ended, you then ask your child to apologize for what she's done, verbally guiding her if necessary: *Say I'm sorry.* Ask her why she's sorry, and help her verbalize what she did that broke the rules.

- **Make amends.** Offer her a hug, show affection, and give positive reinforcement for the first neutral or positive thing she does after that.

You may want to consider some of the arguments below and decide whether you want to routinely use time-out with your toddler.

ARGUMENTS FOR TIME-OUT	ARGUMENTS AGAINST TIME-OUT
It's a time-out for you, too. A time-out can potentially give you a brief time to collect yourself.	**It can require a lot of time.** If your toddler is resistant to comply with time-outs, you could end up spending a lot of time correcting and re-correcting behavior.
It tests toddler independence. Testing her will against yours could be considered a practice run for building self-confidence and autonomy.	**It tests toddler thinking.** Children under 3 have trouble comprehending that someone else could feel differently than they do in a given situation. If your toddler feels a compelling anger toward you, or that she doesn't love you any longer, she expects that you feel exactly the same, which can be upsetting.
It can be effective. If you have an amenable child who wants your approval, time-outs can be an efficient and effective way to modify your toddler's behavior.	**It can backfire.** If you have a highly active child who ignores your admonitions, the time-out can turn into a power struggle, involving hitting, chasing, and frustration. Over time, time-outs become old hat and aren't as effective.

PRAISE AND ITS PITFALLS

It's clear from research that an atmosphere of warmth, caring, and positive parental support builds the strongest and most resilient children. Sometimes parents can get caught in being too negative or too critical of their children, pointing out their mistakes and relentlessly trying to correct their behaviors through punishment or scolding.

It's also possible to err in the opposite direction by piling heaps of praise on children. It's true that lots of praise can help a toddler feel noticed and appreciated, and that might put her in a more cooperative frame of mind. But too much praise can sometimes have an opposite effect and interfere with a child's internal compass that tells her what's "good" and what's

"bad." Exaggerated praise not only isn't genuine, it's also not realistic, which could widen the distance between your toddler's reality and your own.

Dr. Thomas Gordon, pioneering parenting expert and author of *P.E.T.: Parent Effectiveness Training*, believed that children who are continuously showered with rewards by their parents— through praise, awards, candy, ice cream, and other treats—become overly dependent upon parental feedback and rewards. In the real world, they become anxious and concerned about looking good and never making mistakes. Rather than being able to become deeply absorbed in what they are doing, they constantly look up to check that they have someone else's approval, stifling their own ability to savor their own accomplishments.

TIP

Save praise for when it is a spontaneous and sincere response to something that is truly "wow worthy."

TIP

Tantrum pointers: Head it off, stay calm, distance yourself to wait it out, and don't reward to placate.

TIP

The most effective behavior modification approaches are those that teach a child what parents want her to do, not those that punish her for what she does.

ARGUMENTS FOR PRAISE	ARGUMENTS AGAINST PRAISE
It's reassuring. It signals to your child that you are nearby and watching.	**It diminishes self-gratification.** Over time, an overpraised child may lose touch with her own motives and feelings. She could also increasingly crave compliments and become increasingly anxious about whether she is "right" or not.
It indicates attention. Whether negative or positive, toddlers crave attention, and praise delivers that.	**It can interrupt.** Praising your child may draw her concentration away from what she is doing, and distract her from resonating on the natural joy she's feeling about her actions.
It teaches language. Praise reinforces a positive vocabulary: "Way to go!" "High five!" "Good girl!"	**It may confuse.** Does your toddler feel equally as excited about what she's doing as you seem to be? If what she's doing doesn't feel all that praiseworthy to her, then your praise may feel confusing, or it could simply pass over her head like extra static.

Politeness Pointers

Realistically, your toddler will get more of a grasp on "politenesses" (that is, saying *please* and *thank you*) around the time she starts going to preschool. Even then, all training is apt to fly out the window if she feels rushed or overcome with other, more urgent demands for her attention. Effectively communicating in society is a process, not an event.

Even the most outgoing and confident toddlers often clam up in unfamiliar social encounters. Meeting new people and making eye contact with grown-ups could be off-putting or downright distressing. Perhaps the best tip for teaching manners is to relax, be sociable yourself, and let your toddler learn from your behavior rather than expecting much from her right now. We're pretty sure there are no Emily Post awards for toddlers.

However, shopping with a toddler can be a challenging, unavoidable, and exhausting task. Your tot wants something in every other aisle, from crackers to board books, candies to pet toys. Over time, it's enough to make you dread the trip.

Here are some basic tips to encourage polite conversation and make shopping with your toddler more bearable:

- **Plan ahead.** Create your grocery list ahead of time and organize it by aisles so you can quickly roll your cart through the store, rather than roaming back and forth because you've forgotten an item.
- **Time it carefully.** If there's no way you're able to shop on your own, time your trip for when the store is most likely to be empty: early in the week, at opening time, or late in the day when most people are eating dinner. Time the trip, too, for when your toddler is likely to be rested.
- **Feed before you leave.** Make sure he's not hungry when you leave for the store and take along a cup of water, snacks, or a necklace of Cheerios on an elastic string to gnaw on.
- **Set up rules.** Prepare your toddler for shopping with you by laying out a couple basic rules. Examples: *You have to ride in the cart*, or *Only one treat*, or something similar that makes sense to you.
- **Invite her to help.** While she's safely strapped in the cart, give your toddler specific tasks that you know she can handle. Let her hold objects or put them down into the cart for you. Invite her to choose between two apples, two bananas, or to make other simple selections.
- **Make the cart interesting.** A fabric cart protector available online or one with toys sewn on may make the ride more interesting and pleasant. Fasten stroller toys on a chain so she has something to occupy herself that she can't throw overboard.

- **Consider a backpack.** If your child is hard to manage while sitting in a grocery cart, consider using a framed child carrier. It'll take up a lot of room in the shopping cart, but it'll keep her restrained and allow her a birds-eye view of everything that's going on.
- **Use shopping for teaching.** The supermarket is a great place to model polite behavior. Liberally use *please* and *thank you* to demonstrate how to handle the give-and-take of objects and favors.
- **Sort groceries at the checkout counter.** To make your arrival home easier, group cold items together, and canned goods and boxed items in separate bags. When you arrive home, put away the frozen and refrigerated items and postpone the rest until later if your child needs attention or it's time to start a meal.
- **Praise for success.** On the way home, talk with your child about all of the positive things she did to help you with shopping. So long as you don't overdo the praise, it can be a positive motivator. (See page 71 for caveats about praise.)

Communicating with a Toddler

When it comes to communicating effectively with your toddler, it helps to understand that her world is much different than yours. Wonderfully, as she ages her communication skills and willingness to cooperate will improve. Rather than inundating your toddler with too many changes all at once, choose just one skill to work on at a time. Expect a learning curve, a "one-step-forward, two-steps-backward" progression for learning new skills. And in meantime, here are some practical ideas for managing your little "young and restless" star.

- **Move in close.** Get close, touch her on shoulder, and ask her to look at you before saying something important.
- **Speak her name.** No other word has quite the pulling strength of her own name for getting his attention. No need to yell: A low, calm voice should do.
- **Keep it short and simple.** Use a few clear words for making your point. Model what you want. Invite her to try.
- **Make it fun.** When delivering a lesson, convey enthusiasm as if you are presenting an exciting new game. If she appears uninterested and distracted, or doesn't respond, try again later.
- **Time it right.** The best time to try new things is when she's most likely to be cooperative, alert, and playful (such as after breakfast in the morning). Cut slack during the hours you know she's most likely to be tired, irritable, or hungry.

- **Make directions positive.** Rather than always telling her *Not* to do things, express the behaviors you're hoping for as simple, positive commands accompanied by hand gestures: "Walk slowly," "Sit here."
- **Ask questions.** Jump-start your toddler's thinking processes with questions: "Where is your ball?" "Can you close the door?"
- **Don't hover.** Rather than laying out a series of commands for her to follow and constantly showering her with praise or corrections that tend to interrupt her when she is trying to concentrate, simply relax and observe what she's doing. Then describe what you're seeing in concrete terms: "I am going to pick up the ball and put it in the basket. What will you pick up?" "You're helping Mommy put the toys away, aren't you?"
- **Offer help with transitions.** Prepare her for transitions with a gentle warning: "Five more minutes to play, then we'll have lunch." Or offer her two simple options that make her feel she's got some decision power: "Do you want to go inside *now*, or in five minutes?"

TIP

For a list of behavior help by state, visit *www.findcounseling.com.*

Getting to Yes

Whatever happened to your charming and very amenable offspring who is now digging in her heels and deliberately defying you? What could have possibly gone wrong?

Actually, nothing! Your toddler is just trying out her wings as an independent, separate person. One of the greatest rewards of being an individual, it seems, is the power to say *no*. And your toddler will practice using this word on you . . . perhaps even as often as you use the word on her!

But take heart. Here are a dozen parent-tested, practical strategies to help you convert her *no* to a nod:

- **Encourage cooperation.** Give your toddler the most attention when she's being cooperative. Give the least attention when she's being difficult.

- **Use *no* less often.** Consciously cut back on the number of times you use the word *no*, and save it for serious warnings. You might consider delivering the *no* with a clap, both to get your toddler's attention and to make you consider the seriousness of the situation. (Or substitute "stop!" or "danger!" with the police officer's palm-up hand sign for "stop.")

- **Make life predictable.** Meeting her eating and sleeping needs at the same time every day can help stave off meltdowns triggered by hunger and fatigue.

- **Accept limit testing.** Try not to take your toddler's behavior as a personal affront. Her brain is hardwired for standing her ground and repeating the same experiments over and over. Stay calm, and simply help her move on.

- **Be gentle but firm.** Avoid asking questions that generate yes/no answers, such as "Do you want to go inside for lunch?" If she's having fun playing, you can guess what your toddler's response is likely to be. Instead, give several advance notices of an upcoming change, then just *do* it.

- **Use non-verbal correction if effective.** Your toddler is primed to pay attention to your gestures, facial expressions, and body language. Instead of making a big deal of minor misdeeds, try facial expressions, shaking your head, or other non-verbal messages of disapproval if your toddler seems to respond to them.

- **Redirect.** Diversion is a parent's number one toddler-shaping tool! Use her short attention span to your best advantage: Present a more enticing option than what she's into at the moment with a flourish of great excitement.

- **Use the simplest commands.** Don't flood your toddler with lots of verbiage. Use the fewest and simplest words possible for explaining what you are doing or what you want her to do. Examples: "Inside now!" "Walk slowly."

- **Limit options.** Two is the maximum number of choices your little one can handle at a time. Instead of asking, "What do you want for lunch today?" try asking, "Cheese sandwich or peanut butter sandwich?"

- **Minimize rules.** Put only a few simple rules in place that the whole family agrees to, and consistently enforce them. Say, for instance, "It's never okay to hurt others."
- **Be playful.** Make your requests in a conspiratorial whisper, speak in a high, squeaky voice, or pretend you're a puppet. Sometimes turning a request into a game improves the odds that the request will be honored without issue.
- **Keep perspective.** Remember, though unpredictable, the toddler years are a very important time in your child's development. Your toddler is probably going to prove that you have more patience than you thought you had.

From Don't to Do

Toddlers tend to hear strongly worded commands as something to DO. If you yell, "*Stop* running around the pool!" What is likely to register with your toddler is: "*Run* around the pool!" So, rather than telling her what you *don't* want her to do, try rephrasing what to DO:

INSTEAD OF SAYING THIS:	TRY SAYING THIS (WITH HAND GESTURES):
Don't run!	Walk slowly. (Fingers "walking" slowly)
Get down!	Put both feet on the floor. (Two fingers touching palm)
Don't hit!	Pat gently. (One hand patting the back of the other)
Don't yell!	Speak softly. (Pushing-down motion using one or both hands)
Don't touch that!	Look here. (Hands clasped)
Listen to me!	Look at my eyes. (Fingers of one hand pointing toward your eyes)
Don't bite!	Mouths are for eating and kissing. (Point to your puckering mouth)

Harnessing Toddler Power for Change

You can use the powerful forces of your toddler's age and personality to help create positive change in her life. Here's a chart of typical toddler behaviors with practical hints for how to turn them into positive behavior changes.

NEGATIVE BEHAVIOR	HOW TO CHANGE IT
Clingy, wants to sleep in your bed, distressed when feeling rejected	Encourage positive touches, "hug breaks," and lots of positive attention
Into everything, breaks things, plows headlong into unsafe situations	Consistently enforce boundaries with clarity and firmness
Impatient, low tolerance, easily upset when she doesn't get her way	Remove and redirect with short instructions in calm voice
Impulsive, ignores you, distracted by objects, sights, and sounds	Make eye contact, keep commands short and clear
Highly physical, constantly in motion, unable to settle down, resists car seat and high chair restraints	Daily, vigorous play, preferably outdoors, using brief time-outs (30 seconds to 1 minute) for unwanted behavior
Hypersensitive to others' body language, upset at unspoken stress or disapproval	Mirror upbeat attitude; deal with family conflicts after her bedtime
Ignores you and threats of discipline	Consistent, simple commands with exaggerated hand signals: "Sit here," "Get down," "Pat gently"
Throws tantrums, is frequently enraged	Safe distractions: "Would you like to hold my keys?" "Let's go outside!"
Sensitive to change, can't handle transitions, likely to revert to babylike behavior during changes in routine	Familiar daily routines, comfort objects, and rehearse roleplays for unfamiliar situations
Aggressive or socially inappropriate behaviors	Intervene immediately with restraint, using simple commands

NEGATIVE BEHAVIOR	HOW TO CHANGE IT
Territorial and possessive	Ask her permission to touch her things and model good behavior
Oppositional, won't cooperate, bangs head in frustration	Remain calm, ignoring if necessary, then distract
Overreaches physical and mental abilities, tries things that could lead to self-injury	Build up her decision-making power by giving two options: "Do you want this, or that?" and acknowledge attempts at new skills, allowing for controlled risk with close supervision of certain activities

Q & A

Q: When I try to discipline our 2-year-old, she just laughs at me. Yesterday, she smacked the dog in the head with a book and slapped me in the face. I've tried time-outs, but she runs away and starts his hitting all over again. What should I do?

A: Between 24 months and 30 months are the prime time for aggression, and some toddlers are more physical about it than others. They strike out to express their frustration or anger before they have the words yet to express their feelings. If you're the victim of a toddler's aggression, it's hard to hold back from returning the action just to "teach her a lesson." Don't. Hitting, biting, or kicking back only teach her that aggression is okay, but only for grown-ups. Instead, take a breath, state the rule that was broken, issue brief and understandable commands, and then follow through consistently. Read the guidelines offered in "Getting to Yes" in this chapter.

Q: My 17-month-old daughter is a little shy and doesn't like to be "smothered" by our very demonstrative out-of-town relatives. In fact, when they go to kiss her she turns her head and runs away. How can I teach her to be polite while respecting her need for space?

A: Typically, toddlers don't grasp grown-up standards of conduct or feel bound by them. Your daughter is simply acting normal for her age. You can help her to become more familiar with enthusiastic "hello" greetings. Hug her at the front door when you enter after being gone a while and comment: "It's so nice to HUG you! I love hugs!" Collect photos of relatives in an album along with their printed names and share your memories about them. Invite her to engage in brief conversations with relatives with the speakerphone on so you can monitor when she needs to hang up. When visitors come, allow your toddler some time to get used to new faces before she warms up. Having a few toys or her favorite books lined up on the coffee table might help encourage adult-to-child interactions with others. If you accept her needs and boundaries, it's likely your relatives will ease up and respect them, too.

Q: We want our son back! He used to be so easygoing, always smiling and happy. Now at 18 months he's turned into a little demon! He seems unhappy almost all the time and screams if he doesn't get his way. Where did we go wrong? Did we spoil him?

A: Believe it or not, your toddler is more frustrated than you are! He is getting a clear idea of who he is, what he likes, and what he doesn't like, but this awareness isn't matched by his ability to communicate his wishes with you. For example, your son may know that he wants the real glass, the one that you and Daddy use, his sip cup, and he needs it right now, but you don't appear to understand what he's asking for. Trying to explain why drinking from a glass isn't a good idea doesn't help him with his strong, unrelenting desire to get his hands on it.

It helps to understand that this is just a passing phase, and that you will get your son back (even better than before)! Meanwhile, make sure that he's getting plenty of time outdoors to get sunshine and let off steam, feed him protein-rich snacks every few hours to keep his blood sugar level stable, and try to remain calm and consistent without getting overly emotional about it, since at this stage he is learning by your example how to behave.

Q: Our daughter, who is nearly 3, is a great kid. She can be very polite and gentle, but she just doesn't follow directions very well. The teachers at her child-care center have told us that they have to ask her over and over to get her to do something. Is something wrong, or is this normal behavior for a girl her age?

A: Some children simply need to be reminded a few times before they are willing to leave something they're engaged in. There's also a remote possibility that your daughter could have a hearing problem or an auditory processing disorder that makes it hard for her to attend to things being said to her, especially when there is a lot of noise and distractions going on. If this is the case, talk with her teachers about giving her face-to-face directions so they're sure they have her undivided attention.

Also, share the teachers' concerns with your health-care provider, who will want to check your daughter's hearing and may be able to suggest a specialist for assessing whether there is a sensory processing problem. At home, try giving her only easy, one-step directions and then build from there with gentle reminders if she forgets what you've said. Keep her teachers informed that you are doing what you can to help find a solution to her inattention.

Language

Learning how to improve communication is a major task for a toddler. How your child uses facial expressions, gestures, sounds, and words to communicate with you and express his needs and wants are part of his personality and his burgeoning social skills. In this chapter, you'll find lots of practical suggestions for building your relationship together with words, including a brief section on baby sign language to help those parents who are interested in helping their toddlers learn how to do it.

Sometime between 12 months and 15 months most toddlers utter their first word, typically "Dada," followed later, with coaching, "Mama." Beyond that lies a whole new world of learning and exploring sounds and meanings. Suddenly your toddler will be interested in everything: babies, daddies and mommies, birds, bugs, trucks, dogs, rain and snow, and he will approach everything as a first-time traveler in the world.

Single words are your toddler's version of whole sentences. His utterances will carry their own unique spin, such as "nana" for banana, or "kiki" for kitty. It isn't perfect English, but he will use his words consistently over and over for the object or the person he's referring to. After that come two-word sentences, using only the two most important words that are needed, such as "Bye Dada," and "All done." At the same time your toddler will be developing his vocabulary, he's increasingly more interested in listening to what adults are saying.

This chapter is all about speaking, listening, reading, and language skills.

> **TIP**
>
> If you'd like more detailed information about the development of language, try Kenn Apel's *Beyond Baby Talk: From Sounds to Sentences.*

Stages in Language Learning

Since every child's speaking and language skills develop in different ways, use this chart as a general guideline for toddler communication.

AGE	LANGUAGE SKILL
12 months	Tries to use words or word fragments to communicate. May understand simple instructions, especially when parents' words and actions go with them. Practices making sounds. May gesture, such as pointing to a bottle or book. Mimics play actions, such as covering eyes when playing peekaboo.
18 months	Vocabulary of approximately 5 to 20 words. Uses mostly nouns: "doggie," "milk," "cookie." May repeat words over and over. Can follow simple commands when there is a gesture, such when you point and say, "Please bring me the cup." Mumbles to himself and uses nonsense jargon with feeling.
24 months	Vocabulary of about 150 to 300 words, and adds new words almost daily. Can follow simple directions and respond to "Show me your eyes" (nose, mouth, hair). Likes to look at books. Rhythm, volume, and pitch of words aren't well developed yet. May stutter when trying to talk too fast or lisp when trying to pronounce words that have "s" and "z," both usually disappear around age 4 ½.
36 months	Understands more than he can articulate. Vocabulary is 900 to 1,000 words. Says short, three-word sentences: "Me want juice!" Carries on brief conversations with playmates and tries to tell simple stories. Tries using plurals and past tenses, such as "Doggies gone."

Language Learning Starts Early

When you think about it, it's truly remarkable how elegantly a toddler masters his native tongue in such a short time—whether he is learning the complexities and peculiarities of English, Spanish, Chinese, Japanese, or Urdu.

Some experts suggest that the toddlerhood is the best time for learning a second language (when fluency is the goal). Though this is not yet a widely held belief, many parents choose this time to begin teaching a second language. Our thought is that you don't need to worry yourself if you're not actively coaching your toddler on anything but his native tongue. That's optional, and extra language skills can readily be mastered anytime during childhood (or later).

What may surprise you is that the foundation of your child's language skills was being built long before he was born. We now know that the capacity for human communication is built into babies' brains during pregnancy. Even as early as 24 weeks' gestation, some fetuses react to sounds: The sharper the sound, the stronger the baby's reaction. Three months before they arrive, a fetus is already tuned into his mother's voice, language, and rhythms.

Newborns arrive already preprogrammed to react more to higher-pitched female voices than to the deeper sounds of male voices, perhaps because that's what they've been listening to in utero. And they naturally gravitate toward the sounds of human voices. They know the difference between tones that mimic human sounds, gibberish, and real language.

Even very young babies move in response to their parents' language, and slow-motion cameras show that babies' movements synchronize to each word they hear at times when they are alert. Their movements are so rapid (measured in hundredths of a second) as to be unnoticeable to sleepy parents. For example, at the sound of a single word, a baby's head may move slightly to one side, his hip may shift positions, a shoulder may rotate inward, or a big toe may curl.

During the first month of life, babies begin with gentle cooing noises. Four-month-olds can detect statistical patterns in the way sounds go together in languages—theirs and others'—to determine the beginnings and endings of words. They will quickly get bored and stop listening to made-up or unfamiliar languages unless presented with new combinations of sounds. At about 6 months, they start babbling and repeating the same sounds over and over, such as "ba, ba, ba" or "da, da, da." Babbling soon turns into riffs of speech that sound a lot like your baby carrying on a conversation, followed by real words using clear consonant and vowel sequences that are unique to his native language.

Whether you know it or not, you've been a natural language teacher. The singsong way parents talk with their babies by slowing down their speech or stretching out and enunciating sounds melodically over two octaves is perfect for engaging babies and communicating emotions to them. And the way you have sequenced words and coupled words with pointing and gesturing are both a part of the elegant way you've already enhanced your baby's language learning.[1]

FROM "GA-GA" TO "HELLO, GOGGIE!"

As we mentioned earlier, a toddler's "real" words typically are uttered between 12 months and 15 months of age, though each toddler is different. Between 18 months and 24 months, his vocabulary will literally explode. Some precocious tots even master as many as twelve words a day!

Something really incredible is happening inside your toddler's head: He is beginning to understand language and symbolic communication, which allows him to convey thoughts to you through words. With a greater understanding of language, his sense of self as an individual, separate from you and others, starts to change, too, which is expressed by words such as "me" and "mine."

By 24 months, or 2 years, toddlers typically have a vocabulary of about 150 to 200 words.

While most 2-year-olds are pretty much on the same level when it comes to decoding language being spoken to them, the size of each child's vocabulary can vary widely. The majority of children this age will have roughly a fifty-word vocabulary, some may have

as many as two hundred words at their disposal, talk in simple sentences, or even sing the ABC song, but there's no need to fret if your toddler isn't that proficient yet. Language skills will even out over the long haul.

No matter how many words your toddler uses to speak, you're bound to find it exciting and sometimes humorous to observe his powers of expression. He may see his first caterpillar and tell you it's a "doggie," or he may consistently recognize the street where Nana lives.

Between 20 and 30 months, you can expect a huge burst in your toddler's vocabulary and communication skills—more rapid language development than any other time in his life!

During this remarkable phase, his vocabulary will suddenly leap from about 200 words to 1,200 by the time he reaches age 3. At that time, your burgeoning linguist will start applying grammar rules, using plurals and other complex language skills with the fury of a college student cramming for a language exam. Nearly everything he expresses will be understandable by you and others.

By age 4 your child will be remarkably adept at using his native language with everyone, including strangers, who will readily understand his communication.

HOW TODDLERS COMMUNICATE WITH ONE ANOTHER

Although babies and young toddlers may acknowledge one

another, their communications are mostly limited to gestures and facial expressions. During play, communication between toddlers ages 16 months to 32 months is more likely to be unspoken. They imitate one another to create mutual understanding. They communicate by using exaggerated movements, facial gestures, and voice inflections, and, occasionally, brief word exchanges.

Sometime between 18 months and 24 months your toddler may cue into the crying of another child, especially if the child is a companion. He may have a growing awareness of others' needs and intentions, but that will seldom be related to anything more than what's going on right at the moment.

By 29 months to 38 months, your toddler will start to carry on conversations that seem more mature, but as in the past, he will be more likely to use actions and gestures rather than words. As his language ability increases, his understanding of others' feelings and intentions will deepen, too, and you may glimpse moments when he seems to be processing experiences or memories beyond just what's happening in the here and now.

BOY-GIRL LANGUAGE DIFFERENCES

When it comes to mastering language, girls have a distinct advantage. In fact, at birth girls have about 11 percent more brain cells than boys do. The part of the brain devoted to language also matures faster in girls than in boys, too, so little girls typically start talking sooner. And, regardless of gender, firstborns tend to talk slightly sooner than their younger siblings, perhaps because parents have more time to coach them.

By 16 months of age, most boys can use about thirty words, while girls may be using nearly double that number. While your son will point and say, "Doggie," his twin sister could well be expressing, "Look, Mommy, it's a big dog!"

Preschool girls also tend to score better on tests that focus on expressive language, and they are more likely to use emotion words sooner, such as "love," "happy," and "sad." They're also are more likely to use language as a way of collaborating or solving problems. Boys, on the other hand, tend to be more action-oriented, although their passive understanding of language is roughly the same.

Parents appear to play a part in the language differences between girls and boys. When parents, mostly moms, were studied about how they interacted with their 2- and 3-year-old children, it was found that they used different language for boys than for girls. Moms of 2-year-olds tended to ask their daughters more open-ended questions and used longer, more complicated sentences with them.

When parents talked with their sons, they tended to be more directive and used simpler words. Parents of 3-year-olds have also been found to be more likely to limit their conversations to what's happening in the moment with their sons, but they'll start non-play conversations with their daughters, especially in situations that required help.

Are these communications styles different because parents have gender biases? Maybe. But it could also be that their ways of communicating worked best with the genders of their children.

When it comes to starting up conversations with other children, girls seem ahead of the game. A British study of children casually talking with one another in homes found that half of 30-month-old girls participated in conversational exchanges, but only one in three boys did so at the same age. By 36 months, 89 percent of girls were carrying on brief conversations compared to 60 percent of boys.[2]

Building Your Toddler's Vocabulary

There are lots of easy things you can do to help build your toddler's vocabulary. Most parents do them quite naturally in the process of everyday interactions. They repeat words over and over, ask their children to verbalize what they want (rather than throwing a fit), and correct his grammatical errors or offer instructions: "Open the door, Jason. Turn the knob. Push the door open. Thank you!"

Each day offers hundreds of opportunities for helping your toddler expand children's language skills. Here are some ideas for enriching your toddler's expressive skills:

- **Offer a running dialogue.** Simply talk naturally when you're together. He'll start picking up words and how language sounds from exposure to your steady stream of speech.
- **Go eye-to-eye.** Conversing with your child at his level—eye to eye—will send him a message that he's captured your complete attention. Frequently doing that will help to build his confidence, and, at the same time, it might help you to pay closer attention to his cues and what he has to say.

- **Label things.** Name objects and describe your activities as you go along. "Mommy is washing clothes. I am putting the detergent in the washing machine. Okay, now I'm turning the knob. Can you hear the washing machine?"
- **Help connect language and gestures.** Combine gestures with words. When he points at something he wants, help him by expressing what you think he's asking: "You want to drink from your cup?"
- **Expand his words.** Use his words and expand them. If your toddler points to a dog, you respond with, "I see! It's a big, white doggy." He points and says, "Get ball," you follow his model and rephrase in a whole sentence: "You want me to get the big, red ball?" Phrasing your response as a question invites him to express more to you.
- **Give advance notice.** Announce to your toddler what you're planning to do with him before you do it. "I am going to put you in your car seat. We are going to the store to buy groceries."

• **Express feelings.** Learning the words such as "happy," "sad," "mad," or "frustrated" can help your child use language instead of flailing or screaming to express himself. The best way to do that is by openly expressing feeling words: "Mommy feels very happy right now," "You must be feeling angry," and so on.

MAKING MAGIC WITH BOOKS

When you read to your toddler and share stories with him, you're helping to develop his love for language and how it sounds. Learning to listen to stories takes time and practice. As a baby, your toddler probably was more interested in throwing the book on the floor, grabbing it and holding the pages down so you couldn't turn them, talking over you while you were trying to read, and listening for a minute or less. As he ages, hopefully he will let you get on with the story, even if it's only four pages at one sitting.

Books for toddlers come in all shapes and sizes. There are cloth and board books for the transition months between babyhood and toddlerhood, activity books, pop-ups, bedtime favorites, object-naming books, alphabet and number books, and all varieties of newfangled tomes and old classics to interest even the most restless read-to-me kids.

The best book selections for toddlers have minimal words and lots of clear and realistic drawings. Pages aren't too busy or complicated, and stories are about easily identifiable people, animals, or objects. Dialog is brisk and lively and characters develop by what they do.

Humor is something toddlers love, but it needs be very literal, since children this age don't appreciate sarcasm or subtle humor. And it's simply too early for long, drawn-out fairy tales since your toddler's patience and imagination ability remain quite limited.

CLASSIC CHILDREN'S STORYBOOKS

Some stories are destined to become your child's favorites, and he will demand that you read them a hundred times before they're (finally) set aside for another option.

Here's a list of some time-honored classics that parents like and children ask for again and again:

• *Brown Bear, Brown Bear, What Do You See?* by Bill Martin Jr. (Eric Carle, Illustrator): Gentle, rhythmic repetition propels this board-book story through a menagerie of colorful animals, from a white dog to a black sheep.
• *Chicka Chicka Boom Boom* by Bill Martin Jr. and John Archambault (Lois Ehlert, Illustrator): Brilliant colors fill each polka-dot-bordered page on this alphabet journey. The rhymes are irresistible and fun: "A told B, and B told C, 'I'll meet you at the top of the coconut tree.'"
• *Good Night, Gorilla* by Peggy Rathman: Conveyed mostly in pictures, this story follows a

Read-to-Me Stages

AGE	BEHAVIOR
12 months	Views books as objects–something hard or soft, to be chewed, thrown, patted, and to entice grownups to make sounds. Able to listen to only one or two pages being read before getting distracted. May listen better while tooling around the room. Attempts to hold the page when parent tries to turn it. Babbles over parent's voice while being read to or tries to fiddle with parent's mouth. Board books may be manipulated like a toy and may distract while riding in the car or waiting for appointments.
18 months	Though outgrowing cloth and board baby books and ready to enjoy heartier fare, may sometimes still want the *Pat-the-Bunny* experience. Enjoys books as objects to carry around. Wants the same book read over and over. Enjoys books with animal sounds or those with recurring themes, such as the moon, a dog, or balls. May want to "read" to adult in gibberish, even if book is upside down or multiple pages are turned at once.
24 months	Wants to choose bedtime story. Enjoys books with simple rhymes, or story lines about other small children or animals. Responds to simple questions about pictures in a book: "Where's the cow?" May enjoy "reading" catalogs and junk mail inserts. May respond to simple stories to help with separation anxiety.
36 months	May be able to sit still for brief story times at the library or bookstore. Fills in the blanks for nursery rhymes. Asking toddler questions, such as "What do you think happened next?" may spark responses. May catch small reading "tricks," like giving a character the wrong name to see if he is paying attention. Books may be used to help in preparing for separations, dental appointments, travel, moving, and other life experiences.

weary watchman as he walks by the gorilla cage on his nightly rounds at the zoo. The gorilla answers with lots of mischief.

- *Go, Dog. Go!* by P. D. Eastman: Children love the simple, silly phrases about dogs of all kinds, including green dogs, dogs who like skis, and puppy love.
- *Goodnight Moon* by Margaret Wise Brown (Clement Hurd, Illustrator): This enduring (and endearing) childhood bedtime classic centers upon a young rabbit's good-night wishes for every object he sees. Also recommended by this author: *The Train to Timbuctoo.*
- *How Do Dinosaurs Say Goodnight?* by Jane Yolen (Mark Teague, Illustrator): An enjoyable story follows dinosaur children and their bedtime trials.
- *Moo, Baa, La La La!* by Sandra Boynton: Whimsical funny animals carry on with oddball antics, including three dancing pigs who sing "La La La." Also recommended by this author: *Hippos Go Berserk.*
- *Mr. Brown Can Moo! Can You?* by Dr. Seuss: The very serious and squinty Mr. Brown imitates everything from popping corks to klopping horses and invites everyone to join him in the fun.
- *Owl Babies* by Martin Waddell (Patrick Benson, Illustrator): Three little owls worry that their mama won't come back, but she does. This sweet story helps reinforce to kids that mama might not be there, but she'll be back soon!
- *Pat the Bunny* by Dorothy Kunhardt: A touchy-feely classic for babies through preschoolers that invites petting the bunny's soft fur on one page, feeling daddy's scratchy face on another, and other textural experiences.
- *The Napping House* by Audrey Wood (Don Wood, Illustrator): A granny sleeps in her cozy little bed. She is joined by her grandson, a dozing dog, a snoozing cat, a slumbering mouse, and a flea that causes quite a commotion.
- *The Very Hungry Caterpillar* by Eric Carle: A ravenous caterpillar eats his way through the days of the week, from Monday to Sunday, then he spins a cocoon and is transformed to a beautiful butterfly after two weeks.

HAVING FUN WITH READING

Here are some playful things to do with your toddler to help prepare him for reading on his own later:

- **Use your finger.** If you follow along with your finger as you read, your toddler will start to notice the text, and you may soon discover him "reading" books using his own repetitive sounds while dutifully pointing out the words as he tries to mimic how they sound.
- **Make the book his.** Toddlers love their own names. Write "this book belongs to" with your child's name at the front of his book and read that at the beginning of every reading session. Or buy books, available by mail and online, that print your child's name into the story.
- **Use pregnant pauses.** Once your toddler has insisted on

having the same book read to him over and over, pause occasionally and invite him to fill in the blanks. Don't correct him if his words aren't completely on target. The idea is just to keep him involved in the story.

- **Ask good questions.** Rather than reading a book from start to finish, consider stopping to ask questions that will prompt your older toddler to provide answers: "What does the cow say?" "Where did the dog go?" "Where is his mommy?" "Is it daytime or nighttime?" Help him start thinking about cause and effect: "What's going to happen next?"
- **Look for rhymes.** Your child may enjoy learning sound words like "boom" or "moon." Copy the word on a card, draw a simple picture of it, and invite your child to compare the word on the card with the word in his book.
- **Follow story obsessions.** Whether your toddler becomes obsessed with the moon, fairies, or bears, help him expand his repertoire by asking the children's librarian at your local library for other book titles that go with his favorite theme.

The Art of Weaving a Bedtime Tale

Telling stories is a great way to promote your child's language abilities. Parents have been telling their children stories of one kind or another since beginning of civilization.

It's easy to see why: Storytelling can stimulate, educate, entertain, and reassure toddlers and young children. And it's a pleasant, relaxed way for busy parents to set the tone for bedtime.

Bedtime tales mean a great deal to a child. Made-up stories don't need to be long or elaborate. What really matters is the undivided attention your toddler gets from you, despite your busy life.

There are many folktales and stories from the past that are so good in the retelling that they can be pulled out and used over and over. With toddlers' limited attention span, bedtime stories need to be simple, short tales. Consider making up a story about an animal with the same name as your child then build a continuing saga about the main character and his friends. Or try making up adventures of various farm animals with clever names. Your child can supply the sound effects. What matters most to your child is your willingness to spend a few extra minutes of together time with him each night, creating fun, imaginative adventures.

Here's one way to start your story: "Once upon a time there was a little rabbit who decided to go for a hop in the woods because it was such a lovely day. No sooner had he started out than Mr. Squirrel scampered down a tree and said, 'May I come, too?' Well, Mr. Rabbit and Mr. Squirrel soon met Mr. Raccoon, who said, 'Maybe there will be good things to eat along the way. May I come along?' . . ." and you're off and running.

The child who hears custom, just-for-you stories eventually will jump in and start adding details as his language abilities improve, and in time he may start making up stories on his own with you as his audience. You can invite others in the family to help you in the storytelling. You might be surprised at what he'll come up with! Be sure to write them down for posterity's sake.

Storytelling is fun both for you and your children, but you also are learning a lot about your child's individual qualities. Stories also give you a chance to learn more about your child's sense of humor and also what scares him. Ultimately, there will come a day when your young one will proudly say, "Let me tell you a story this time."

Creating Your Own Toddler Books

One way to have fun with your 2- or 3-year-old is to create homemade books together—one-of-a-kind originals. Early books can be made of pictures that you've clipped from magazines or images you've printed out from the Internet. Invite your toddler to glue them onto hole-punched pages that can be tied together with colorful yarn.

Once your toddler acquires better scribbling skills, you can invite him to add his own artful creations using crayons or nontoxic markers. Toddlers are so proud of these early creations, and they can make great keepsakes for relatives.

Snap candid photographs of your toddler peeking out from under the bed, peering out from behind a chair, wrapped in clothes in the closet, or doing other silly things. Show him playing hide-and-seek with other family members, petting the dog, having a picnic together, sitting on Grandpa's lap. Create hand-printed or computer-generated captions to go with the snapshots.

You can use these homemade books the same way you would use a traditional book to prepare your toddler for the arrival of a new baby, for instance, or a move to a new home, an upcoming vacation, or other change. If possible, illustrate the book with your own drawings while your toddler watches, or use photographs you find in magazines or printed from the Internet.

If you enjoy scrapbooking, consider creating an enduring, personalized book for your toddler to look at over and over. For a fee, online sites such as Kodak (*www. kodak.com*) and Shutterfly (*www. shutterfly.com*) create library-quality, bound photo books that are available in a huge array of colors, patterns, sizes, and formats, such as preformatted ABC books that use pictures of your toddler with your unique captions.

Later on, you may be able to nudge your child to use story making as a way of processing life events. He may thrive on creating and repeating stories that circle around events that have frightened him, about making new friends, or describing the imaginary world of monsters that live in the closet at night that could help him feel less afraid.

Should You Teach Your Toddler to Read?

The Internet is filled with written accounts and videos by parents bragging about how their little Jennifers and Jasons have memorized words using multimedia programs purchased from infomercials: "Look how my 3-year-old can now read a whole book by himself!" Other parents are disappointed by the programs, when they invested $50 to more than $200 only to discover that toddlers refused to cooperate or found them boring.

Whether or not to coach young toddlers to read is hotly debated among parents and early childhood teachers.

One of the concerns expressed by reading experts is that children using these programs are only learning to "perform" memorized words to get approval and praise from parents, but that the same children could become flummoxed or anxious when they later encounter unfamiliar words and haven't acquired the skills for decoding them.

Parents who use early-reading programs argue that young children are more open to learning at this stage when their behavior is so moldable, and reading now will give them a leg up later when they enter formal education.

If you want to start your toddler on the road to reading but don't want to invest in pricey programs, borrow free materials to enrich your child's pre-reading experiences from your local library. (Your library also may have electronic versions of books that have a read-to-me option). You can also access no-cost, online videos and podcasts that combine graphics, alphabets, and animal sounds in brief phonics lessons.

> **TIP**
>
> Alphabet magnets might seem attractive, but they are a choking hazard.

Baby Sign Language

While babies and toddlers ardently want to communicate their needs and wishes to their parents, sometimes they can't do it very easily because their ability to speak lags behind their ability to think and visualize what they want. (Your toddler's hand-eye coordination also develops earlier than his ability to speak

does.) One way to help your child communicate is to teach him some basic sign language to help him express himself, particularly if he is experiencing any communication delays.

Just as toddlers "talk" with one another using gestures and body language, you can communicate with your toddler in a similar way—not just with words. Hand gestures, body language, and other expressions work well. (Throughout this book we suggest coupling simple hand gestures with words to deliver important messages to your toddler, such as "Stop" and "Don't bite.")

Learning baby signs, starting as early as 8 months of age, usually begins with a basic vocabulary of three to five signs. Words are usually used along with the signing to encourage the child to practice speaking the words for the signs. For starters, simple signs are used to represent common words such as "eat," "sleep," "play," and "cookie."

Some parents believe that giving their toddlers this physical outlet for communication helps to lower their children's levels of frustration and reduces tantrums. They also say that by enabling their children to communicate more precisely, their toddlers seemed to feel a sense of accomplishment and satisfaction over their improved relational skills.

Some studies appear to demonstrate that babies and children taught to sign end up with larger vocabularies and more advanced learning skills than their peers, and better parent-child communication and better focus. What's not clear, though, is whether children who spent the same amount of time doing enriching, fun activities and actively sharing conversations with their parents might show similar gains.[3]

A variety of books and DVDs are available for parents for teaching signing, and most libraries carry a few titles. Video signing demonstrations with babies and toddlers can also be found online.

Q & A

Q: Our daughter is about to turn 3, and she has a huge vocabulary, but she has trouble saying the letter S. She uses her tongue instead of her teeth to make the sound, and it comes out like a "th" sound, like "thnake" for "snake." Should I worry?

A: The S sound often takes the longest to figure out, and some children don't master it until they are 6 or 7 years old. If she can correctly pronounce other sounds, such as "ch" (as in chocolate), "sh" (as in should), and "th" (as in this and that), the chances are very good that she will outgrow it. The "s" and "th" sounds are really almost the same sounds except for tongue position. It's better not to make her say it right, as it might only make her self-conscious. She'll figure it out on her own. (Some children at this age also stutter, and they'll usually outgrow that, too.)

Q: My son is 18 months old and he seems really frustrated when he tries to talk. He'll try to get the words out and then just clam up and not talk at all. I've tried to help him learn new words, but he just shakes his head "*no!*" and doesn't want to have anything to do with it. Is this typical, and at what point should I speak to my pediatrician about language delays?

A: Not to worry! How quickly each child masters language skills is unique to the child. Some children appear to invest all their energy in mastering physical skills at the cost of slowing down to learn words and speaking. It's important not to pressure him into expressing language if he's not ready. Instead, just keep a running dialog going with him about what you're doing—"I'm going to cook dinner," "Here's your milk," "We're going to ride in the car"—so that he's constantly surrounded by words and intonations. Also, instead of watching television, spend "talking" time with him, such as by joining him on the floor while he's playing with toys or getting outside to look at the world of nature. If he doesn't seem to hear you or respond to his name when you call, and he can't see you, your pediatrician needs to check out his hearing and responsiveness to ensure he's still on track.

> **TIP**
>
> While grocery shopping, show your toddler the words on packages, then ask him to help you pick out items.

> **TIP**
>
> Singing simple children's songs, like the ABC song, is a great way to enhance your child's language skills.

6

Play

Lambs gambol, kittens leap and pounce, calves cavort, and toddlers play. Whether it's making a toy car roll across the floor, pushing knobs on an activity center, opening and closing cabinet doors, pulling books off the shelf, dumping clothes out of the laundry basket, or pulling the dog's tail—to a toddler, it's all in great fun.

Sometimes play can be creative, like making something new— squishing clay into a shape, making paint colors go on a piece of paper with your hands, or stacking blocks so they make a tower. And at other times, play offers a chance to learn the give-and-take of interacting with other children.

The nature of play is that it is spontaneous and in the moment. It mostly arises out of a toddler's "what if?" attitude: "What if I roll this toy on the floor?" "Under the couch?" "Toss it down the stairs?" "Put it on the shelf?" "Drop it in the toilet and pull the handle down?"

What play *isn't* to a toddler:

Having to do something someone else makes you do, like being made to "share" by handing over your prized dump truck or doll to another child, being told to "go play" because Dad is on the telephone and he wants you not to bother him, being made to pick up toys when you have trouble understanding what you're being asked to do or remembering what comes next, or having to sit still or do something "educational" just because someone else thinks it will be good for you later.

When it comes to playing, more is going on than meets the eye. Your toddler isn't simply enjoying himself, he is also getting lots of new information about others and his world, learning how to think, and be creative. You can just watch how his lightning-fast mind encounters something new and novel. He will approach something, home in on it, reach out to touch it, and pick it up, and then start his patting, pounding, smearing, pushing, pulling, or dropping it—his way of getting to know how things work.

During play sessions, your toddler's physical skills, and his ability to communicate and to think beyond just the present are all given a workout. In fact, play is such an essential part of learning that it has often been labeled "children's work." All the skills your toddler needs to master during this important stage in growth are built into his moments of intense exploration.

This chapter gives you a window on what is most likely to interest your toddler at any stage and gives you all sorts of ideas for ways of expanding play possibilities and enjoying fun times together.

Learning from Play

Playing is the main way that toddlers learn new skills. While he's having fun, he's learning important things about objects and other people, too, including the following:

- **The nature of objects.** During play, your toddler is in the process of actively figuring out how objects work: how to stack them, knock them over, hide them, and find them again. At the same time, he is learning that objects (as well as people) are unique and separate from himself.

- **Cause and effect.** Pouring, sifting, gluing, painting, squeezing, coloring—all these teach your little scientist about the qualities of materials and how they work. When he mixes, stacks, pours, and puts things in and takes them out of containers, he's in the process of learning about in and out, more and less, large and small, empty and full, and so on.

- **Music and rhythm.** Simple nursery rhymes and songs, banging things together, listening to lullabies and children's songs, and clapping and moving to music introduce your child to how music and rhythms work, which can help with communication, too.

- **Language.** Being read to, watching puppets, listening to language, pointing to pictures, naming animals and colors, pretend playing, and talking about what he's doing help to sharpen his thinking, memory, speaking, and attentiveness. (See more on language skills in Chapter 5.)

- **Being with others.** Your toddler may play better with older children and not be very interested in children his age, but he is still getting a chance to practice important social skills, including gesturing, taking turns, sharing, and negotiating for what he wants without upsetting his playmates.

- **"Stick-to-itiveness."** Block and toy stacking, putting away and pulling out, and finding missing toys sharpen his concentration skills, and help him learn how to chain one action after another, follow directions, and solve problems.

- **Body skills.** Moving around teaches him about his body, and his boundaries, and gives him more confidence in himself. Active play enhances your toddler's body skills and builds the groundwork for later gracefulness and athleticism. (More on building body skills in Chapter 2.)

Props for Play

As your toddler matures, his play becomes more sophisticated. Here are your toddler's play skills by age along with suggestions for toys and activities according to his age.

AGE	PLAY SKILLS	PLAY MATERIALS
12 to 14 months	Making noises and sounds	Music boxes and pull-string music makers Jack-in-the-box Noise-making activity centers CDs of children's songs and lullabies for relaxing or dancing Rattles and musical balls
	Pushing, pulling, throwing, and banging objects	Soft blocks and balls Stacking boxes and cups Pots, pans and lids, wooden spoons Board books for opening and closing Hand-sized toys for manipulating and hide-and-seek games
	Pretending	Toddler-friendly objects that mimic grown-up things: keys, cell phones, remote controls Dolls and stuffed animals
15 to 17 months	Climbing and swinging	Safe, toddler-scale indoor or outdoor play set, sandbox
	Imitating	Small broom, vacuum, lawn mower, wheelbarrow, or grocery cart Plastic tub for "washing" dishes Small wooden carpenter's bench with hammer and pegs

PROPS FOR PLAY (CONTINUED)

AGE	PLAY SKILLS	PLAY MATERIALS
15 to 17 months	Matching shapes	Simple sorting toys
		Stacking rings
		Large wooden puzzles with fat grippers
	Identifying	Picture books
		Enlarged family photos inside a stick-and-seal photo album
18 to 20 months	Stacking and building	Large cardboard bricks
		Large blocks and snap-together kits
	Drawing and simple art projects	Washable nontoxic crayons and markers with large sheets of plain newsprint
		Play dough (see recipe on page 113)
21 to 24 months	Art and music	Bubble-blowing toys
		Pudding or nontoxic, tempera-based finger paints
	More advanced pretending	Dolls with doll-sized stroller and high chair
		Stick horse
		Appliance box "playhouse"
		Dress-up clothes (hats, gloves, shoes, beads, glasses)
	Pre-reading	Picture books
		Simple (4 to 5 pieces) wooden puzzles
		Audio books with accompanying picture books
25 to 30 months	Sorting	Puzzles with large pieces or knobs
		Shoeboxes, clear containers, and old purses for sorting and storing small toys and objects
		Easy-to-open purses with carry handles or backpack
		Pants and jackets with large pockets for carrying things

AGE	PLAY SKILLS	PLAY MATERIALS
25 to 30 months	Advanced pre-reading	Large wooden alphabet letters in colors
		Simple storybooks with a plot
		Talking activity center
	Water playing	Bubble blowing ring and liquid
		Pitchers, measuring cups, buckets, and containers
	Moving around	Beanbags
		Toddler-sized ride-on toys
		Small wagon
		Swings and climbers
31 to 36 months	Learning about music	Sturdy, lightweight CD player/radio
		Pots and pans, pot lids, wooden spoons
		Toy or real piano, xylophone, flute
		Cardboard appliance boxes with cutout doors and windows
	Pretending and imitating	Toddler-sized kitchen or store
		Wooden- and plastic-wheeled toys and airplanes
		Other pretend-play props
		Kitchen tools such as big spoons (with and without holes), funnels, gelatin molds, and cookie cutters
	Collecting	Toddler-sized baskets with handles
		Rocks, shells

TIP

Store all art supplies in a closet in a clear plastic bin with a lid.

Television and Toddlers: Good or Bad?

Face it: At one time or another, most families use their television sets as a temporary entertainer for their kids. A 2003 Kaiser Family Foundation report found that on a typical day in the United States, 68 percent of all children under age 2 use screen media. Of those, 59 percent watch television, 42 percent watch a video or DVD, 5 percent use a computer, and 3 percent play video games (yes, at age 2 or younger).

The report estimates that 74 percent of all children under age 2 watch television every day, and more than one in four (26 percent) have televisions in their bedrooms. Toddlers averaged 2 hours and 5 minutes of screen time daily.[1] Surprisingly, the report also found that approximately 20 percent of 2- to 7-year-olds have televisions in their bedrooms—about 6 percent fewer than the 2-and-under age group.

We've already heard of reports that link TV watching with childhood obesity. Increasingly, marketers are targeting very young viewers with their sales pitches for toys and junk food, encouraging our children to demand products at younger and younger ages.

According to the American Academy of Pediatrics (AAP), kids in the United States are exposed to more than forty thousand commercials each year. From junk food, fast-food, and toy advertisements on kid-centered television networks to appealing promos on the backs of cereal boxes, product marketing inundates kids of all ages, wherever they turn. Almost half of the ads are for breakfast cereals, and about a fifth (or 1 in 5) are for fast-food restaurants.

For toddlers, the line between regular programming and commercials simply doesn't exist. Advertisers' disclaimers, such as sugar-loaded cereals being "*part* of a nutritious breakfast" go right over their heads (and often over the heads of grown-ups, too). Marketers count on young viewers asking for products that are visually associated with fun and happiness, and surveys show that toddlers as young as 18 months demand products they see advertised on commercial television.

A 2006 report of the Institute of Medicine (IOM) entitled *Food Marketing to Children and Youth: Threat or Opportunity?* concluded that current food and beverage marketing practices put children's long-term health at risk. It pointed a finger at high-calorie, low-nutrient snacks, fast foods, and sweetened drinks that could be connected to early-onset diet-related chronic diseases.

HOW MUCH TV IS TOO MUCH?

The AAP's position is that children under 2 years of age should not be exposed to television at all, and that children older than 2 not be allowed to watch more than 1 to 2 hours of quality (non-commercial) programming per day.[2] The AAP's recommendation rests on numerous studies that appear to show that television watching can negatively affect children's language development during this critical time of brain development.[3]

Pediatricians and child experts aren't worried so much about what television exposure does to young children as opposed to what it *doesn't* do.

A toddler glued to a screen is *not* talking and playing with his parents and other children, being read to, singing, dancing, or playing. He's not actively engaged by young children's primary sources for acquiring sophisticated communication and imagination skills. A young television viewer is also not actively exploring the dimensions of his world, something his brain needs for creating and defining neural pathways. Nor is he getting the vigorous exercise, preferably outdoors, that helps him build strong muscles and bones and further develop his physical coordination and agility.

A flickering screen is no substitute for natural sunlight that helps children's bodies to produce critical vitamin D and to regulate healthy sleep-wake patterns. And its flat, moving images can't ever come close to delivering the benefits of a healthy lifestyle that human contact and interaction brings.

A 2007 study conducted by Dr. Marina Krcmar and her associates at Wake Forest University tested how well toddlers learned language from popular children's programming such as *Teletubbies* versus language presented by live adults. The results? Real people beat the TV screen. In fact, toddlers younger than 22 months of age derived very little word acquisition from television word teaching.[4]

In 2010, researchers at the University of Montreal reported on the impact of television exposure at age 2 on academic performance later on. The study included more than 1,300 children. The study found that the more time toddlers spent watching TV, the more likely they were to experience a decrease in classroom engagement and math success, and an increase in sedentary lifestyle, body mass index, and victimization by classmates.[5]

Drawing upon a national sample of "heavy-television" homes, another study found that 35 percent of children from birth to 6 years live in homes in which the television is always on (or most of the time), even when no one is directly watching.

Daniel Anderson, a researcher at the University of Massachusetts, found that when adult television shows were played in the background, the play episodes of 12-, 24-, and 36-month-old children were about half as long as when the television was turned off. Television reduced the children's focused attention by about 75 percent, and instead of being able to concentrate on what they were doing, the children skipped from one toy to another.[6]

Even though most parents are convinced that educational

television shows, videos, and DVDs will help to make their offspring smarter, research shows a different result. For instance, researchers from the Children's Hospital in Boston and Harvard Medical School found no evidence of learning benefits for babies and toddlers from watching TV during the first 2 years of life.

Advertising for baby learning products such as Baby Genius, Brainy Baby, and Baby Einstein give the impression that their products encourage discovery and inspire learning in children. But researchers from the University of Washington and Seattle Children's Hospital Research Institute found that baby-coaching DVDs and videos not only are not beneficial, but they may even be harmful. Babies and toddlers under age 2 who watched them understood fewer words than those who didn't watch. Those who spent the most time watching TV had lower language and visual-motor skills by the time they reached age 3.

That's not to say that *all* television viewing is bad, but there are serious limitations for toddlers. Children's educational television may help a child with basic alphabet and number skills, or teach concepts such as "over" and "under," "big" and "small." Later on, television may help to enrich preschoolers' and grade-school children's understanding of nature, wildlife, and other things about the world. But in this case, more is not better. It's best to stick to the AAP guidelines and restrict or limit toddlers' exposure to television.

TIP

According to the AAP, children under 2 years of age should not watch television at all, and children 2 and older should watch only 1 to 2 hours of non-commercial programming per day.

TELEVISION GUIDANCE

But we parents have to be realistic! Your toddler is likely going to watch some television, and you may even use a children's DVD once in awhile to temporarily occupy her.

If you decide to let your toddler spend time watching television, here are suggestions for keeping a handle on it:

• **Get the good stuff in first.** Provide your toddler with opportunities for talking, singing, and playing with you, vigorous outdoor exercise, and improving hand-eye coordination (fine motor skills). Allow television only when all of your toddler's needs for active engagement have been met, and for strictly limited amounts of time.

• **Make viewing a "together" time.** Use television watching as an opportunity for interacting with your child and asking questions. Keep the mute button on your remote control at your fingertips for silencing commercials ("Oops! Here comes a commercial!") and use the quiet breaks for talking about what the two of you are watching. Or record programs and fast-forward through the commercials.

- **Declare a quiet zone.** Don't keep the television running for background noise or to keep you and your toddler company. Since it interferes with both toddler and adult sleep patterns, ban sets from bedrooms. Declare mealtimes and pre-bedtime hours as TV-free times to help your toddler settle down for sleep.
- **Don't use viewing as a bribe.** Using television viewing as a reward for good behavior and withholding it for bad behavior may be a convenient short-term solution. But in the long term, it may make watching TV seem more valuable to your child than it should be.
- **Be aware.** Be conscious of how background television sounds may affect your toddler's concentration and play. Stick to selected age-appropriate videos and public television rather than commercial programming that could be delivering messages you don't want. Watch shows together and talk about them during breaks.

Playing with Other Kids

Playing with other children isn't just about handling toys; it's also about what happens during playtime. Between 10 months and 24 months of age, your toddler will start to show signs of enjoying being around other children. He'll smile, and he'll make sounds and gestures when another child gets close that tell you he's having a good time.

Having the chance to interact with another child can be exciting. In fact, toddlers from 17 months to 36 months are more apt to laugh and smile at their siblings or playmates their own age than they do for their parents.[7] But some toddlers can become upset or fearful when other toddlers invade their territory.

Once your toddler reaches around 33 months, he's likely to be more attracted to playing with his older siblings or other children than with you.[8] Don't feel rejected: Other children are simply fast-moving, unpredictable, and *interesting*.[9] Toddlers with the best sharing vocabularies are more likely to have learned how to express their desires using language from their parents or siblings.

British researchers listened in on how toddlers ages 12 months to 45 months communicated with similar-aged friends who were playing together at home.[10] Toddlers 18 months and younger simply weren't able to carry on true conversations in which both parties conversed. Instead, they carried on more basic exchanges, or what the researchers called "proto-conversations."

One toddler would say "here," and pass a toy to the other, who would accept it. Or one child would make a move, such as reaching out to grab a toy being held by the other, who might respond with an adamant "No!" Occasionally a toddler would use "my" or "mine" when another child tried to take something away from him. Playmates showed physical aggression by grabbing objects held by another child, or they might hit the other child when resources, such as toys, food, or objects, had to be shared.

By 24 months, fewer than half (less than 40 percent) of 24-month-old toddlers could carry on conversations with one another. After 24 months, toddlers, especially girls, began to use "my" and "mine" when they were about to share something, and it was during that 24- to 36-month stage that simple conversational exchanges were used.

Between 30 and 36 months, increasingly more toddlers understood and the verbalized possessive words "my" and "mine" in their conversations with other children. While no 18-month-olds could use words such as "have" and "got" to show ownership, half of 36-month-olds made reference to "having" objects. And sometimes older toddlers used words like "want" and "need," such as "I *want* the toy!" or "I *need* that car!"

No matter the age, it's important to stay pretty close to your playing toddler. Having "his" grown-up nearby and in sight can help to make your toddler's early forays with other playmates more fun than foul. You may be able to model interesting things to do, and you can also stand guard to make sure no one gets grabbed, knocked over, bitten, or hurt.

Playtime and Sharing

While grown-ups generally have a clear set of rules about how children are supposed to play with other children, such as being polite, saying please, and being nice to others and willing to hand over a toy to keep another child happy, toddlers operate under an entirely different set of rules.

When it's time to play, conflicts with other children are bound to arise. Usually it involves a toddler's not wanting to share his toys or other belongings. When battles erupt between a toddler and other children, they're usually over who has ownership rights over what.

These disagreements are typically acted out physically with clinging to the toy, trying to pull it away from another child, and hitting, biting, or crying when one child feels thwarted. These conflicts tend to peak during the 24- to 30-month age range. When they become better at communicating with gestures and words, toddlers start to calm down.

According to your little toddler attorney, the Law of Possession might go something like this: "If I have played with a toy, it's mine." Or it might be: "If I get my hands on it, it's *mine*, and nobody is allowed to take it away from me."

Your youngster will immediately try to guard a ball, a ride-on toy, or another desirable object with any means at his disposal—particularly if he thinks another child has designs on it. From his limited point of view, being asked to hand over a toy to another child is an outrageous request, comparable to someone trying to force you to hand over the keys to your new car to a stranger so he can drive off with it. In his childlike way of thinking, what's his is *his*, and, for that matter, what's *theirs* should be his, too!

These conflicts arise out of your toddler's awakening understanding of the connection between people and possessions. Most toddlers younger than 24 months don't grasp that personal objects—toys, clothing, and so on—can be owned by particular people. As he nears his 36-month mark he will develop the understanding that his possessions are different from those belonging to you or others.[11]

It's not uncommon for preschoolers and older children to have conflicts about ownership. Around age 5, though, your child will probably figure out on his own how to use different strategies for independently settling those differences of opinion. Hopefully you'll get a chance to watch your child civilly negotiating with another child as they try to arrive at a compromise without pulling, grabbing, or hitting.

WAYS TO ENCOURAGE SHARING

Here are some simple things you can do to introduce the sharing concept to your child and his little playmates:

- **Offer one-on-one opportunities with other children.** The best way to learn how to share is by having experiences with other children. That's best done with only one other child in a controlled, quiet setting, rather than in a loud, rambunctious group, such as playgroups and birthday parties—that is, unless you're a skilled early childhood education teacher and trained in how to jump into the fracas to make peace.
- **Be prepared to step in.** When someone's being overly possessive, it takes being fast on your feet and the ability to come up with exciting, new options to attract a child out of the conflict.
- **Encourage "pseudo" sharing.** Invite your toddler to "show" his toy to another person— perhaps an older child or an adult—without actually having to relinquish it.
- **Fence 'em off.** One separating strategy for conflicts is to sit on the floor with your legs extended straight like a human fence between warring parties until things can cool down. It helps to have a handful of some other interesting toys to present in hopes of drawing up momentary peace between warring parties.
- **Model the behavior you want.** Make a big deal of sharing objects with your child: "Would you like to hold my keys? I will share them with you." "Mommy is sharing." "Look how Jennifer is sharing!" "Thank you for sharing." "It makes Mommy smile when you share."
- **Help him master sharing words.** Teach him new words for sharing, such as "mine," "yours,"

"got," "have," and "give." Even a simple sock puppet can engage your toddler briefly in "Here, take this," and "Can I have that?" concepts.

- **Play a simple sharing game.** Sort colored blocks or small toys with your toddler: "Mine . . . yours . . . mine . . . yours . . . share!" (Give one of yours to him). Repeat the cycle, then hold out your hand, say, "Share!" and wait for him to give you one of his. "Now, I will share with you! We are taking turns! Yayyy!"

Playful Pets

Most toddlers are entranced by animals. It's hard to resist a dog's wet, sniffing nose or a cat's swishing tail. Pets definitely attract a toddler's attention, and, fortunately, most know how to submit to toddler love when it's showered on them.

Sometimes pets' names are among the first words that a toddler speaks, and he will imitate words such as "go for a walk." He might enjoy watching dogs play, and going for a walk is good for exuberant toddlers, too.

Teaching your toddler to be gentle, kind, and caring with a pet can help him apply those feelings later toward other children and adults.

Toddlers can derive tremendous joy from watching the creatures in their house go about their daily antics. Your child may want to help care for animals, so give your child an easy job, such as pouring a cup of pet food into the dog's bowl. He may prefer to personally feed the pet every single morsel, one nibble at a time. Your toddler can also pick up the cat's empty water dish and help put it in the sink. He may be eager to help some more, so be sure to teach him to keep his hands out of animal food bowls and litter boxes.

Your toddler may want to imitate the way you groom your pet with a brush, but it may be best to avoid this, lest he hurt the animal by handling the brush or comb unskillfully.

PET SAFETY

The primary issue with toddlers and animals is making sure that your pet doesn't bite, scratch, or hurt your child. Sometimes a toddler's antics and his high-pitched voice can incite dogs to view them as playthings or prey, which could lead to nips, gnaws, or being jumped on and knocked over.

Your pet's safety is important, too. Now that your toddler is up and walking, he's capable of chasing, grabbing, and squeezing household pets, which can hurt them or incite them to bite or scratch in self-defense. Squeezing or sitting on a small animal, such as a hamster, guinea pig, or rabbit, could kill them.

Here are some tips for helping your toddler get along with household pets:

- **Demonstrate good pet handling.** Show your toddler how to slowly approach a pet from the side, and to gently stroke his head. Words, such as "easy," "gentle," or "nice" with demonstrations may help.

- **Enforce the no-no's.** Don't let your toddler pull tails or ears, poke at eyes, kick, or bother a pet who is eating or sleeping. Keep him away from the litter box or animal feces in the yard or sandbox.
- **Encourage play.** Your toddler may enjoy simple games with pets, such as fetch, blowing bubbles for your dog to chase (see recipe on page 113), or kicking around a ball, but adult supervision is important.
- **Create a pet retreat.** Dogs and cats need a place to retreat from being annoyed by a child, such as a crate or a perch that keeps your child out or that he can't reach. You may need to use a safety gate to distance your child from your pet so that he can rest and restore.
- **Exercise caution.** Granny's pooch may seem cute, but he could attack a curious child. Make rules about not getting near a possessive pet.

Let's Pretend!

Between 18 months and 36 months, your child will voluntarily begin to travel into the world of imagination and pretend play, which signals an important step in his development.

During the second year your toddler will start play-acting by pretending to drink from a cup or carrying on a conversation on his toy cell phone. He will become increasingly more driven by imagination. He'll be scared of evil monsters or pretend to be one himself, spin into a tooth fairy, become a growling dog or clawing cat, or don a cape and imagine he has superhuman powers. He may try to comb his hair with a ballpoint pen, pretend to nap only to pop right up with a grin, gently lay a teddy bear down to sleep and cover him up with a blankie, or push blocks or toy cars across the floor while making vroom-vroom sounds.

It used to be thought that young children couldn't tell the difference between reality and fantasy, but newer research suggests that children are very adept at telling the difference between what's real and what isn't. Your child's joy and giggles at pretending, his fake and his real cries, his knowing looks as he glances up at you in the midst of his imaginings, and the sheer drama of his actions are all signals that he's straddling two worlds on purpose and clearly understands the difference.

You can encourage your child's ability to pretend by doing things, such as coaching him to feed his favorite stuffed hippo with a spoon, putting it in a toy stroller for a walk, or snapping a bib around its neck. Waterproof dolls can be dumped in the tub for a scrub. Talking with your toddler as he plays, giving him feedback about what you see him doing, and asking him to describe his actions are ways to encourage his language and social skills.

Lots of toy commercials on television and in magazines might make you think that every child must have his own battery-powered, ride-on vehicle, cell phone, or toddler laptop. Even without all those brightly colored props, your toddler is going to get his imagination going without a single toy. You know this is true: From shoe boxes to wooden spoons, sticks to rocks—*anything* can and will be recruited as a play toy.

Some kinds of setups and play areas promote more dramatic play than others. Those that have a private, cavelike feel, such as being under a table covered with a sheet, being inside an appliance box with holes cut for windows and a door, or, being inside a plastic children's playhouse with entrances and exits are more likely to help your child with his pretending. Play props can encourage pretending, too, often better than toys can, so keeping a basket full of hats, gloves, scarves, capes, and other items can help to evoke pretend moments.

Moms and dads can help to encourage their children's imagination, too. One study found that mothers who engaged with their toddlers in pretend play produced children who quickly mastered how to do that, while the children of mothers who didn't showed more limited progress in acquiring imaginative skills.[14]

Older children can teach your toddler a thing or two as well. Studies show that playing with moms tended to be more reality-based and less imaginative (feeding a dolly or putting her to bed) than when they played with other children, which spurred their imaginative abilities onward. One study found that 17- to 20-month-olds who played with other children showed more creative and unusual uses for toys and other objects than those who didn't have that exposure to other children.

An older brother or sister is great for introducing 2- and 3-year-olds to superheroes, princesses, and other imaginary characters. These will help pave the way for your toddler's journey into the world of pretending that intensifies as he nears the 3-year mark.

35 Cures for Toddler Boredom

If you're having one of "those days" when you can't think of anything to do but mope around the house or turn on the TV to pass the time of day, try one of these quick pick-me-ups with your toddler (or refer to "Forty Fun Body Builders" in Chapter 2 for more ideas):

1. Play hide-and-seek.
2. Collect rocks and sticks in a basket.
3. Make homemade play dough (see recipe on page 113), or sacrifice a can of refrigerated biscuit dough for the sake of play.
4. If your toddler is 2 or older, together you can briefly watch dog, cat, or baby antics online or sing along with previews and samples of toddler music

online. (However, avoid this activity if your toddler is younger than 2.)

5. Build a playhouse or choo-choo out of a cardboard box.
6. Give your toddler a gentle piggy-back ride.
7. Pull out a quilt and lay it on the floor with lots of pillows, then look at a book together.
8. Play "post office" by putting junk mail in a cardboard box with a slot cut in the top.
9. Draw big lines and circles with thick chalk on concrete.
10. Talk or toot horns through a paper towel tube.
11. Kiss the clean bathroom mirror wearing lipstick.
12. Make a shoebox train for toys.
13. Play with a flashlight inside a table "tent" covered with a sheet or blanket.
14. Fingerpaint using instant pudding on a tray or rimmed baking pan.
15. Paint the bathtub with big painters' brushes and water tinted with food coloring.
16. Try rolling down a grassy hill.
17. Play peekaboo.
18. Bang on pots and pans.
19. Have a tea party on the floor with small sandwiches and juice.
20. Play in sand with water, spoons, and molds.
21. Put lids on small plastic storage containers, and try stacking them like blocks.
22. Loosely wrap yourself in toilet paper like a mummy.
23. Help sweep and mop the kitchen floor.
24. Push animals around in a play stroller, then rock them to sleep and put them to bed.
25. Gently bounce belly-down on an exercise ball.
26. Make a few beanbags out of an old pillowcase and then play throwing games.
27. Peer through a magnifying glass.
28. Peel stickers off of clothes or stick them all over paper.
29. Talk to sock puppets.
30. Go to the library and look at picture books.
31. Scribble with dry-erase markers on a mirror
32. Sing along with children on musical CDs or listen to a bedtime story.
33. Learn about the days you and your toddler were born.
34. Make an edible necklace of O-shaped cereal on a string.
35. Throw a parade with marching music, pot lids, and wooden spoons.

Making Room for Play

Being surrounded by tall people can affect your toddler's sense of mastery over his world—a world completely adapted for much larger people.

The chairs, stairs, sinks, toilets, beds, shelves—the entire house—is designed for the comfort of people over 4 feet tall, so your toddler has to continually adjust himself to your world similarly to the way that disabled persons are forced to adjust to the architectural barriers built for the benefit of the physically able majority.

Where do you begin readjusting a home to make it more comfortable for your young child? The answer is his bedroom. Adults take walls for granted, but to a child, walls are for kicking when you're mad, for bouncing balls off of, and for posting favorite pictures or artwork.

Make good use of wall space by painting a section or a whole wall with chalkboard paint, which allows for drawing with chalk that can also be erased. (Just make sure your child knows the difference between crayons and chalk, as well as "his" special wall versus the other walls in the house!) You can also securely mount an unbreakable, full-length mirror that lets your child look at himself and see reflections. Or decorate with bright, intriguing, and easily removable wallpaper.

STORING AND DISPLAYING

The best way to display toys for easy access (and cleanup) is on open shelves or by using soft-sided bins in a closet, with just a few select toys at a time. Shelves make everything easy to find and they make cleanups easier, too. You can teach your toddler early sorting skills by encouraging him to share in the cleanup: "Let's put the trucks here, the dolls here, and the books here." Multicolored shelves and bins are exciting to look at, and with a little ingenuity and some paint, you can turn a shelf cubbyhole into a dollhouse or play garage.

A good way to keep your child interested in his room as a play place is to rotate toys and books every few weeks. Excess toys can be stored in a transparent bin in the closet, well out of your toddler's reach while the shelves stay pared down to a few good toys. Display picture books open and standing on the top shelf so that your child can readily see the covers. Colorful plastic or ceramic clothes hooks screwed into the wall at a child's height can be used for hanging clothes.

To make your toddler's room even more interesting, make the room feel more customized by hanging bright mobiles, colorful kites, or a length of brightly colored, patterned fabric from one end to the other at ceiling level. Be sure everything is age-appropriate to avoid choking hazards in the event objects fall down.

A low, sturdy table and chair will be useful for playing with hand toys, pounding on clay, or trying chalk and crayon skills and finger painting. Also consider a low shelf for picture books, and a small, covered mattress and floor pillows for story time.

Art Play

Busy toddlers don't yet have the coordination or patience for big art projects, but there are lots of simpler, everyday creative experiences that you both can enjoy together. Making art can help your toddler refine his hand and arm skills, and help him to learn that by doing one thing he can make something else happen—"I drag a crayon across paper, and a line shows up," "I rub my hands in paint and make patterns," "I squeeze clay and it makes shapes."

Supplies for Toddler Art

Here's a list of materials you'll need for art play with your toddler:

Dad's old shirt, sleeves cut off and worn backward, to protect clothes from paint smears	**Construction paper** for scribbling and folding (dark colors for chalk drawings)
Oversized coloring books for *not* staying in the lines	**Inexpensive art tablet** for stickers and scribbling for older toddlers.
Textured and colorful papers— junk mail, old magazines, butcher paper, and so on—for art projects	**Photo albums with self-stick pages** for making personalized books (or just to practice peeling and unpeeling)
Paper grocery bags for making masks and as painting surfaces	**Masking tape** for gently holding down paper and for posting artwork
Thick crayons, easier for a toddler to hold, or crayon pieces slowly melted into multicolor disks in a muffin tin	**Nontoxic, washable tempera paints** for painting in the bathtub or on paper grocery bags
Liquid starch for mixing with tempera paint to make finger paint	**Fingerpaint paper,** shiny on one side
Handheld chalkboard and thick chalk for scribbles and doodles	**Spray bottle with squeeze handle** for bathtub play and plant watering
Magnetic drawing toy (Magna Doodle, Etch A Sketch) for a different kind of drawing	**Painters' brushes with thick handles** for painting watercolors on the bathtub or painting tempera on paper

SUPPLIES FOR TODDLER ART (CONTINUED)

Watercolor tin for painting on dry paper, wet paper, and paper towels	**Stickers** to occupy him when he's fussy in the car and to stick on his sleeves as a distraction
Sponges for bathtub play and painting projects	**Absorbent paper towels** for painting projects and cleanups
Old, clean cotton socks for making hand puppets	**Washable marking pens** for scribbling on paper or grocery bags
Rimmed cafeteria tray or roasting pan for keeping water and paint in one place	**Nontoxic glue stick** for sticking things on paper and boxes (with supervision)
Cardboard boxes for storing, sorting, and painting	**Textured objects** such as sponges, crumpled newspapers, and wide-tooth combs for making patterns on painted paper.

GETTING ART STARTED

Here are some tips for sharing art moments with your toddler. Just remember that his attention span is short, so be efficient with the time he will stay occupied. Close supervision is needed to keep art from spreading where it doesn't belong.

- **Go green.** Make sure that the art materials your toddler uses are nontoxic, don't give off noxious fumes, and are completely washable.
- **Set up in advance.** Get everything prepared while your toddler is not around, such as when he's taking a nap.
- **Cover up.** Cover the floor with newspapers, or an old shower curtain you can rinse off, and cover your toddler with one of Dad's old shirts.
- **Stay close.** Finger painting can

quickly turn into shirt, face, and wall painting. Create a "toddler safe" zone to ensure that your little Picasso doesn't expand his palette beyond acceptable boundaries.

- **Focus on the process, not the product.** Rather than obsessing about salvaging pieces of your toddler's art, instead pay attention to his joy in the creative process by filming and photographing him hard at work.
- **Think big and chunky.** Small hands work better with big materials. Examples: large commercial paintbrushes, fat chalk, and chunky crayons.
- **Don't get stuck.** Rather than messing with goopy glue or too-tacky tape, use a piece of shelf liner, sticky side up, and invite your toddler to create a collage with colored pieces of yarn, torn gift wrap, and pictures from magazines and junk mail.
- **Go with the flow.** Stay at it

for longer than a few minutes, and expect to spend more time cleaning up than doing the actual project.
- **Enjoy yourself.** Put on casual clothes, relax, and join your toddler in his art zone with some spontaneous play of your own.

QUICK CRAFT RECIPES

Here are some simple recipes for making your own art materials from scratch.

Bubble Solution
¼ cup liquid dishwashing soap, such as Dawn or Joy
¾ cup cold water
5 drops glycerin

Mix ingredients together in a wide-mouthed bowl. For blowing bubbles, use a small plastic bubble blowing wand, or make your own out of floral wire or pipe cleaners formed into circles. (Note: Glycerin can be found in most pharmacies and sometimes in craft stores.)

TIP

Homemade bubble solution will produce better results if you make it in advance—the older the solution, the better the bubbles.

Fingerpaint
½ cup liquid starch
½ cup liquid tempera paint

Mix ingredients in a cup or invite your toddler to do the mixing himself, with your supervision.

Jell-O Joy
4 large packages of Jell-O (any flavor, or different colors)
Plastic dishwashing tub or baby bathtub

Prepare the Jell-O as directed on the package, using separate dishes for each color. Refrigerate until gelled, then bring to room temperature before using. Line a part of the kitchen floor with an old shower curtain or small tarp. Put a container in the center and invite your (undressed) toddler to squish the Jell-O between his fingers, spoon it into small plastic containers, put his feet in it, and make a mess (but be careful about slipping). Vanilla pudding could be used instead of Jell-O.

Play Dough
1 cup water
½ cup salt
2 teaspoons cream of tartar
1 to 2 teaspoons food coloring
1 cup all-purpose flour
2 tablespoons vegetable oil
⅛ teaspoon almond, vanilla, or lemon extract, optional

Combine the first four ingredients in a large saucepan. Cook on low heat, stirring with a wooden spoon until the mixture is warm. Gradually stir in the flour (to avoid lumps) and oil until the flour begins to thicken and the mixture begins to pull away from the sides of the pan. Roll and cut into desired shapes. Bake finished pieces at 200°F for 45 minutes or until hardened and no longer sticky, then cool completely. As an alternative, air-dry dough on a plate for about 3 days, rotating the plate for even drying.

Buttermilk Art

Dark construction paper
¼ cup buttermilk
Sponge paintbrush
Fat colored chalk

Tape down the construction paper and moisten it well with buttermilk. Invite your toddler to draw pictures with the chalk on the paper. Pictures will take a day to dry.

Music Play

Your toddler is attuned to hearing, even in utero. After birth, his heart rate will slow down when he hears familiar music you played before he was born. Yes, he's really paying attention. Even though he was born loving to hear your voice, he is even more attuned to listening to your singing, even if your singing isn't so melodious.

The magic of music is the emotional connection it makes with your toddler. Music can also help him experience the rhythms of others and of different cultures. Paradoxically, music has one of two effects on babies and toddlers: It can arouse them and make them more excited, or it can calm them and help to soothe them.

Parents often ask: Does exposing a toddler to Mozart raise his IQ? "The Mozart Effect," as it was dubbed in 1993, was based on a rather poorly conducted study of college undergraduates. The study found that students who were briefly exposed to Mozart temporarily increased their spatial abilities. There was a media frenzy about the results, ultimately leading to the idea that listening to classical music would make babies smarter.

Listening to music or singing doesn't make babies or anyone else smarter, but it can help elevate their moods. And it doesn't matter what the music is—any kind will do. So Barney singing with his friends works equally as well as Wolfgang's concerto.

MOVIN' AND GROOVIN'

You can communicate your love of music to your toddler in lots of ways. If you hum while you do household chores, encourage him to beat out rhythms with a spoon on a pot lid, put your iPod on a player and dance to it together, or play familiar lullabies on a repeating CD when it's sleepy time so that he experiences the relaxing joy of music.

Help your child learn more about music with simple children's songs, such as "Eensy Weensy Spider," "Twinkle, Twinkle Little Star," and songs you make up while you push your child on the swing or drive around in the car. However you do it, letting your child experience music is enjoyable.

You can help your toddler learn to recognize rhythms by tapping two blocks together or clapping as the two of you listen to music together. You can add counting as a part of the rhythms and motions of music: "one, two, three; one, two, three . . ."

As he matures, your toddler may come to love the sense of mastery he feels from learning to operate an iPod or CD player himself. Special safety rules are in order. Keep the player well out of your child's reach unless you're there to supervise. And use a safety outlet that won't allow the device to be plugged in or unplugged except by an adult.

Here are some practical ideas for sharing music with your toddler:

- **Collect CDs and DVDs.** You can often find used children's music, songs, and stories on CDs and favorite DVDs at thrift stores and yard sales. Or, you can borrow them for free from the library; plus, online booksellers offer a huge collection of sing-along records.

- **Release your inhibitions.** Clear away space in the living room or den, and move to the music with your toddler as if no one is watching. You might tell him: "Let's each do what the music tells us to do." A few suggestions to get you started: "Carnival of the Animals" by Camille Saint-Saens, "The Peer Gynt Suite" by Edvard Grieg and "Nutcracker Suite" by Pyotr Ilyich Tchaikovsky.

- **Get out the sound makers.** Musical instruments are good for developing hand skills. Collect handheld rhythm instruments, such as drums, tambourines, maracas, and cowbells, or make your own from coffee cans, oatmeal boxes, dried beans in a lidded container, and metal mixing bowls.

- **Practice clapping.** Invite your toddler to try all the kinds of different sounds that he (and you) can make by just using your bodies. Try clapping softly and loudly, slow and fast, with flat or cupped hands, and so on.

- **Use props.** Make moving to music even more fun by adorning scarves, hats, Hula-Hoops, and streamers. (Be sure to record your musical event!)

- **Combine art and music.** Use music to inspire storytelling or as a backdrop for art creation.

- **Teach listening skills.** Spend time listening to the "music of nature"—birdsong, flowing water, wind, or sounds of the city—and try imitating them.

- **Encourage vocal awareness.** You and your toddler can feel your vocal cords move up and down as you sing high and low notes. Try imitating each other's sounds.

Party Time!

Toddler birthday parties can be great fun, or they can be total disasters. They could go either way. To stack the odds in your favor, start by planning ahead with an eye toward a playful time. Consider the timing of the event as well as the length of it.

Try to plan it for a time when your child will be well rested and fed. Opt to have a cake lighting ceremony with relatives or a casual backyard party with just a few friends and neighbors. Exquisitely themed parties are best reserved for when your toddler is 3 or older, when all of those special touches are more likely to be appreciated. But for now, your toddler just wants simple activity.

To make your little guests happy, give them the freedom and space to roam around and try out different things. For an indoor party, consider a series of "experience stations" that allow each child to wander between different activities at his own pace.

For one station, cover a toddler-height table with paper and a "splat mat" underneath. Use it as a center for making objects out of salt dough (see recipe on page 113). Make a second area with a crawl-through tunnel or a refrigerator-carton playhouse. A third area could house soft foam balls, beach balls, or lightweight playground balls, fun for throwing and kicking around. Props could include real hats for trying on.

If you decide to go outdoors with the party, consider using a toddler-scaled playground ("tot lot") that's fenced in. Weather permitting, the guests could wear bathing suits and play with sprinklers in a toddler-sized wading pool or Slip 'n Slide. (Constant supervision is required.)

Of course, you could also have the party at a commercial destination, such as Chuck E. Cheese's, the zoo, a children's gym, or a McDonald's with a children's play area. That will make party giving much simpler, and you'll have less preparing, less cleaning, and less hassle, but it will cost you. Some commercial party places allow you to supply your own cake or party favors.

PARTY TIPS

Here are some ideas for making your toddler's birthday party a success:

- **Enlist helpers.** Try to have one helper for each child. Older children may work if you coach them ahead of time on what they need to do. Ask someone to take pictures or video for you.
- **Keep the guest list and the party short.** An hour or two is enough excitement for most toddlers.
- **Time it right.** Try to have the party when kids are apt to be well rested, such as 10 a.m. or 3 p.m.
- **Make it casual.** Dress for comfort.
- **Open gifts later.** It may offend eager parents and relatives who want proof of your toddler's elation, but it will sidestep overeager (and, by this time,

probably overstimulated) toddlers who want to help open gifts and territorial disputes over those gifts.

- **Offer an easy menu.** Consider small portions of foods that are easy to eat and easy to prepare, such as grilled cheese, peanut butter and jelly sandwiches, or pizza squares. Sides could include snack crackers, soft pieces of fruit with dips, and juice boxes.
- **Give simple goodie bags.** Give each toddler a little party bag of

inexpensive gifts on their way out, such as sheets of stickers and other art supplies that won't pose a choking or safety hazard.

> **TIP**
>
> For toddler birthday parties, avoid structured games, balloons and piñatas, and clowns or other costumed characters that could frighten.

Play Safety

Finding a safe public playground for your toddler can be a challenge! While slides, swings and jungle gyms might be ideal for school-aged children, they're dangerous for toddlers who are impulsive and have little awareness of their physical limitations. Your toddler's using the wrong equipment could translate into black eyes, bumps, bruises, and even broken limbs and serious head injuries.

According to the Consumer Product Safety Commission (CPSC), more than 200,000 children are taken to emergency rooms because of playground-related injuries. In 2008, monkey bars accounted for the majority of injuries to toddlers needing emergency care.

A good playground for toddlers and young children has a soft foam surface under the play equipment that dries quickly after rain to cushion falls. The youth play area should be stationed well away from the toddler zone.

Features could include: small, low swings with backs and safety belts, crawling tunnels, low structures for safe climbing, a small, low sliding board with a safe ladder and high sides, trees for shade in the summer, and possibly sprinkler-style fountains for supervised water play. Nearby restrooms are a plus.

Your toddler will need your constant supervision and continuous reminding about basic safety rules, such as not walking in front of or behind swings, since he can't understand the pendulum effect and could be struck while passing. It's also good practice to not let your toddler twist a swing or push an empty swing.

He will also need your supervision on sliding boards. Slides are only for coming down, not for climbing up. He'll have to wait until other children are out of the way at the bottom of the slide, and he might need your help in dismounting the equipment.

BACKYARD PLAY EQUIPMENT

If you decide to install a backyard play set it's important to compare units with an eye toward safety. When shopping for a swing set, choose something that not only will appeal to your toddler right now, but can be adapted and changed as your toddler grows and his physical capabilities change.

Equipment should be sturdy in construction. Be sure to follow the manufacturer's installation instructions. Swings and climbing equipment need to be sturdy and securely anchored in concrete so they won't tip over. Avoid buying used equipment.

The surface under the equipment should be soft and cushiony in case your toddler and his friends fall. Check to ensure that wood used in play structures has been treated only with nontoxic preservatives.

Here are some basic guidelines for installing backyard play equipment.

- **Play-set spacing.** All items should be at least 6 feet from a fence or wall.
- **Play-set height.** Equipment should be no higher than 6 feet from top to ground. Play platforms should be no higher than 4 feet from the ground, and they need guardrails to prevent falls over the side.
- **Swings.** The safest swings for toddlers have bucket-shaped seats and safety belts. Swings should be at least 24 inches apart and 30 inches from support posts. Avoid swing chains fastened with open S-shaped hooks. Chains can come loose with vigorous swinging.
- **Sliding board.** A toddler slide should have a gradual incline of no more than 30 degrees. It should have sides that can be gripped.
- **Surfacing.** The surface under the equipment should be soft with no compacted dirt, rocks, or tree roots. Use play sand, wood chips, sawdust, tree bark, or rubber mulch for absorbing dismounts.

> **TIP**
>
> It's best to avoid large backyard trampolines. They're dangerous for children of all ages, and some insurance companies refuse to insure a home that includes a trampoline on the premises.

Q & A

Q: My 3-year-old daughter, Erin, turned into a prima ballerina about 6 months ago—at least in her own mind. She won't wear anything but her pink tutu and leotards. She performs arabesques for strangers in the supermarket, and hates it when people say things like, "Are you going to be a ballerina when you grow up?" She thinks she is a ballerina right now. She can't get enough of ballerina picture books and watching Angelina Ballerina DVDs. What gives?

A: You're not alone! Your daughter is going through a typical toddler phase. Pretend play helps toddlers feel more empowered as they become aware of their weaknesses and dependence. Pretend play helps toddlers develop vocabulary and links thoughts with actions. It will produce some of your child's most creative moments, so it's healthy for her—and for you. Learn all the nomenclature of her obsession so you're speaking the same language, and don't be afraid to ask questions and join her in the fun.

Q: I am the dad of an 18-month-old boy. I work late hours and worry that I will not know my own child. I am concerned that I will hurt him if I play with him. What can I do to bond with my toddler during the precious time we have together?

A: Studies show that, regardless of gender, a child needs to know his father, as it helps with identity formation. Play enhances the bond between you and your toddler and lays the foundation for a lifetime of mutual intimacy. Give yourself time to transition from work to home, so that when you are home,

you're in the mood to play. Also, be sure you're not arriving home in the middle of his bedtime routine, as you've disturbed the routine and now your child is less likely to go to bed if he knows Dad is in the house.

Minimize distractions by relinquishing your cell phone, pager, and other work gadgets. If there is time for play, get down on the floor with your child, keeping in mind that toddler play is more exploratory than purposeful. Toddler attention isn't very long, so be prepared to switch gears as needed. Get involved with rituals that make routine seem like playtime. As you become more familiar handling him and knowing what makes him laugh, you will know when he's in the mood for a game of hide-and-seek under the dining table or when he would rather have you read to him.

TIP

For age-appropriate games and other advice specifically for fathers, see our companion guide *Great Expectations: Becoming a Dad* by John Carr.

7

Sleep

Sleep is really important for overall health and well-being, and children need more sleep than grown-ups do. However, as long as there's something interesting going on (and there always is!), your toddler is going to resist getting his Z's.

This chapter is all about toddler sleep and the ways you can get around a battle of wills and get some space and privacy for yourself at night, too.

Toddler Sleep

As you found out during your child's infancy (if not sooner), being sleep-deprived makes people clumsy and cranky, and lack of sleep can cause long-term harm to learning and memory. Studies have found sleeplessness can weaken the body's immune system, making sleep-deprived people more susceptible to viruses. Overtiredness can even contribute to obesity.

But figuring out how much sleep your toddler requires is far from an exact science. There's no clear agreement among child development experts about exactly how much sleep is optimal

for toddlers. Not only do sleep needs appear to vary genetically, sleep requirements gradually change over time. Newborns need approximately twice as much sleep as adults do, while 1-year-olds need 3 hours more than 3-year-olds do.

There's another reason there is no "magic number" for the amount of sleep hours that individuals need: People, including toddlers, can accumulate sleep "debts," needing more or less sleep on a given day depending on how much they've gotten in preceding days. This doesn't mean that you can "make up" sleep hours you've lost, but it does mean that sleep deprivation can, over time, affect sleepiness during waking hours, and how readily your toddler (or you) can fall asleep, and also it can cause accumulated negative effects.

So, figuring out exactly how much sleep your toddler needs requires a little intuition plus a pinch of trial and error. If he has frequent episodes of being cranky or clumsy, a too-late bedtime is probably to blame. If he's simply refusing to settle down for a morning nap and is chipper without it, he could simply have outgrown that particular naptime.

The undeniable truth is that you can't force anyone, including your toddler, to fall asleep or stay asleep. You can, however, set the stage for healthy sleep by establishing consistent routines that include regular, predictable bedtimes and naptimes.

KEEPING THINGS CONSISTENT

Whether it's eating, exercising, or sleeping, predictable routines are key to your toddler's sense of well-being. They help him anticipate what's going to happen next. And consistency can help ease your toddler's anxiety, too, whether it's daily separations, such as bidding good-bye at day care or the nightly separation of saying good night when it's bedtime. Eating and sleeping by the clock can also help to reduce meltdowns.

Keeping things regular offers psychological benefits; having rhythmical, predictable days and nights are hardwired into the genes of all living creatures. During the first year of life, a baby's hormones naturally will synchronize with

How Sleep Changes by Age

Sometime between 9 months and 18 months, most toddlers will transition from two naps a day to one after-lunch siesta. Typically, the morning nap will be dropped first, while the afternoon nap will continue. Most children phase out of napping completely at around age 5, but sometimes highly active toddlers stop sooner.

Again, how much sleep your particular child needs may be different, or vary according to his sleep debts or other things going on in his life, such as illness. Here's a general guide:

AGE	NUMBER OF NAPS, DAILY	AVERAGE TOTAL HOURS SLEEP, DAILY
12 to 17 months	1 or 2	12.5
24 months	1	11.4
36 months	1	10.8

the light and dark cycles of his environment. Light exposure and darkness cue the 24-hour hormonal cycles of wakefulness to tiredness, and without regular light exposure the sleep cycles of humans (and animals) become erratic. So when you think of your child's sleep routines, think beyond the hour before bedtime or when naptimes happen. Instead, try to keep in mind his whole 24-hour cycle.

Quality sleep, quality awake time, exposure to sunlight, times of activity, and sleep cycles are all intertwined. Nutrition quality is also connected to sleep: Eating higher fiber and quick-digesting foods, such as fruits, berries, and cereals in the morning or afternoon, and saving slower-digesting, higher-fat foods, such as meats and cheeses, for dinnertime may help your child stay full overnight and encourage soiled diapers in the morning or afternoon, instead of the middle of the night.

CREATING A SCHEDULE

If you've been winging it with your child's schedule and want to make the move toward more consistent days and nights, the best way to start is by planning his schedule around his natural wake-up time. Most toddlers are pretty consistent about waking up early, no matter what time they go to bed the night before. Other than having blackout shades and hoping your toddler won't notice the sun has come up, there's not much that can be done to alter those early-morning wake-ups.

Even though you could try inching bedtime later by 15-minute increments each night to see if that entices him to sleep later in the morning, most parents discover that postponing bedtime doesn't help. Their toddlers continue to wake up at the same early hour, but then they're tired and cranky until they get a nap the next day.

To figure out a good go-to-bed hour, use this formula: On average, a 1-year-old needs about 12 ½ hours of sleep per day, with around 10 or 11 hours of sleep at night and the remainder as one or two naps during the day.

Even though you have little control over when your child wakes up from a nap or what time he wakes up in the morning, you can set his bedtime according to how much sleep he will need in a 24-hour cycle. If your 1-year-old wakes up at 6:30 every morning and takes an hour-long nap every day, you'll want to start your bedtime ritual at about 6:15 and plan to have lights out by 7:00.

Sunlight is also known to play a powerful role in harmonizing wake-sleep patterns. Plan for ample outdoor time each day, and sunlight can help regulate your toddler's sleep hormones. You can also encourage stronger night-and-day patterns by dimming lights and turning off any television sets in your home in the hours that precede bedtime. It doesn't matter who is watching it—the flashing-light stimulation that television sets emit stimulate the human brain into thinking it's daytime, which could be affecting your sleep, too.

SAMPLE SLEEP SCHEDULE FOR A 1-YEAR-OLD

Time	Activity
6:30 a.m.	Wake up, change diaper
6:45	Breakfast
8:00	Morning activity (preferably outside)
9:30	Morning nap, if your child still needs one
10:30	Snack, then activity
12:30 p.m.	Lunch
1:00	Nap, followed by snack
2:30	Afternoon activity (preferably outside)
5:30	Dinner
6:45	Bath
7:00	Tooth brushing, pajamas
7:10	Settle-down time: dim the lights and enjoy your before-bed quiet time routine
7:15	Lights out, parents out of the room

FROM WIRED TO TIRED

Research shows that toddlers who go to bed earlier—between 7:00 p.m. and 7:30 p.m.—actually sleep more and have better-quality sleep than toddlers who are put down later.

Don't be fooled if it's close to bedtime but your toddler doesn't seem tired. Get the bedtime routine rolling anyway. Toddlers often become more and more hyper when they're tired, and that wide-awake hyperactivity could be masking overtiredness. What sounds like a happy laugh can quickly turn into mania and meltdown if your toddler starts clumsily bumping into things, falling down, and dissolving into tears. The irritation of extreme tiredness could be winding your toddler tighter and tighter until he becomes frantic, high-pitched, and on the brink of breaking down.

The trick is to start your toddler's rituals earlier—a drink, a snack, a chance to go potty, saying good night to everybody. He doesn't need any extra opportunities for energy release, such as roughhousing, running, jumping, climbing, or blowing off steam. He just needs signals and your help in turning his system off so he can relax. Once you slow him down, you can see the sleepiness taking over.

When your toddler moves into the "pretend" phase as he nears age 3, then practicing "pretend bedtime" may help him feel more agreeable about going to sleep when bedtime rolls around. Make a nest or use a toy baby bed so that dolls or toy baby birds can pretend to go to sleep, too. As your child gets older he'll be better able to talk about what getting tired feels like.

AFTER LIGHTS OUT

Repeating the same rituals each night before bed will help your child mentally prepare for encroaching bedtime. You can create pre-bedtime rituals that feel comfortable for the two of you. The only essential elements are bathing, getting into jammies, and brushing teeth.

One important note of caution, though: Control how long the ritual lasts—30 to 60 minutes from bath to bed is a reasonable time frame to aim for.

As your toddler approaches 3, he will get better at trying to delay the inevitable. One solution can be to shorten other parts of the routine so that you're still meeting the 30- to 60-minute total. For instance: "You can keep playing in the tub, but we will only have time to read one book tonight."

Once all the formalities have been done and it's time to dim the lights, consider doing something restful that you both enjoy. Here are some ideas:

- Sing a lullaby.
- Say good night to things in the room.
- Say a prayer.
- Share positive moments of the day.
- Share a childhood memory.
- Rock and snuggle for a few minutes in a bedroom rocking chair or glider.
- Is his favorite stuffed animal tucked in? Is the night-light turned on?
- Then, it's "lights out" and nighty-night.

After dark, toddler imaginations can run wild. Cartoon characters, child-sized dolls, and those classic horror-movie standbys, clowns, puppets, and decorative masks, can all morph into terrifying figures once the lights go out. A simple, functionally designed room is not only cheaper, but it could be more restful to your toddler, too.

Sleep Training

Sleep training is any kind of behavioral intervention used by parents to alter their children's sleep habits. It has two goals: to help children fall asleep by themselves at nap- and bedtime, and to put children back to sleep without parental help if they wake up. Parents ideally begin this training in their children's infancy.

Research suggests that consistency is the only effective tool in sleep training. Researchers at the journal *Sleep* reviewed dozens of sleep studies (for infants aged 2 months to 11 months, from 1970 to 2005) and divided the strategies into these five categories:

1. **Extinction.** Also known as "crying it out," parents put the infant to bed at night, for instance, and didn't respond again until morning, unless the child was ill or in danger, though in some cases parents stayed in the room with the baby.
2. **Graduated extinction.**

Sometimes called Ferberizing, named after Dr. Richard Ferber, this method is similar to extinction. The difference: Parents went in to soothe the child on a fixed schedule of progressively longer intervals, for instance every 3 minutes, then every 5 minutes, then every 10 minutes.

3. **Positive routines and a faded bedtime.** Set nighttime routine, wake-up time, and naptimes were established; then, the baby was taken out of the crib for a certain amount of time if he had problems sleeping. Then the parents put the child to bed at a later-than-usual bedtime while maintaining the consistent wake-up time, with the bedtime being moved up earlier in 15-minute increments until it becomes early enough for the baby to get a good night's sleep.

4. **Scheduled awakenings.** Parents recorded the baby's nighttime wake schedule for a while (for example, one complete night), followed by waking the baby 10 to 15 minutes before he would predictably wake up (for example, on the next night). Parents gradually increased the time between scheduled awakenings to nudge the child toward longer and longer sleep periods.

5. **Parent education.** For this strategy, parents were simply taught about the importance of sleep, consistency in routine, and to put the child down to sleep in a "drowsy but awake" state to encourage independent sleeping.

Research showed that *any* one of the above strategies could be effective in altering babies' sleep patterns. It wasn't just the specific strategy that got results, but the fact that parents applied it *consistently.*

And parents using a strategy—any strategy—reported increased confidence in their parenting skills, decreased stress, and higher marital satisfaction. One study found a 45 percent decrease in maternal depression.

So what's your sleep strategy? (For more information on sleep, see the companion guide *Great Expectations: Baby Sleep Guide* by Marcie Jones and Sandy Jones.)

Navigating Nighttime Wakeups

There's getting your toddler down to sleep . . . and *then* there's convincing him to stay asleep long enough for him (and everyone else in the house) to get enough rest.

It's not unusual for toddlers to wake up during the night, even if they used to be world-class sleepers. And until your child is articulate enough to explain himself, you won't always be able to figure out why he's waking up. He may have had a vivid dream or been woken up by a stomachache, or a headache from emerging molars. Then again, he could simply be having a hard time putting himself back to sleep once he wakes up, which usually happens when sleeping cycles shift between light and deep sleep.

You want to comfort and help him if he needs you. But you also want to be mindful about it and not arouse him even more, or reward him for nighttime wakeups by being oversolicitous with hours of rocking, soothing, or feeding as ways of encouraging him to fall back to sleep.

For getting through middle-of-the-night wake-ups, try:

Pause first: When you hear that all-too-familiar, middle-of-the-night shriek, take a look at the clock and give him at least 3 minutes to settle down on his own. Sometimes babies and toddlers cry, whine, or shriek in their sleep. Avoid rushing in only to find he's lying down and probably would have gone back to sleep if you hadn't opened the door and aroused him.

Then act: If tired cries continue, and he's clearly becoming more and more awake, or his cries are unusually shrill and prolonged or it sounds like he's in pain, then of course you want to respond and see if you can figure out what the problem is.

Does he have a soiled diaper? (That one should be obvious.) Is something making him uncomfortable? If the answer is yes, fix the problem as quickly and unobtrusively as possible, then go. Keep the room as dim as you can. Don't talk, just stay calm. Change his diaper, or if he feels warm or you suspect he's in pain, take his temperature and give your doctor's recommended dose for discomfort and leave.

If you can't find a problem, but the sight of him is breaking your heart and you simply can't leave the room, try hugging him while he's standing up, then gently easing him back into a lying-down position.

Again, unless there's a dirty diaper, vomit, or another problem that can't be solved by any other means, avoid making your intervention a stimulating or rewarding experience by turning on the lights, talking to him, picking him up, or taking him out of the crib, which will only increase the chances that he'll repeat his wake-ups later.

TIP

Never use a crib tent to confine a roving toddler. His head could become trapped between the frame of the tent and the railing.

MIDNIGHT BATHROOM CALLS

Just when you've gotten your child to sleep, another new kink in the hose comes along: Potty training. Your toddler will soon figure out that "I gotta go potty" is his "Get out of jail free" card! During the day, the minute your child says he has to go to the potty, of course you rush him there.

You don't want to undo all of that progress. Take your child to the bathroom, but don't let potty time turn into the late show. Put a night-light in the bathroom so you don't have to turn on the lights completely. Don't say more to your child than you have to. Give him a minute or two to get the job done, then escort him back to bed with no fanfare.

If he's out of bed multiple times, without actually putting anything in the potty, don't be afraid to put your foot down and declare the potty card null and void.

SEPARATION AND SLEEP TROUBLES

Some toddlers begin to have problems going to sleep due to separation anxiety issues, as early as 6 months and up to 15 months. Separation anxiety should abate by age 2, when toddlers are able to understand that you will come back after you go. If severe upsets and separation anxiety persist, the problem could be something else— an anxiety disorder, problems with transitions.

Parents can help young toddlers through a separation anxiety phase by providing consistency. Again, routines will help your child anticipate what comes next. When it's time to separate, it helps to not get too emotionally worked up—even if you're torn up inside with guilt about leaving your child at day care, or in his crib or toddler bed. Good-byes and good nights should be short and sweet, with

reassurance that everything is okay through your facial expressions, body language, and demeanor. (Read more about separation issues in Chapter 3.)

NIGHT TERRORS

Night terrors are a sleep disorder that happens during a phase of nondreaming sleep, when a toddler or child seems to be startled awake by fear. Your toddler may suddenly sit bolt upright, shrieking, gasping, and thrashing, or he may wake up in a sweat. Children ages 2 to 6 are most prone to night terrors, and they affect about 15 percent of all children.

The terrors usually happen during the first hour of sleep. While some episodes may be triggered by stress, fever, or overtiredness, it is also thought that there may be a genetic predisposition to them. Note: Night terrors are not the same as nightmares. Nightmares usually happen at a different stage of sleep, and children and adults who have them don't remember them.

Thankfully the night terrors usually last only a few minutes, though some hours-long episodes aren't unheard of.

Experts suggest not attempting to wake a child from a night-terror episode. Being woken up may actually be more frightening and disorienting than the episode itself. Simply stay close by, grit your teeth, and keep him from falling out of bed or hurting himself until the episode subsides. Most likely, he won't completely wake up, but will instead fall back into a deep, gentle sleep. If you're still concerned, discuss these wake-ups with your toddler's pediatrician.

NIGHT WEANING

Usually, nighttime nursing is the last to go in the weaning process. If you're nursing your toddler off to sleep and you enjoy it, then that can be a cherished moment that the two of you share together. But if you feel it's time to stop nursing, then the easiest solution is to have someone else put your child to bed for a while. (It's good for your child to get used to the idea that other people can put him to bed, too.)

If you're the only one available for bedtime duty, though, then you have no other option but to kindly, gently, and lovingly draw the line. Wear something he can't get into, such as a turtleneck.

When he cries, fusses, complains, and beats your chest as if it's a broken vending machine, say "no" firmly, then rock and cuddle him while he expresses his feelings. It may take him longer than usual to settle down for the first few nights, but eventually it will happen.

Though he may protest, again be sure to put him down before he is completely asleep. You're not giving him any less love or closeness, and after you've put in a year (or more) of breastfeeding, nor do you need to feel guilty about deciding that you don't want to continue any longer. The positive thing is that you're helping him learn how to soothe himself to sleep without a crutch. (For more information on weaning, see the companion guide *Great Expectations: The Essential Guide to Breastfeeding* by Marianne Neifert.)

From Crib to Bed

Unless you're expecting another baby and will need to recycle your toddler's crib, there's really no need to rush him out of his familiar sleeping quarters. Cribs have the great advantage of being fully protected on all sides, and, let's face it, its cagelike properties prevent nighttime and pre-dawn roaming.

Your toddler is ready for a bed with no bars once he becomes agile and big enough to climb out of the crib, which is usually around age 3. As soon as he has figured out he can shift his body weight to get up and over things, and he's tall enough to get a leg over the top of the crib rail, it's just a matter

of time before he makes his first successful crib escape.

To ensure your child is safe inside his crib, it's important to lower the mattress to the very lowest level and take out any crib bumpers, pillows, or other items that could be used as stepping stones—everything, that is, but the one small stuffed animal or blanket that your child is especially attached to when he pulls up to stand at the bars.

After your child has successfully climbed out once, you can be sure that he'll try again, even if he got hurt the first time. Unfortunately, unless you happen to catch him in the act of actually throwing a leg over, you may not know your child is big enough to climb out until the fateful day when you hear a thud, followed by a scream, or your stealthy toddler inexplicably appears in your bedroom in the middle of the night.

Once you notice your child starting to get that escape-artist urge, put some padding under his crib—an extra layer of rug padding, or interlocking foam floor panels—and go toddler bed shopping. A nice perk of some toddler beds is that a crib mattress will fit into them. They also come in some adorable shapes, like little racecars, castles, and so on. It doesn't matter what style of bed you get, but remember that toddlers are too young for bunk beds or lofts because of the risk of falls or head entrapment on the ladders or sidebars.

Another option is to skip the toddler-bed stage altogether and move your child right into a regular twin bed—just be sure to have bed rails on both sides to prevent falls.

A downside to toddler beds is that keeping the child in the bed is more of a challenge now that it's a lot easier for him to get out, and it's not safe to have your toddler roaming the house at night.

Hundreds of baby sleep books and articles essentially say the same thing: Stay nearby—either in the room or outside the door—and gently yet firmly put your toddler back in bed again and again while avoiding interaction that might stimulate him more or risk turning the whole thing into a game. This back-to-bed ushering may actually take hours for the first few nights, but consistency is key. Ultimately, your child will get the message.

If your toddler turns into a midnight wanderer, you may need to figure out a way to stop him from exiting his room. Re-employ the baby monitor and install a baby gate across his bedroom exit. Make sure the room is kid-proofed, with bookcases bolted to the walls, drapery cords safely secured, and accessible windows fitted with window guards. If you're not going to use a gate, put a dimmer switch on your hall light (or use a night-light in the hallway) and keep a latched gate on the stairs so there's no danger in turning the wrong direction on the way to your room.

If he makes it to your room, resist the urge to let him into bed. Without speaking, walk him back to his room and replace him in his own bed. When your child is old enough to understand, if he's still fixated on being in your bed, you can make an exception and let him in your bed when it's light outside, as long as he stays quiet and still. This may earn you a few valuable minutes before you have to get out of bed on weekends.

> ### TIP
>
> A calming CD of lullabies or soothing music played when your toddler is extra-tired and falling off to sleep may help him associate the music with being relaxed and drifting off to pleasant dreamland.

Establishing a Sleep Schedule

As a parent, you need to take charge of your toddler's routines. It's your job to set limits and teach your child to sleep independently. A sleep schedule can help. Here's how the nightly routine might look:

• Get cleaned up and dressed for bed.
• Relax the body and mind.
• Be still long enough to let sleep happen.
• Rest long enough to be restored for the next day.

Sounds simple, doesn't it?

It isn't. Not only do toddlers have trouble with their nighttime, go-to-bed skills, but a lot of adults do, too. About 60 percent of American adults report frequent problems with falling asleep. According to a survey conducted by the National Sleep Foundation, 20 percent of 1-year-olds wake up regularly overnight, while 76 percent of parents wish they could change their child's sleep habits.

It helps to approach independent sleeping like any other skill that your toddler learns, whether it's drinking from a cup or mastering self-toileting. You'll need to figure out some strategies and have realistic expectations about success and backsliding.

Testing limits is what toddlers do. The same drive that prods your toddler to inch his finger closer to whatever you tell him not to touch while simultaneously watching for your reaction will also drive him to test your limits at night.

The trick is figuring out when your child really needs you versus when he's simply using the situation to get your attention in the night. If he asks for one more story or song, will you comply? Exactly how many times can he ask to get up to use the potty before you draw the line? If he throws something out of his bed and cries to get it back, will you go in to fetch it? And just when you've figured out that you're being played and you're not going to fall for a certain trick again, your toddler could well come up with a new strategy.

It's not always easy to tell when a toddler is tired. Sometimes he may rub his eyes, get whiny, or flop around. Other times he may be exhausted but still seem wide-awake. Though we can use general guidelines suggested by experts, it can still be hard to judge exactly how much sleep your child needs.

Special Bedtime Issues

BED SHARING

Throughout human history, children and families all bundled up and slept together for warmth and protection. There were no electric lights or central heating, nor separate bedrooms for everyone. All shared the same room (or the same cave), and monsters weren't something toddlers imagined, but truly frightening things lurking in the dark that were life-threatening.

Children are hardwired to not want to sleep alone, and it makes sense since humans are mammals, and therefore, pack animals. Besides, grown-ups' beds are a lot more comforting than cribs with bars. They're snug and warm, smell like Mommy, and probably have better-quality sheets and blankets, too.

Despite how appealing it is to your toddler to stay up as long as possible or jump into bed with you, there are some very good reasons why your toddler should be trundled off to bed at a decent hour and sleep in his own bed.

First, there are your own needs to think about. After a long day of working, tending to the household, and chasing after a toddler, you deserve the peace and quiet of your own bed and a restful night so that you can do it all again tomorrow. And letting your child into your bed could potentially undermine his confidence. Instead of consistently helping him to see his bedroom and bed as a cozy retreat for relaxing and resting at the end of the day, you might inadvertently be reinforcing the notion that there really *is* something scary about his own bedroom and sleeping alone.

Still, some parents share a bed because the whole family enjoys it. As long as everyone is getting enough sleep and no one minds, there's nothing wrong with it. But if you're bed sharing just because you brought your child into your bed one night and now don't know how to get him out, or if your child is sneaking into your room, that's a different story.

Moving a child from the family bed to a room and crib of his own is never easy, and it gets progressively more challenging the older the child gets (at least until middle-school peer pressure sets in).

If your child has been sleeping in your bed and has never slept alone, start with him napping in his own room and bed. Make getting to the crib in time for naps a priority—don't let morning errands run long and risk having him fall asleep in a car seat or stroller for that dreaded mini-nap that fuels him up for the rest of the day.

When naptime arrives, rock or snuggle with your toddler until he's almost asleep and then put him down, giving him a few reassuring pats if you want. Then leave the room to give him a chance to settle.

As tempting as it may be to rock him into a limp sleep, then put him down and sneak off, he'll be even more upset when he wakes up to find that you're gone and he doesn't know where he is or how he got there.

If he cries a tired, complaining cry, give him a reassuring pat, say night-night, and give him a chance—at least 15 minutes—to settle. The point is for him to learn to go asleep on his own, and staying in his room sends the message that you don't have confidence that he can do it, and also that somehow it's your job to usher him off to sleep.

SLEEP AFFIRMATIONS

When you close the door, your toddler may surprise you by

just fussing a little while before dropping off to sleep. If he becomes wide-awake, his cries don't abate, and he's standing up in his crib, you have a choice to make: either staying out of the room and letting him cry himself to sleep, or going in and intervening.

Here are some sleep reminders for when you're transitioning your toddler from your bed into his:

• You can't fall asleep for him.
• You are not hurting your child or your relationship with him by insisting that he sleep in a crib.
• Sleeping in his own bed or crib isn't harmful.
• Sleep deprivation is unhealthy for you, him, and the rest of the family.
• Sleeping alone is something that everyone has to learn sometime, and it becomes progressively harder to learn the older a child gets.

Sleep may be more difficult for your toddler if he has already transitioned from a crib to a toddler bed but there has been a change in the family—a new baby sister or brother, for instance. In that case, stay in his room. Sit in a nearby chair, and when he gets out of bed, gently but firmly reposition him back in his bed again.

The first time he gets out, give him a verbal reminder: "Sleepy time." After that, don't look at him, talk, or interact. Sometimes it takes more than an hour of putting him back into bed, but don't give up prematurely. If you do, it signals that he can win the bedtime battle if he just keeps at it. Remember: You make the rules, and you know what's best. Consistency is key.

> **TIP**
>
> Going to sleep with a bottle of formula can cause milk to pool around your child's teeth, leading to decay. If your child must have a nighttime bottle, use water.

Q & A

Q: My son has always been a GREAT sleeper. He usually goes down around 7:30–8:00 p.m. and he'll sleep until around 7:00 a.m. Lately, however, he's been waking up in the middle of the night and refusing to go back to sleep. He will scream at the top of his lungs, and when I go in there, he asks to eat. I'll take him downstairs, and he cries to watch one of his favorite shows. This has happened on and off now for a week. I'm pregnant with our second and am exhausted all the time. Any advice?

A: Your son is manipulating you and you need to draw the line— fast. Toddlers are all about trial and error as they try out different options to figure out what works to get what they want, which is admirable for them but may not be so great for you. While you may be okay with late-night snacks and TV the first or second time, weeks or months of this is not going to be good for anyone, especially not with a new baby on the way.

Your toddler needs his rest, and you need yours. He needs to eat the healthy food you serve him, not hold out for a better offer. (For more on picky eaters, see Chapter 8.) And eating after he's brushed isn't good for his teeth, either.

If he's going to bed at 7:30, that's really not very long after dinnertime. If he wakes up at night, give him a chance to calm himself down. If he doesn't, go in once, make sure he's not in danger, give a hug, then say goodnight. Don't turn on lights, pick him up, talk to him, or let him get up, and don't offer him more than a sip of water.

The screaming may seem horrible to you, but it's not "I'm-in-danger" screaming. It's screaming from not getting something that he wants that, incidentally, happens to be bad for him. If he was screaming to have candy for dinner you wouldn't give in, and you wouldn't feel guilty about it. This is the same deal.

And note that the screaming may get worse before it gets better, because he will try to replicate whatever it was he did that got him treats and TV in the past. Stay consistent, and don't fall for it!

Also, if you're worried about how your new baby is going to affect your close relationship with your child, rest assured that he will adapt as children have for millennia, and there's no need to try to "make up" for the separation that's coming in advance by coddling him in the night. You both need your rest, and it's your job to make sure that happens.

Q: I know that children wake up early, but how early is too early? My son was waking up at 6:30, which was bad enough, but lately he's been getting up even sooner than that—on 5 a.m. some days. Then he'll be cranky and takes a two-hour nap at 8 a.m. What can I do?

A: If your child is waking up at 6 a.m. and is chipper and raring to go, and goes on to have an upbeat and active day, that's one thing. You may not have a choice but to adjust your own sleep schedule accordingly. But if he's waking up when it's still dark and before he's had a chance to get a good night's sleep, that's another story.

Your child can't read the clock, of course, so you can help differentiate night and day with your routine. Decide what a "decent hour" would be— say, 6 a.m. If it's earlier, though, treat this wake-up as if it was the middle of the night. Wait and see if he can put himself back to sleep.

Blackout curtains or light-blocking shades may help to trick him into thinking it's nighttime. For older toddlers who are able to grasp simple rules, an alternate rule is that it's not time to get up until it's light outside, and if he gets up before that, then he needs to play quietly in his room.

As we've suggested earlier, you can also try working with his bedtime. Sometimes being overtired can result in broken sleep, and an earlier bedtime can help. But with some toddlers, that can backfire, making your 5 a.m. riser a 4 a.m. riser. Or you can experiment, making his bedtime 15 minutes later on successive nights, until it's about an hour later than usual.

Both the earlier and later bedtimes are worth a try, but don't be shocked if neither makes a difference in your child's wake-up time. Early wake-up times are often an unchangeable reality of life with toddlers. If that's the case, then the most workable solution is to turn off the television at night and go to bed an hour or two earlier yourself.

> **TIP**
>
> The lavender fragrance is thought to promote relaxation. Try putting a small drop of pure lavender oil (available at health food stores) at the foot of your toddler's crib sheet.

8

Nutrition

Welcome to the Toddler Café!

One of life's great pleasures is having a meal with your family. If you're a first-time parent whose idea of dinner is standing in the kitchen eating takeout, toddlerhood offers an opportunity for you to discover or rediscover the fun of preparing simple, fresh food. You can revisit all of those foods that you used to eat when you were younger, and create new family favorites while you learn your child's tastes.

However, the simple pleasures of feeding your child also come with concerns and controversies. First, you might start with some basic questions about food and health: How can you tell if a child is eating enough? How do you get a picky eater to try new foods? And just how is it possible to shop, prepare, and eat while there's a toddler who demands all of your attention?

Then there are always other nutrition issues that crop up: Could fatty-acid supplements really help

boost your child's brain power? How will you know if your toddler has a food allergy? Are vegetarian diets healthier for kids? Should you worry about sippy cups made of the wrong kinds of plastic, or fish contaminated by PCBs?

This chapter will help you find answers to old and new questions and how to make sure your toddler is well nourished. For in-depth information about child nutrition and a bevy of wholesome, easy recipes for making your own baby food, be sure to consult the companion volume *Great Expectations: Best Food for Your Baby & Toddler* by Jeannette L. Bessinger with Tracee Yablon-Brenner.

We'll start with food safety, the basic tools you need to feed young toddlers, followed by what to feed an older toddler, and finally, how to manage important lifestyle issues, including practical tips for how to shop, prepare, and eat meals with a toddler.

Parents' Biggest Toddler Eating Challenges

Parents worry a lot, but when it comes to the health and nutrition of their toddlers, they say they worry most about:
- Figuring out which foods have the most nutritional value.
- Having a finicky child who rejects healthy food and won't try new things.
- Identifying food contaminants such as pesticides, pollutants, and certain plastics.
- Managing an active kid while trying to shop for or prepare food.
- Raising a child at a healthy weight.
- Getting a wandering toddler to sit down long enough to share family meals.

Why Is Nutrition So Important?

It's hard to believe that while food is so plentiful, inadequate nutrition could be such a huge problem. But that's the case, sometimes because of severe poverty.

Obesity is a huge problem for U.S. children, too. One in seven children is obese in this country, and in 2008, the U.S. Centers for Disease Control and Prevention reported that about 14.6 percent of 2- to 4-year-old children were obese.

More often than not, our children's nutritional deficiencies are the result of time-stressed parents not taking the time to shop wisely or prepare healthy meals when it's faster and easier to rely on fast foods and prepackaged snacks despite their lack of nutritional value.

Convenience foods are an easy habit for a toddler—or anyone—to get into. Why sit down to eat when a drive-through can deliver a meal that any toddler would be happy to gobble down in the backseat? And why buy fresh fruit that will probably go bad when fruit leather lasts forever?

The biggest problem is that for a food to be mass-produced, it needs to be loaded with more fat, salt, and sugar than any home cook would have the nerve to add. And yet these are just the foods that our national tastebuds have become accustomed to.

TIP

Let your child have access to water all day, but limit milk or juice to mealtime.

Toddler Nutrition 101

Fresh food simply prepared provides good nutrition (and flavor) for people of all ages.

There are some healthy eating habits that you can teach your child early on by modeling the right behaviors. Bring home only quality foods, share family meals together, and avoid foods that deliver empty calories. Ingraining these early food habits could have a lifelong impact on your child's health.

Granted, shopping for and preparing fresh foods takes more time, energy, and effort than pulling up to a drive-through window or punching buttons on a vending machine, but if you make good nutrition a priority, you'll soon develop time-saving steps and routines that make the process easy and enjoyable. In addition, you'll redevelop a taste for good foods and will have a natural aversion to many of the low-nutrient, high-fat, high-sodium, super-sweet foods so many of us eat.

The good news is: Your toddler is only beginning her lifetime of gustatory adventures. You get to introduce her to new taste experiences and the joy of eating, one small serving at a time.

There's also the fulfillment of having a hand in creating new family rituals around meal sharing that she will fondly remember later. It's not just about the food, but the experience of sitting down, talking, and sharing a meal together.

RECOMMENDED DAILY ALLOWANCES FOR TODDLERS

For your baby's first year, breastmilk or formula made up most of her calories. After her first birthday, your toddler is able to eat virtually anything an adult can, as long as the food doesn't pose a choking hazard. She also should switch to drinking cow's milk and water for hydration, so this is a convenient time to replace the baby bottle with a sippy cup if you haven't already.

Because switching from formula to milk is an important rite of passage for young children, you should be aware that regular cow's milk has a very different nutritional profile than infant formula. For instance, cow's milk is low in iron and can negatively affect the body's absorption of iron. In addition, consuming more than 3 cups of cow's milk a day can irritate the intestinal tract in some children, causing small amounts of bleeding, which leads to gradual blood loss through the stool and possibly anemia.

Milk should be limited to roughly 16 ounces per day for this age and split up into frequent, small servings.

Daily Nutrition for Toddlers

Calories: 1,000 to 1,300
Protein: 16 g
Vitamin A: 1,000 IU / 300 mcg
Vitamin C: 40 mg
Vitamin D: 200 to 1,000 IU
Thiamin (Vitamin B1): 1,000 IU / 300 mcg
Riboflavin (Vitamin B2): 0.8 mg
Niacin: 9 mg
Vitamin B6: 1 mg
Folate: 50 mcg
Calcium: 800 mg
Iron: 7 mg

Each of these nutrition guidelines is important for toddlers' everyday health, and we'll explore each one of them.

Calories/Servings by Age

The American Heart Association offers general guidelines for estimated daily calories and recommended food group servings for babies and toddlers.[1]

	1 year	2-3 years
Kilocalories[a]	900	1,000
Fat, % of total kcal	30-40	30-35
Milk/dairy, cups[b]	2[c]	2
Lean meat/beans, ounces	1 1/2	2
Fruits, cups[d]	1	1
Vegetables, cups[d]	3/4	1
Grains, ounces[e]	2	3

[a] Calorie estimates are based on a sedentary lifestyle. Increased physical activity will require additional calories: 0 to 200 kcal more a day if moderately physically active; 200 to 400 kcal more a day if very physically active.

[b] Milk listed is fat-free (except for children under the age of 2 years). If 1%, 2%, or whole-fat milk is substituted, this will utilize, for each cup, 19, 39, or 63 kcal of discretionary calories and add 2.6, 5.1, or 9.0 g of total fat, of which 1.3, 2.6, or 4.6 g are saturated fat.

[c] For 1-year-old children, calculations are based on 2% fat milk. If 2 cups of whole milk are substituted, 48 kcal of discretionary calories will be utilized. The American Academy of Pediatrics recommends that low-fat/reduced-fat milk not be started before 2 years of age.

[d] Serving sizes are 1/4 cup for 1 year of age, 1/3 cup for 2 to 3 years of age, and 1/2 cup for 4 years of age and older. A variety of vegetables should be selected from each subgroup over the week.

[e] Half of all grains should be whole grains.

TIP

Try the following ideas for getting meals on the table when you have a toddler: (1) Entertain her in a high chair, (2) Make meals using a slow cooker, (3) Use a baby backpack or Snugli if your toddler isn't too heavy, and (4) Let her snack while you prepare the meal.

Calories

Toddlers have small stomachs, and most need to eat about once every 2 ½ to 3 hours. A typical eating schedule for child is 3 meals a day plus two or three snacks a day. Snacks often account for up to 20 percent of their daily energy and nutritional requirements, so it's important to put together snacks that are both nutritious and appealing.

Meals should be offered at about the same time every day, with snacks offered 2 to 3 hours prior to mealtime. Snacks should be used to satisfy hunger, but never used to reward behavior, calm a child, or dry tears.

Generally toddlers' growth rate is much slower than that of 1-year-olds. As a general rule of thumb, you can figure a serving to be about 1 tablespoon of any food type per each year of your child's age. So a 3-year-old's serving would be 3 tablespoons of food. However, this is just a general guideline. Your child's appetite is your more reliable guide.

Protein

Protein is found in every part of the body, from the hair to the toenails. Protein helps the body repair old cells and build new ones, so it's an essential element for health. Protein can be found in abundance in meat, eggs, nuts, tofu, dairy products, legumes.

Sometimes parents worry that their toddlers aren't getting enough protein because they refuse to eat meat, but a child doesn't need to eat meat to get enough. A toddler will get a full day's supply of protein just by drinking 2 cups of milk per day.

The only children who are at risk of not getting enough protein are those who are on vegan diets, which contain no animal products at all.

Keep in mind that your child doesn't have molars yet, so pieces of meat larger than pea size will pose a choking hazard. Try small amounts of thinly sliced eggs or cheese, or deli meats such as meatloaf, liverwurst, sausage, or hamburger.

Do not give your 12- to 18-month-old pieces of meat or fish that haven't been thoroughly cooked and finely chopped. Avoid nuts, other than nut butters or spreads. Toddlers aren't able to chew them properly.

Vitamin A

Important for building good vision and a healthy immune system, vitamin A is fat-soluble and commonly found in liver, fish, fish liver oils (cod liver oil), eggs, dairy products, leafy, dark green vegetables, and deep orange fruits and vegetables. The recommended daily allowance for vitamin A is 1,000 IU or 300 mcg, or about the amount found in a tablespoon of cooked carrots, a tablespoon of mashed sweet potatoes, or one to two tablespoons of chopped steamed spinach or kale.

Vitamin C

Probably best known for supporting a healthy immune system, vitamin C (or ascorbic acid) helps in healing wounds, tissue growth, and bone production. It is a powerful antioxidant and is needed for enzyme reactions and cell protection. It also helps the body cope with physical and emotional stress. Good sources of vitamin C include broccoli, Brussels sprouts, cantaloupe, oranges, sweet red peppers, and tomatoes.

TIP

Steam or stir-fry greens and vegetables, as boiling them often destroys their vitamin content.

Vitamin D

Vitamin D helps build bones by contributing to calcium absorption and bone health. It also aids in disease prevention, the building of teeth and hair, and contributes to cell growth and activity and organ regulation. It is the only vitamin that can be manufactured in the body. Good food sources include mushrooms, Atlantic mackerel, salmon, herring, sardines, cod liver oil, and eggs.

Probably due to a lack of sun exposure, about 12 percent of toddlers in the United States don't get enough vitamin D. The Food and Nutrition Board (FNB) at the Institute of Medicine of The National Academies recommends that children between ages 1 and 3 get 200 IUs a day; however, the American Academy of Pediatrics feels that the recommended daily intake should be between 400 and 1,000 IUs, and that children who do not drink at least a quart of fortified milk per day should be given supplements.[2]

How much sun a child will need to manufacture adequate vitamin D on her own depends on the latitude where you live, the season, and how lightly the weather permits you to dress her. If dressed but not wearing a hat, a light-skinned child will need about 2 total hours of sun exposure per week; in a bathing suit, a half-hour of sun will do.[3] Babies and young children with a medium skin tone will need an estimated average of 168 minutes (or 2 hours and 48 minutes) per week of sun exposure while dressed without a hat, and dark-skinned toddlers may need 3 to 12 hours of sun exposure weekly to produce adequate vitamin D supplementation.[64] If you are concerned about the link between sun exposure and skin cancer, consider vitamin D supplements instead.

Thiamin (Vitamin B1)

Thiamin helps with carbohydrate metabolization, energy production, and healthy skin. It also supports the nervous system. Good food sources of thiamine include whole and fortified grains and cereals, pork, nuts, seeds, and salmon.

Riboflavin (Vitamin B2)

Riboflavin is important for energy production and support of the nervous and immune systems, and necessary for tissue repair and healthy eyes. Soy products, meats, and vegetables, including peas, asparagus, beet greens, spinach, and okra, are good food sources of this vitamin.

Niacin (Vitamin B3)

Important for energy production, metabolism of fats, and maintenance of healthy skin, niacin also supports the nervous and digestive systems. Good food sources include liver, chicken, milk, eggs, avocados, sweet potatoes, nuts, seeds, and mushrooms.

Vitamin B6

This vitamin helps with metabolizing proteins, building red blood cells, and maintaining blood sugar and healthy skin. Good sources of B6 include fortified cereals, chickpeas, beef, turkey, brown rice, buckwheat flour, and halibut.

Folate

Also known as folic acid, folate is a water-soluble B vitamin best known for its importance during pregnancy in helping prevent anemia in the mother and neural tube defects in the fetus. Folic acid works closely with vitamin B12 in the synthesis of protein as well as the production of DNA and is a key player in development of red blood cells. Good food sources of folate/folic acid include beef liver, legumes, dark leafy greens, and citrus fruits.

Calcium

Calcium is essential for building and maintaining bones, as 99 percent of it is stored in the bones and teeth. The American Academy of Pediatrics has stated that the average dietary intake of calcium by children is well below the recommended levels, which means that they will not develop optimal bone mass, and which can put them at risk for fractures. Toddlers need about 500 mg per day, or about two servings of vitamin D–fortified milk.

There are other great sources for calcium besides milk, including other dairy products, such as hard and soft cheeses, yogurt, and sour cream. Other nondairy sources include salmon, sardines, leafy greens, broccoli, peas, Brussels sprouts, and almond or sesame butters. There are also calcium-fortified orange juices and other calcium-fortified foods.

The amount of calcium in many prepared foods can vary depending upon the brand. For example, one type of cheese could supply only 5 percent of a child's daily allowance of calcium (about 50 mg) while another might offer 30 percent (or 300 mg). Reading food labels can help ensure that your toddler is getting enough calcium.

Iron

As your toddler grows, the amount of hemoglobin in her blood increases. That's what gives blood its red color. Iron is an important compound in the formation of hemoglobin, but if your child isn't getting enough iron (called iron-deficiency anemia), then less oxygen is reaching her cells and tissues, affecting their function.

The symptoms of anemia from the lack of enough iron may come on gradually, but sometimes there are no visible symptoms. An anemic toddler may appear tired with dark circles under her eyes, she may seem sluggish, have a rapid heartbeat, seem more irritable than normal, or have a poor appetite, brittle nails, or a sore or swollen tongue.

The only way to know for sure if your toddler is anemic is through a simple blood test to measure hemoglobin, the substance that gives blood its red color and delivers oxygen to blood cells. Never attempt to treat your child's suspected anemia yourself with iron supplements without first consulting your doctor, since too much iron can be poisonous and could even deadly.

Red meat, including ground beef, provides one of the most easily absorbed types of iron, but there are other sources for iron, too. Try dark-meat poultry (thighs and drumsticks), egg yolks, leafy green vegetables including spinach and kale, brown rice, dried fruits, nut butters, blackstrap molasses (which can be stirred into milk), and iron-fortified breakfast cereals.

How Much Is a Healthy Serving?

It's easy to worry about whether your toddler is getting enough vitamins and nutrients every day. Even though she is starting to look less like an infant and more like a child, she doesn't need as much food as when she was a baby. That may surprise you.

She doesn't need as much food because her rate of growth has slowed down significantly. As a general rule of thumb, you can figure that one serving is equal to about 1 tablespoon of any food type for each year of age, so a 3-year-old serving of unsweetened applesauce would be 3 tablespoons. Keep in mind that this is just a general guideline; let your child's appetite be your guide.

You can mix and match among foods to give your toddler variety, and interesting flavors and textures. For some ideas, pick and choose from the chart below.

TYPE OF FOOD	BEST EXAMPLES	SERVING SIZE
Breads, grains, and pastas	Brown rice; whole-wheat or multigrain bread, tortilla, bagel, or English muffin; whole-wheat or multigrain pasta, barley, bulgur, or quinoa	½ slice of bread; 4 to 5 tablespoons rice, pastas, or grains

TYPE OF FOOD	BEST EXAMPLES	SERVING SIZE
Beans	Black, butterbeans, great northern, kidney, lima, navy, pinto; black-eyed or green peas; lentils	¼ to ½ cup per day
Cold cereals	Low-sugar O-shaped cereal, unsweetened shredded wheat	½ cup
Dairy products	Cheese (cheddar, cream cheese, American, cottage, mozzarella, ricotta, provolone), milk, sour cream, yogurt (plain)	2 cups milk per day; 1 chunk of cheese the size of a large, halved grape (cut smaller) or 3 thin slices; ¼ to ½ cup of cottage or ricotta cheese; 1 cup yogurt; 1 teaspoon sour cream
Eggs	Boiled (and chopped or sliced), egg salad, scrambled	½ egg, never raw
Fish and seafood	Cod, flounder, lobster, salmon (wild Pacific, fresh, frozen, or canned), sardines (canned), scallops, shrimp	2 ounces
Fruits	Apricots, banana, cantaloupe, citrus fruit, kiwi, mango, papaya, tomato, watermelon, or canned, unsweetened fruit packed in its own juice	2 to 3 tablespoons every day or every other day
Hot cereals	Oatmeal (steel-cut oats are best), wheat cereal, grits	1 to 2 tablespoons
Meats	Beef (lean), chicken (skinless), lamb, pork, veal	2 ounces
Nuts	Almond, cashew, or peanut butter (1 teaspoon at a time)	1 tablespoon
Vegetables	Beets, bell peppers, broccoli, carrot, collards or dark salad greens, green beans, kale, onions, spinach, squash, sweet potatoes, zucchini	2 to 3 tablespoons per serving

Carbohydrates, Fats, and Proteins

The foundation of a healthy diet is a combination of carbohydrates, fats, and proteins. According to current information, carbohydrates should make up the bulk of the diet, about 45 to 65 percent of daily calories. Fats should amount to 30 to 40 percent of daily calories, and proteins should account for 5 to 20 percent of daily calories. Let's take a look at each of these foundation items, called "macronutrients."

CARBOHYDRATES

Carbohydrates are one of the major energy sources for the human body. The body breaks carbohydrates down to turn them into usable energy. The process produces tiny molecules of sugar (blood sugar or blood glucose) that are absorbed into the bloodstream to supply energy for running the body's cells. The body will either use its manufactured sugar right away, or it will store it in the liver and muscles for later use.

When it comes to your toddler's health, not all carbohydrates are created equal. Some carbohydrates support good health, others don't.

Simple carbohydrates are sugars that the body uses as fuel. In food terms, it is any starchy, white food. Think of cornstarch, white sugar, or white flour—sticky and gluey. Examples of simple carbohydrate products include white bread and bagels, white rice, white potatoes,

most baked goods, candies, candy bars, and most energy bars. These carbohydrates will give you or your toddler a quick energy lift, but they'll also abruptly leave your system, causing an energy "crash" and creating hunger pangs for more carbohydrates.

Complex carbohydrates, the "preferred" carbohydrates, are absorbed slowly by the body during digestion because they contain protein and/or fiber. Complex carbohydrates help your body retain fluids and provide long-lasting energy. They can be found in fruits, vegetables, beans, and whole grains, such as whole-wheat bread and pastas, brown rice, steel-cut oats, beans, and nut and seed butters.

> **TIP**
>
> The proteins in kiwi fruit and strawberries can cause strong allergic reactions in some toddlers.

Why Some Sugar Isn't So "Sweet"

Sugar is used for making cakes, cookies, candies, soft drinks, juice drinks, and sweetened cereals. But it is also found in other places, too: in breads, canned and packaged soups, ketchup, crackers, peanut butter, tomato sauces, frozen pizzas, cured meats, and salad dressings. These sugars go by

Carbohydrates Quicklist

Remember that for toddlers' safety, foods should be cut into ¼-inch dice, strips, or shreds. All foods should be cooked, steamed, roasted, or pureed. To help demystify "preferred" carbohydrate sources, refer to this quicklist.

Vegetables	Carrots, bell peppers, green beans, okra, pumpkin, squash, sweet potatoes, zucchini
Fruits	Apples and unsweetened applesauce, bananas, blueberries, grapes (seedless halves), mandarin oranges, mango, pineapple, raspberries, tomatoes
Whole grains	Amaranth, millet, oats, quinoa, and other whole-grains

many names, such as dextrose, maltose, fructose, lactose, sucrose, corn syrup and high-fructose corn syrup, honey, fruit juice concentrate, sorbitol, brown sugar, and molasses. Some of the new, natural sugars you might find on labels include agave syrup, stevia, and brown rice syrup.

The sugar that we know—the white, granulated kind—is made up of both fructose and glucose. Fructose is the critical element in high-fructose corn syrup (HFCS). At least one TV commercial says that HFCS is "okay in moderation," but the problem is that HFCS now appears in a staggering array of packaged foods: breakfast cereals, pizzas, fruit and sports drinks, ketchup, fruit yogurts, and crackers and breads. That's just the beginning of the list, and even very young children are ingesting far too much HFCS in relation to healthy carbohydrates supplied by fruits and vegetables.

Read the fine print on ingredient labels. Foods will often show sweeteners in their various forms among the top ingredients in many commercial products. Ingredients are listed in order of their importance in the food, so the foods with higher amounts of sugar will list sugar or a sugar derivative at the beginning of the ingredient list. People who ingest higher-than-recommended amounts of sugar run the risk of developing weight problems, diabetes, high blood pressure, heart disease, and more. Mounting research points to too much sugar (in its many forms) as a culprit in these health problems. Controlling your toddler's (and family's) sugar intake is a great step to improving everyone's nutritional status.

Most young children consume too much juice. One study found that children who drank 12 ounces or more of juice daily were more likely to be shorter in stature and obese.[5]

The American Academy of Pediatrics and the American Academy of Pedodontics both recommend real fruits over fruit juices (see chart below), and milk or water as beverages. Juice, if offered at all to young children, should be limited to ½ cup per day and served in a cup, not a bottle. It should never be taken to bed or carried around during the day in a container, since that allows children's teeth to be bathed in juice sugars, making them more vulnerable to decay. Also, buy beverages that contain 100 percent fruit juice. Beverages labeled as juice drinks can contain 10 percent fruit juice or less.

TIP

Limit your toddler's juice intake to no more than half a cup per day of 100 percent real fruit, no-sugar-added juice.

Whole Fruits vs. Fruit Juices

Whole fruits are better for your toddler than their juices. Since juices typically require multiple fruits to make a single cup of juice liquid, they concentrate juice sugars *and* they're missing the pulp, fiber, and trace minerals of fruits. And, too much juice could cause bloating, gas, and diarrhea.

Here's a comparison of the carbohydrate counts of raw fruits versus their juices:

FRUIT	AMOUNT	GRAMS OF CARBOHYDRATES
Whole apple	1 medium	21
Apple juice	1 cup	28.97
Whole grapes	1 cup	15.78
Grape juice	1 cup	37.85
Whole orange	1 medium	15.39
Orange juice	1 cup	25.05
Whole pear	1 medium	25.66
Pear nectar	1 cup	39.40

FATS

Fat has gotten a bad reputation that isn't fully deserved. It used to be thought that fats were all "bad," but now we know that some are needed by the body, and others are "bad" and can make the body sick.

Good fats are found in your child's brain and body. About 95 percent of your toddler's brain growth occurs between birth and 18 months of age, and her brain is 60 percent fat by weight. Between 30 percent and 40 percent of her calories need to be supplied by fat. But what kinds?

There are four basic kinds of fats, from healthiest to least healthy: monounsaturated, polyunsaturated, saturated, and trans fats.

Monounsaturated fats are considered the healthiest source for fats. Typically, they are liquid at room temperature and turn cloudy when refrigerated. The best sources for these fats are in plant-based oils, such as cold-expelled, extra virgin olive oil. Olive oil and other fats in the monounsaturated fat category have been found to lower rates of heart disease and colon cancer in later life as well as to reduce the risk of diabetes and osteoporosis in adults. In addition, extra-virgin olive oil is higher in vitamin E than other oils. Canola is another monounsaturated oil. Additional sources for these healthy fats are avocados and nuts, which can be made palatable for toddlers by grinding almonds, hazelnuts, sesame seeds, or pecans into nut butters and serving a thin layer on breads, fruits, or vegetable pieces. (Whole nuts can be a choking hazard.)

Polyunsaturated fats stay liquid at both room temperatures as well as at cold temperatures. Their primary sources are sunflower, corn, soybean, and flaxseed oils, and they can also be found in foods such as walnuts, flaxseed, and fish. This fat family includes the omega-3 group of fatty acids, which the body can't produce on its own and which are thought to be powerful inflammation fighters. Good food sources of polyunsaturated fats include fish, whole wheat, peanut butter, bananas, and sunflower seeds.

Saturated fats remain solid at room temperature and melt only at high temperatures. Saturated fats are found in animal products such as red meat, poultry, and fish, tropical vegetable oils such as coconut oil and palm oil, and food products made with those oils. Most toddlers get their fats from the saturated fats found in dairy products, such as whole fat milk, yogurt, and cheeses.

> ## TIP
>
> Store all vitamins well out of reach of your toddler, as too much vitamin A can be toxic and iron poisoning is a leading cause of death by poisoning for children under the age of 6.

Trans fats are considered the least healthy of all fats. They are created by heating liquid vegetable oils in the presence of hydrogen gas, a process called hydrogenation, which makes them less likely to spoil—very good for food manufacturers but very bad for human bodies. The primary sources of partially hydrogenated vegetable oils are shortening, some brands of margarine, and processed foods that have been manufactured with shortening or margarine. (Packages will list partially hydrogenated oils as part of their ingredients on their labels.) Foods that typically contain these unhealthy fats include crackers, candies, cookies, snack foods, fried foods, baked goods, and other processed foods. Trans fats are thought to raise low-density lipoproteins (LDL or "bad" cholesterol), which increases the risk of coronary heart disease, as well as lower high-density lipoproteins (HDL, or "good" cholesterol).

Healthy Fats Quicklist

Remember that for toddlers' safety, nuts and seeds should be shaved, ground, or turned into butters or pastes and served as a thin spread (never by the spoonful). Ideally, nuts and seeds should also be unsalted. To help demystify "healthy" fat sources, refer to this quicklist.

TYPE	SPECIFIC ITEMS
Oils	Canola oil, flaxseed oil (unheated), grapeseed oil, olive oil, peanut oil, sesame oil, soybean oil, walnut oil
Nuts	Almonds, brazil nuts, cashews, hazelnuts, macadamias, pecans, peanuts, pine nuts, pistachios, walnuts (all unsalted)
Seeds	Ground flaxseed; pumpkin seeds; sesame seeds, oil, and tahini (sesame paste); sunflower seeds
Other	Avocados, olives (black or green, pitted)

Of special note: The membranes surrounding nerves and brain cells contain omega-3 and omega-6 fatty acids. The human body cannot manufacture either of these substances, so they have to be obtained from foods. While most people get lots of omega-6 fatty acids, children who are picky eaters may be deficient in the omega-3s.

Food sources for omega-3 fatty acids include oily fish (such as salmon and anchovies), ground walnuts, flaxseed, pumpkin seeds, canola oil, and soy products. Other sources for omega-3s include special eggs produced by feeding hens omega-3 fatty acids, meat from grass-fed cattle, and special mayonnaise that has fatty acids added.

PROTEINS

Protein is found in every part of the body, from your toddler's hair to her toenails. It helps the body repair old cells and build new ones, so it's essential for health. Proteins are broken down into amino acids. The body can't make all of the amino acids it needs, so some must be supplied by foods.

There are two kinds of protein that the body uses: complete and incomplete. Complete proteins are found in meats, poultry and fish, soybeans (read more about soy on page 152), and quinoa. Incomplete proteins don't contain all of the amino acids the body requires but are found in vegetables, beans, nuts, grains, and fruits.

Sometimes parents worry that their toddlers aren't getting enough protein because they refuse to eat meat, but most U.S. children get adequate protein from their diets. For example, it's fairly easy for your child to get enough protein if she drinks 2 cups of milk a day, has ¼ cup of ground beef or turkey, half an egg, or ¼ cup of cheese.

The only children who are at risk of not getting enough protein are those who do not eat meat, eggs, milk, or other combined proteins to make them more complete. To make a complete protein, combine incomplete proteins, such as rice with peas, corn with lentils or beans, or milk with wheat cereal.

Protein Quicklist

Remember that for toddlers' safety, foods should be cut into ¼-inch pieces, or in strips or shreds. All foods should be cooked, steamed, roasted, or pureed. Eggs should be fully cooked. To help demystify the best protein sources, refer to this quicklist.

FOOD TYPE	SPECIFIC ITEMS
Beans	Kidney, lima, navy, pinto, and soybean products (including vegetarian patties, tofu, and tempeh)
Meat	Beef, buffalo, chicken, lamb, pork, turkey, veal
Fish	Pollock, salmon, sardines, snapper, tilapia, trout
Dairy products	Cheese (cheddar, cottage, goat, Monterey Jack, mozzarella, provolone, ricotta, Swiss), milk, sour cream, yogurt (plain)
Eggs	Boiled, scrambled
Nut butters	Almond, sesame, peanut (unsweetened, unsalted)

Fish to Eat, Fish to Avoid

Fish and other seafood can play an important role in a good diet, since they are high in protein and low in unhealthy fats, making them a great alternative to red meat. The safest fish to eat are those with virtually undetectable amounts of mercury or methylmercury, including: American shad, anchovies, Altantic croaker, Atlantic haddock, butterfish, catfish, clams, cod, crab, crawfish, flounder, hake, herring, mullet, North Atlantic mackerel, ocean perch, Pacific mackerel chub, pollock, salmon (including canned), scallops, shrimp, sole, spiny lobster, squid, tilapia, trout (freshwater), whitefish, and whiting.

Some fish contain heavy metals or other toxins. Many of these toxins are thought to accumulate over time, and they may alter children's brain development. PCBs, for instance, have been linked to learning and memory problems in children, and heart problems and possibly cancer in adults.

Avoid these types of fish: king mackerel, shark, swordfish, and tilefish. Also beware of tuna. Fresh and frozen tuna come from bigger fish with much higher levels of mercury, so avoid serving tuna to your child, whether cooked or raw as sushi.

If you have a source for licensed, locally caught fish or like to catch your family's meals, you can follow local and state fish advisories by going to *www.epa. gov/waterscience/fish/states.htm*. For a reputable nongovernment source, try Seafood Watch, with a free online seafood search, downloadable pocket guides, and smart-phone application from the Monterey Bay Aquarium. Visit *www.montereybayaquarium.org*.

Of course, be aware of your child's likelihood for developing food allergies, including for fish and shellfish. See the warning called "Food Reactions" at the beginning of this chapter.

> **TIP**
>
> When possible, avoid fish sticks and frozen, battered shrimp, since those often contain breading and trans fats.

The Soy Controversy

Soy comes from soybeans (edamame beans), and it is widely used in the United States (soy sauce, miso, tofu, and so on). Soy milk began to be used a century ago in the U.S. for controlling diarrhea in babies. By the 1980s it began to be a popular substitution for cow's-milk-based formulas when babies had allergic reactions to them. Tofu, tempeh, and miso are considered excellent

> **TIP**
>
> Avoid soft imported cheeses—such as Brie, feta, Camembert, Roquefort, and bleu—that are usually made from unpasteurized milk.

sources of protein, dietary fiber, vitamin B6, and iron. Soy products are often used by vegetarians and vegans as good substitutes for meat.

On the negative side: Soy can cause allergic reactions in toddlers, such as intestinal inflammation, skin rashes, and, possibly, asthma-like symptoms including respiratory problems, wheezing, and runny nose. With severe allergic reactions, soy can result in serious problems with nutrient absorption (malabsorption syndrome) and severe intestinal inflammation including ulcers along the GI tract and bleeding. The cure for all of these reactions is simply removing soy from the diet.

Isoflavones in soy products have been found to mimic human hormones, such as estrogen. Soy is also thought to interfere with healthy thyroid-pancreatic functioning and the absorption of vitamins A, D, E, and K. The hormonelike properties in soy could potentially affect children's reproductive health later on. The Center for the Evaluation of Risks to Human Reproductive Health (CERHRH) has stated that the risk of soy effects cannot be dismissed, and some European health agencies are suggesting that young children should not be exposed to soy-based foods.

Soy is available in many forms, and it is used in a variety of food products, including milks, hot dogs, vegetable-based hamburgers, cereals, and flours used in doughnuts and similar products. Experts suggest that parents monitor the quantity of soy foods their children consume. Although small amounts of soy appear to be safe, you may want to limit your toddler's intake of soy milks and other soy-based products until research is clearer regarding its safety and long-term effects.

Other Important Nutrients

Most vitamins are nutrients your toddler must get from food because her body doesn't produce them on its own. The best vitamins come from foods and not from chewable vitamins or tablets.

VITAMIN B12

Vitamin B12 is an important contributor to nerve and red blood cell health and to energy levels. This vitamin is found only in animal foods, and good sources of B12 include clams, beef, turkey, chicken, crab, salmon, fortified cereal, trout, and herring.

VITAMIN E

Along with other vitamins, E helps boost immune function and assists in preventing disease. It helps protect the body against heavy-metal toxicity and carcinogens. Vitamin E also fights the free radicals that are destructive to cells. Good sources of this vitamin include vegetable oils, wheat germ, nuts, green leafy vegetables, and whole grains.

VITAMIN K

This is another important component of the blood. It is needed for blood clotting and healthy healing. Vitamin K is made from intestinal bacteria. Good food sources include Brussels sprouts, broccoli, scallions, and leafy greens such as kale, collards, spinach, turnip greens, beet greens, and mustard greens.

PROS AND CONS OF COMMERCIAL VITAMINS

If your toddler is eating mostly healthy foods, then it's very likely she's getting all the nutrition she needs without the need for extra vitamins. But if she's a picky eater, or eats a lot of sugary processed foods and drinks a lot of juices, then you may want to consider giving her a daily dose of vitamins.

Most parents assume that the U.S. Food and Drug Administration (FDA) regulates how vitamins are manufactured and sold in the United States. However, that's not the case. Manufacturers themselves are responsible for ensuring that a dietary supplement is safe before it goes on the market, which means unsafe vitamins could be sold. Manufacturers do not need to register their products with FDA nor get FDA approval before producing or selling them, but product labels have to be truthful and not misleading.

Vitamins are made up of several different components—enzymes, co-enzymes, and cofactors—that must work together to have their intended effects on your toddler's body. The majority of commercial vitamin supplements found in supermarkets and pharmacies contain synthetic vitamins derived primarily from coal tar derivatives. Although they may mimic vitamins from natural food sources, in some cases they may not perform as well as those that occur naturally.

It's important to look at the fine print on the label to ensure that the vitamins you're giving your toddler are made from real foods, which will be listed there. Many synthetic vitamin C supplements, for example, contain only ascorbic acid or a compound called ascorbate, which contains less acid. In reality, ascorbic acid represents only a portion of vitamin C complex. So, in this case, look for rose hips and other food sources used for making the vitamin.

In 2007, Consumer Labs, an independent, consumer laboratory that tests the purity and consistency of commercial vitamins and the accuracy of their ingredient labels, found widespread quality variations, with more than half (52 percent) of the brands tested either including lead (a contaminant), breaking apart improperly, or containing significantly more or less of the ingredients claimed on the labels.[6]

One brand of children's vitamins was found to contain 216 percent more than its labeled vitamin A, delivering potentially toxic levels to children younger than 8 years of age.

In addition, some children

develop allergic reactions to their vitamins. Symptoms are wide ranging, from more irritability and fatigue than usual to coldlike symptoms that don't go away, such as a clear nasal discharge, sneezing, sniffling, wheezing, and even asthma, or skin reactions such as otherwise unexplainable itching and skin rashes, and sometimes sleeping problems.

For safety's sake: Keep all drugs, including vitamins, in childproof cabinets your toddler cannot reach. Avoid taking vitamins and other medications in front of your child, because she may be tempted to copy you. Don't keep medications in your purse or night table where she could get into them, and never call vitamins "candy" or encourage repeat dosages of children's vitamins, even if they're packaged like candy. Bottom line: Whenever you're in doubt about the quality of your child's multivitamin, consult your health-care provider for recommended brands and amounts.

TIP

Store vitamins out of your toddler's reach, administer the proper dosage yourself, and watch to make sure the dosage is ingested.

TIP

Limit your toddler's daily salt intake to no more than 2 grams (or about a third of a teaspoon).

Feeding Your Younger Toddler

Between 12 months and 18 months, your toddler will begin to chew with a rotary movement of her jaws. Her hand and mouth coordination are starting to improve, and she's interested in trying to hold and manage a spoon. She can sit alone easily and is interested in socializing with others, so she may like the idea of joining family meals, even if only for a short time.

By the time she reaches 3, she'll be a lot neater and more civilized and able to sit down on her booster seat at the table with the family, fork and spoon in hand to share what everyone else is eating. But until that happy day, you're going to need a durable (and washable) high chair, a supply of bibs and sippy cups, and lots of patience. Even though your 1-year-old may appear ready and able to learn how to feed herself, it will involve lots of messy practice and clean-ups.

Opinions have changed for what makes good food for children at this age. In the past, it was thought that a toddler's delicate stomach couldn't manage adult foods. Now, the sky's the limit, and it's thought that toddlers enjoy trying out a variety flavors and textures, just as children and adults to. Any food that's non-alcoholic and not too salty will do, as long as it's soft enough or in small enough pieces that it won't cause choking.

Simple flavors work best. For a child's tablespoon-sized servings, any vegetable that is boiled, steamed, or microwaved until tender, then cooled and mashed or finely chopped will work. Plus, with such ease of preparation, nothing's lost if she decides to turn her nose up at it.

BASIC FEEDING TOOLS

There is some basic gear that no parent of a toddler should be without. Here's what you need:

- **High chair.** Your child should always be seated and strapped down when eating to avoid messes, choking, and falls. A chair with removable, washable coverlets, an easy-to-install tray, and lockable wheels is a godsend.
- **Spoons.** Once your child gets to the "I'll feed myself" toddler stage, her fingers may be the best utensils, followed by a short, thick-handled spoon and rounded fork set. There shouldn't be any sharp points or edges, and all should be dishwasher safe.
- **Bowls and dishes.** The steeper the sides of the bowl, the easier it will be for your child to scoop up food. Even though you can buy fancy warming dishes or ones with suctioned bases, the most important features are that they are unbreakable, and dishwasher safe, and contain no nooks and crannies to harbor dried food and germs. Steep-sided rice bowls,

salad bowls, and ramekins will have a life beyond Baby.

- **Quick chopper.** There was a time when moms had to prechew their children's food if they were concerned about choking hazards. Now baby fare comes prechopped and blended to make it more digestible and appealing. Until your child sprouts her first set of premolars for grinding tough stuff (generally around 24 months), you'll need to chop up her food into roughly ¼-inch pieces. A simple 1- or 2-cup mini-chopper will do the job.
- **Microwave.** Many parents swear by microwaves as timesavers, but they do heat food unevenly, leaving pockets of scalding heat that could burn your child's mouth. If you decide to microwave food for your toddler, heat only small portions for 15 to 30 seconds, then stir the food with a clean finger to make sure it's evenly warmed. Scrambled eggs or instant oatmeal will need more time to cool down than they took to cook in the first place.
- **Bibs.** The best versions come with a trough at the bottom to contain spills and keep your child's clothes clean and dry. Most of those tidbits can make an appetizing "second course." Disposable bibs come in handy for travel and eating out. In a pinch, a snack bag clip, hair claw, or clothespin can be recruited to fasten a dish towel or a cloth napkin around your toddler's neck.
- **"Splat" mat.** If you worry about your toddler's meals ending up on your floors, a thick shower curtain

cut to extend one foot beyond your child's high chair, or a square of thick, vinyl sheeting can be used for a good moisture-proof catchall. Just don't trip on it!

- **High-chair toys.** Toys with strong suction cups that fasten onto the high-chair tray are a handy distraction while you're preparing food and put an end to the "drop it over the side and watch Mom pick it up" game.

Shower-curtain rings, spoons, paper-towel tubes, or balls of foil can be makeshift distracters.

- **Dining room digs.** Restless toddlers may not be able to sit through a family meal. Consider adding some interesting toys in a bin in your dining area so she can play on the floor nearby and everyone can finish the meal in peace.

Feeding Your Older Toddler

Once a toddler's "I'm my own person" phase hits, food strikes are common. Refusals could also apply to anything green, mushy, or any other particular food quality your toddler has decided, at least for now, are offensive to her sensibilities. No cajoling, threats, or silliness can change her mind.

A super-busy toddler may only be interested in grabbing food on the go, or she may be ravenous for a day or two followed by several days of less appetite. She may squirm and complain to be let down almost from the minute she's strapped into her high chair, or decide she's only interested in playing with her food or throwing it overboard instead of eating it. (Lucky dog!)

Toddlers' small bellies are designed for frequent grazing in small quantities. Typically, they need to refuel every few hours to keep running at peak efficiency.

Food Reactions

About 20 percent of the population is allergic to something, and food allergies and sensitivities in toddlers are common.

- If your child coughs, wheezes, or develops breathing problems after eating a food, it could be a sign that he's having a severe allergic reaction. Go to the emergency room right away.
- If your child develops hives or skin rashes or blisters, a clear runny nose, or digestive problems within 3 to 12 hours after eating a particular food, that could be a milder sign of a food allergy. If your child is losing weight, seems pale or listless, gags frequently, or has very loose or very hard stools for more than a few days, it's definitely time to notify the doctor.
- Talk with your child's doctor about what's happening, and consider keeping a food journal to see if you can spot the culprit. Cow's milk, soy, wheat gluten, nuts, eggs, and acidic fruits and vegetables such as citrus, tomatoes, and strawberries are all common allergens.

The easiest way to work through a finicky-tot situation is to take a relaxed attitude. No healthy child will allow herself to starve. As long as she isn't losing weight and is otherwise healthy, there's nothing to fear.

WHEN YOUR TODDLER WON'T EAT

Here are some reasons why toddlers snub food:

- **Natural feeding patterns.** Toddlers naturally tend to stock up on food during their active, daytime hours, and their appetites diminish in the evening.
- **Drinks.** If your child is tanking up on milk or juice, the chances are really good that her appetite for food will be affected.
- **Snacks.** Loading up on snacks within 2 hours of a meal could affect her hunger.
- **The "I wanna do it!" phase.** She may refuse to eat from a spoon because she wants to feed herself with her fingers, which for her is a lot easier and more pleasurable than using a utensil.
- **Texture preferences.** Some toddlers prefer mushy textures to crunchy ones. Sore gums from an erupting tooth may also be causing chewing discomfort.
- **Hunger cycles.** Appetites may be small on some days and big on others. An oncoming illness such as a cold can affect appetite, too, and an ear infection could make swallowing painful.
- **More serious causes.** If your child is losing weight, seems pale or listless, gags frequently, or has chronic diarrhea or constipation, then there could be a more serious physical problem going on that needs your health-care provider's attention.

TRICKS FOR TREATS?

As you will soon realize, mealtime may not the best time to try to mold your toddler into the genteel and polite child of your dreams. You want your tot to clean her plate, to eat her vegetables before dessert, and to start using a child-sized fork or spoon instead of her grubby hands.

You decide to get tough and to lay down "the rules," but that inevitably escalates into your issuing ultimatums, pleading, and arguing when she doesn't get with your program. Instead of getting polite compliance and "yes, ma'am," you get mealtime drama, lots of fiddling, and back-arching accompanied by an adamant "no!"

It's very tempting (and easy) to slip into using food and treats to get your toddler to do what you want her to, and or to threaten to

> **TIP**
>
> Your toddler may reject foods offered at the table on a plate in favor of foods packaged in fast-food containers. Consider putting your own nutritious foods inside and see what happens.

withhold food and treats for the same reason, as in: "No ice cream for you today because you had a temper tantrum in the store."

One study of 20- to 24-month-olds found that 12 percent of parents resorted to bribery to get their toddlers to eat. The tactic is just another way of putting pressure on your child to consume food, when what's more important is that she learns to heed her own "I'm hungry," and "I'm satisfied" signals.

From a toddler's point of view, a grown-up's denial or reward of food seems very arbitrary, since she doesn't fully grasp what you consider "good" or "bad" behavior and what that has to do with being given something to eat or being denied a promised treat.

So, she may not make the connection between acting out in the store and having food withheld. Plus, using food for bribes could spur bad eating habits later on.

> **TIP**
>
> The food industry spends more than $10 billion per year advertising to children. Ninety-five percent of the ads are for fast food, soft drinks, candy, and sweetened cereals.

> **TIP**
>
> Stews and soups, lasagna, meat loaf, and pasta sauces are great places to hide finely minced or pureed vegetables.

Your Family Food Makeover

Research shows that if there are only healthy food choices in toddlers' homes and that's what they're offered to eat all of the time, they are more likely to choose those food options even when they're away from home. On the other hand, if there's lots of grazing on salty snacks, sugary between-meal treats, or heavy desserts then those preferences will stick with toddlers, too, wherever they are.

It's really not that hard to make over your family's food choices when you compare how similar a toddler's diet is to an adult's diet.

> **TIP**
>
> Raw oysters are not recommended for children because they can carry water contaminants.

Food Choices for Active Older Toddlers

An abundance of food options can be used for mini meals and quick bites for active older toddlers any time of day. Many of these are not intended for younger toddlers, who could choke on them:
- Cold, unsweetened applesauce mixed with plain, full-fat yogurt and sprinkled with cinnamon

- Baked or stir-fried zucchini strips marinated in Italian dressing and sprinkled with seasoned bread crumbs and Parmesan cheese

- Bite-sized pieces of baked sweet potatoes

- Small, bite-sized pieces of cantaloupe or strawberries

- Frozen bite-size blueberries

- Whole-wheat bread with a thin layer of natural, creamy peanut or almond butter and topped with banana slices

- Mashed pinto or black beans seasoned with ground cumin

- Mashed, cooked sweet potatoes or winter squash formed into small bite-sized balls and rolled in cereal crumbs

- Scrambled or boiled egg in bite-sized pieces

- Chopped, seeded watermelon, peaches, and other soft fruit

- Cottage cheese with crushed fruit

- French toast made from egg and milk and grilled in canola oil or butter

- Mini-sized whole wheat or buckwheat pancakes spread with all-fruit jam

- Cheese slices melted on half of a whole-grain English muffin

- Mini whole-wheat waffle sandwich with peanut butter and mashed banana filling

- Instant oatmeal made with a choice of diced, dried raisins, cranberries cherries, or fresh blueberries

- Thin strips of bell peppers served with a pureed cottage cheese and dill dip

- Steamed broccoli, cauliflower, or carrot pieces coated in melted butter or healthy margarine and sprinkled with Parmesan or other shredded cheeses

- Peeled cucumber strips served with ranch dressing

- Cold yogurt "parfait" in with layers of plain yogurt, cereal, and berries or mandarin orange segments

- Banana strips dipped in plain yogurt and rolled in crushed cereal and frozen on a cookie sheet

- Half a whole-grain pita pocket stuffed with ricotta cheese and thin slices of peeled apple

- Ready-to-eat cereal mixed with dried fruit in a sandwich bag for travel

- Half a whole-grain waffle, spread with plain yogurt and thinly sliced peaches

- Toasted pita triangles for dipping in hummus or pureed bean dip

- Whole-grain bread fingers spread with olive oil and toasted for dipping in mild salsa

- Mini whole-grain toaster waffle cut into fingers for dipping in unsweetened cinnamon applesauce

- Whole grain bread slices cut into shapes with cookie cutters and spread with peanut butter, whipped cream cheese spread, or pimento cheese

- Lettuce leaves topped with thin turkey or ham strips and shredded cheese, rolled up like a tortilla

- Mini toasted pizza made from half of a whole-wheat English muffin spread with tomato paste and topped with mozzarella cheese heated in the toaster oven and cut into 1-inch squares

- Mustard spread on a slice of deli turkey and wrapped around a breadstick

- A grilled, thin-sliced turkey or ham with Swiss cheese sandwich using whole-grain bread and cut into quarters

- Quesadilla strips made from a warmed whole-wheat tortilla, and heated fat-free refried beans, and topped with chopped tomatoes and shredded cheese

- Small pieces of pizza made from whole-grain pita bread topped with steamed veggies (in ¼-inch dice) and shredded cheddar or mozzarella cheese

- Sweet-potato or rutabaga "fries" roasted in canola oil and sprinkled with salt-substitute seasoning or dill weed

- Whole wheat crackers spread with avocado guacamole and mild salsa

- Shredded raw carrots and chopped raisins moistened with low-fat or olive oil–based mayonnaise and spread on whole-wheat bread

- Waffilla: Whole wheat tortilla sandwich spread with shredded cheese and low-fat refried beans, toasted in waffle iron, and cut into small triangles

- Homemade vegetable soup made with organic vegetable or chicken broth

- Creamed soups using steamed vegetables pureed in milk, served in a cup.

Sample Side-by-Side Menus

SAMPLE TODDLER MENU	SAMPLE ADULT MENU
Breakfast Scrambled eggs Cheerios Cup of milk	**Breakfast** Scrambled eggs Toast Cup of milk
Snack Banana Cup of water	**Snack** Banana Water
Lunch Berries Cup of hummus and thin slices of pita Cup of milk	**Lunch** Berries Hummus pita sandwich Drink
Snack Pretzel sticks	**Snack** Pretzel sticks
Dinner Lumps of liverwurst Minced broccoli Cooled, mashed baked potato Cup of water	**Dinner** Steak Broccoli Mashed potato Water, wine, coffee, or tea

If you're ready to do a family food makeover, one of the best ways to get started is to plan ahead what your toddler and your family are going to have at the beginning of each week. Think ahead about healthy breakfasts, lunches, and dinners, and the nutritious snacks you'll need at your fingertips. Creating a formal grocery list and sticking to it will feel like a positive step in the right direction and will keep you from falling for less-than-healthy foods on impulse.

Arrange your list according to where you plan to begin and end in the store. Select your market carefully. These days you're not limited to big-box superstores or chain groceries. Now you can shop at whole foods and health food stores, farmers markets, and other alternatives for fresh meats and produce. And there's no need to stop there: Some families are growing their own produce, including urban dwellers, so don't feel limited by your options.

But if you're walking through the typical food store, your top priorities should be nutritious, healthful, body-building foods found along the perimeter of the store, such as fresh meats, poultry, and fish, colorful fresh vegetables and fruits, and dairy. Whole-grain breads and cereals and brown rice also play a part in supplying needed vitamins, minerals, and fiber while also providing sustained energy.

Let's be clear: a healthy diet doesn't mean an austere one. It doesn't mean a low-fat or fat-free one, either. Toddlers' brains and bodies need fat to thrive. Full-fat milk and dairy foods can contribute much-needed vitamins such as potassium and vitamin D to help to maintain strong bones and teeth.

However, according to the American Academy of Pediatrics (AAP), not all toddlers need to drink whole milk. Children often get their fat intake from non-milk sources, and those who are at risk for overweight or obesity, or those whose families have a history of high cholesterol or heart disease, can use reduced-fat and even skim milk starting at 24 months of age. Recent studies have shown that toddlers who drink reduced-fat and nonfat milks develop normally.

Mealtime Guidance

Here are some tips for encouraging your toddler to eat:
- **Plan ahead.** When possible, plan your toddler's meals in advance.
- **Diversify.** Offer between two and five food choices per mealtime (one per snack).
- **Scale down.** Serve just a few room-temperature tablespoons at a time.
- **Start with fingers.** Young toddlers like pinching up their food from their high-chair tray.
- **Bowl tricks.** For a spoon feeder, serve a couple of different foods next to each other in a small, unbreakable bowl.
- **Be colorful.** Strive for a variety of colorful foods. First comes room-temperature finger foods, such as berries, liverwurst, soft pieces of peas, or Cheerios with a sippy cup of water on the side. Follow with messier foods that have more complex flavors.
- **Recycle.** Offer rejected food again. It may take three or four times before she's willing to try it, or she may never like some foods.
- **Share the fun.** Join your child at mealtimes, and make it a relaxing and enjoyable time to be together. Sit with her and be very excited about what you're eating.
- **Don't be a neatnik.** Let dinnertime be messy. There's always a bath and tooth brushing before bed.

The Vegetarian Toddler

Vegetarian toddlers can easily meet their protein needs by eating a varied diet, as long as they consume enough calories to maintain their weight. In the past, the common opinion was that foods had to be carefully combined to make sure that toddlers got "complete" proteins with every meal. But that opinion has changed, and it is now thought that a mixture of proteins throughout the day is sufficient.[6]

Many common foods can quickly add up to provide sufficient protein for your toddler. Good food sources include: beans, lentils, nut and seed butters, chickpeas, green peas, whole-grain breads, leafy greens, potatoes, and corn.

Monitor the following nutrients if your toddler is vegetarian or vegan: vitamin B12, riboflavin, vitamin D, calcium, iron, and zinc.

VITAMIN B12

Since B12 is found only in animal foods, lacto-ovo vegetarians (those who eat milk and eggs) can get their daily allowances through dairy products and eggs. Vegan children can try soy products within limits (see soy discussion on page 152), veggie burgers, nutritional yeast, and some breakfast cereals. Some toddlers may need a vitamin B12 supplement.

RIBOFLAVIN

Also known as vitamin B2, riboflavin helps convert macronutrients (carbohydrates, fats, and proteins) to energy and helps support tissue repair. Soy products (see discussion on page 152), green peas, asparagus, beet greens, spinach, and okra are good food sources of this vitamin. Vegan toddlers can also try almond butter, yeast extract spread (such as Vegemite), and fortified breakfast cereals.

VITAMIN D

Most of the best vitamin D sources are found in animal foods, but with moderate amounts of sunlight (about 20 minutes per day on the hands and face), most light-skinned children can manufacture sufficient amounts of vitamin D internally. However, if ultraviolet rays are blocked by air pollution, your child is dark-skinned, or you follow a vegan diet, supplementation may be necessary. Vegetarian toddlers can get their vitamin D through cow's milk, soy milk, and some fortified breakfast cereals.

CALCIUM

Calcium, as discussed earlier, is found in the body, mostly in bones and teeth. Vegetarian toddlers typically get ample calcium in their diet from dairy products. Vegan toddlers can try beans, blackstrap molasses, Chinese cabbage, collard greens, ground nuts (be aware of nut allergens), kale, and turnip greens.

IRON

Getting sufficient iron is important for all toddlers, especially if they don't eat meat. Vegetarian and vegan toddlers can get adequate iron from dried fruits, baked potatoes, mushrooms, cashews, dried beans, spinach, chard, tofu and tempeh (again, see the soy discussion on page 152), bulgur, and iron-fortified foods such as cereals, instant oatmeal, and veggie "meats."

Using iron cookware can also increase iron intake, and combining vitamin C–rich foods (citrus fruit or juices, tomatoes, or broccoli) with iron sources can help your toddler's body absorb iron better.

ZINC

Zinc supports normal growth and development in toddlers, and supports immune system function and the healing of wounds. Because there are rich plant-based sources of zinc, most toddlers of all dietary persuasions typically get about the same amounts of zinc through diet.

However, vegetarian and vegan toddlers tend to eat more amounts of foods that are high in phytic acid (whole grains and legumes), which blocks the absorption of zinc. Eating miso soup or miso paste with zinc-rich foods will help enhance zinc absorption. Other things you can do to reduce the phytic acid in grains and legumes is by soaking them for at least 3 hours or overnight, then discarding the soak water, and by eating yeasted grains, such as whole-grain breads.

> **TIP**
>
> The American Dietetic Association recommends that vegetarian toddlers 2 to 3 years old need about 16 grams of protein per day, and vegan toddlers need 18 to 21 grams.

Choking Dangers

Most choking fatalities among toddlers are caused by nonfood items. These might include small parts from toys, pen and marker caps, marbles, coins, magnets, watch batteries, and deflated latex balloons. Although it's fairly rare for tots to suffer a fatal choking accident from food, it's important to always play it safe. But where does a parent begin? Right here.

> **TIP**
>
> Consider enrolling in a CPR course offered by your local Red Cross chapter, community college, or safety agency.

FOODS TO AVOID

There are some foods that might
seem to be no-brainer no-nos for
toddlers, such as hard candies. But
a few old-favorites foods, such as
cheese chunks, are also potential
dangers. Avoid serving foods
that break into chunks (Vienna
sausages and toddler meat sticks);
thick, sticky foods (peanut butter);
or foods that could plug a child's
windpipe (carrot coins or hot dog
slices). Taking these precautions and
preparing toddler-friendly portions
takes the scare out of these foods.

- **Nuts, seeds, and popcorn.**
  Whole and chopped nuts, pumpkin
  and sunflower seeds, and popcorn
  can cause choking in children
  under 3. Nuts should be crushed,
  flaked, or pureed into butters.
  Never feed spoonfuls of nut
  butters, such as peanut butter,
  to your child. Use smooth rather
  than chunky versions and spread
  them in a thin layer on crackers,
  bread, or thin slices of fruits or
  vegetables.
- **Hot dogs.** Their rounded shape
  and flexibility form a perfect
  airway plug and they are very
  difficult to dislodge once they
  get stuck there. They, and finger-
  shaped sausages and "toddler"
  meat sticks, are equally as
  dangerous. Either serve in small
  pieces (¼-inch dice) or avoid
  altogether.
- **Hard vegetables, crunchy
  fruits, and chunky cheeses.**
  Raw carrots, whole grapes, raw
  or cooked corn, cherry tomatoes,
  raw green beans, and cheese
  chunks also pose a risk unless
  they're diced or shredded.
- **Chewing gum and hard or
  sticky candies.** Toddlers
  shouldn't be given gum to chew.
  They'll swallow it, and they
  could choke on it. Round or
  hard candies such as gumdrops,
  butterscotch candies, caramels,
  marshmallows, and jelly beans
  should be avoided, too, since they
  can form a perfect seal in a tot's
  small windpipe and cut off her air
  supply.

GAGGING AND SWALLOWING PROBLEMS

Children who have swallowing
problems often are extremely
picky eaters. They frequently may
gag on food or throw up during or
after eating and will reject foods
that are difficult for them to chew
and get down. The problem could
be poor tongue, jaw, or throat
muscle tone and coordination,
or the problem could also be a
chronically inflamed throat from
gastroesophageal reflux (GER)
disease, in which food travels up
the esophagus and digestive acids
cause burning sensations in the
throat.

If you suspect either of these
problems, your toddler's doctor
is the best person to advise you
on how to help your child. Some
university medical schools have
pediatric gastroenterologists
(children's gastrointestinal
specialists), and many communities
have physical, occupational,
and speech therapists who have
training in helping children with
these issues.

Until you find a solution, you

may want to offer nutritious pureed foods or fruit or fruit-and-veggie smoothies served in cups with wide straws, along with child versions of vitamins and minerals in liquid or appealing, chewable forms that would normally be supplied by a well-rounded diet.

SAFETY TIPS

To make foods safer for your toddler, follow these tips:

- **Cut small strips.** Cut round, slick foods, such as hot dogs, toddler meat sticks, celery, and cucumbers, into short, matchstick-sized strips, and shred carrots.
- **Chop up chunks.** To reduce the threat of choking, cut cooked potatoes, carrots, beets, string-free celery, meats, or fish—anything in large chunks—into small, bite-sized (¼-inch) pieces.
- **Debone.** Carefully remove all bones from fish, chicken, and meat before serving.
- **Remove pits and seeds.** Remove seeds and pits from plums, peaches, grapes, olives, and other seeded foods.
- **Give food a fork test.** Cook foods until they're easily pierced with a fork.

Signs of Choking

Choking occurs when something blocks your child's airway. If she can speak or cough loudly, her airway is only partly blocked—do not try to open the airway. Instead, phone 911.

Signs of choking in the child with a completely blocked airway:
- The child suddenly begins to cough, gag, or have high-pitched, noisy breathing.
- The child holds her neck with one or both hands.
- She has bluish lips or skin.

ACTIONS TO RELIEVE CHOKING IN A CHILD

When a child 12 months or older is choking and can't breathe or speak, you must give abdominal thrusts (the Heimlich maneuver). The Heimlich maneuver pushes air from the child's lungs, like a cough.
1. Kneel or stand firmly behind him and wrap your arms around her so that your hands are in front.
2. Make a fist with one hand.
3. Put the thumb side of your fist slightly above the navel (belly button) and well below the breastbone.
4. Grasp the fist with your other hand and give quick upward thrusts into her abdomen.
5. Give thrusts until the object is forced out and she can breathe, cough, or talk or until she stops responding.

If the child becomes unresponsive, shout for help or call 911, lower the child to the ground, and start CPR. If someone else is present, send that person to call 911 while you start CPR.

For information about giving CPR, visit *www.americanheart.org*, before an emergency happens.

> **TIP**
>
> Children who are at risk for food allergies should wait until at least age 3 to try foods that are potential allergens.

Q & A

Q: I'm worried about my 1-year-old. He seems ravenous all the time! He refuses baby food and cries and complains until we feed him "table food" like the rest of the family. He has a bigger appetite than my 4-year-old daughter! Should I stop him from overeating? How much can one toddler eat? I don't want him to be overweight.

A: Your child is equipped with an elegant, built-in program that tells him when he's full and when to stop eating, so it's important to allow him to regulate how much he eats (or doesn't). Toddlers' appetites vary a lot, and some children aren't interested in eating, while others have huge appetites, especially when they're going through a growth spurt and mastering how to crawl and walk. What's important is to supply your child with healthy food choices, such as palatable meats, fruits, vegetables, and whole-grain cereals, pastas, and breads, instead of allowing him to load up on snack foods that are nutrition deficient, greasy, salty, or loaded with sugar, high-fructose corn syrup, and other sweeteners, or chemicals and preservatives.

Q: Our 14-month-old daughter has suddenly become a very picky eater. She's getting downright finicky, and she's not much into meat. One day she may love pasta and cheese, and the next day she may refuse it, mash it into her high chair tray, or drop it on the floor. Any advice?

A: Most kids do become picky at about that age. And they also continue to grow and thrive, even when they have eating strikes. It's hard to know in advance what will work for them from one day to the next. The best idea is to look at nutrition from a weekly or monthly perspective, rather than a daily one. There's no need to get into a battle of wills. Just give her healthy choices, and remove her from the chair if she starts dawdling and dropping food overboard, a sure sign she's finished and getting bored. Teach her to say "all done" and to hand over her bowl as a substitute for giving everything to the dog.

Q: Our son was normal weight at birth, but his growth curve slowed way down from 3 months onward. He was breastfed the first year and started solids at 4 months. Now, at 28 months, he weighs only 21 pounds, 6 ounces. He doesn't eat much and often skips meals, but otherwise, he's active and seems healthy. Medical tests don't show anything wrong with him. What can we do to make sure he's well nourished?

A: First, check on your size and the size of your child's other parent. If either of you is petite, he's likely reverting to his genetic code. If your son chokes or gags frequently and seems to only want to eat pureed foods, he may have a swallowing problem that needs to be looked at by a specialist. That said, it's typical that kids his age to turn into picky eaters, only wanting cheese, French fries, or other quirky food choices. Try serving him small meals every few hours, measured in tablespoonfuls and centered around his favorite foods, with new things introduced alongside them. If there are no issues with dairy, try sprinkling some of his foods with grated parmesan cheese, or serving veggies with a tasty cup of dip of herb-flavored yogurt or diluted nut butter. Also keep an eye on beverages, as they can affect appetite. A chewable vitamin pill can help to ensure he's getting all the vitamins and minerals he needs until his appetite picks up.

Q: Our daughter is 3 and she has been having diarrhea every few days. Her doctor told me to give her clear liquids, applesauce, and banana. Isn't there something else she can eat besides that?

A: Diarrhea in toddlers has lots of causes. It can be aggravated by lots of things, including teething, allergies to milk products, fatty foods, too much juice, viruses, taking antibiotics, and so on. Follow your doctor's advice about what to feed your toddler, but inform the doctor if your daughter's problem doesn't improve, or she appears to be unwell and to be losing weight. Ask about her drinking Pedialyte or other beverages designed to replace lost electrolytes and minerals. The BRAT diet, which stands for bananas, rice, apples, and toast or tea, is often recommended for diarrhea. Applesauce has pectin that helps to solidify stools. Bananas have the same effect. You might also consider serving her warmed chicken or beef broth. After her diarrhea eases up, your toddler's intestinal tract may be aided by yogurts with probiotics that help to replace the intestines' friendly bacteria that have been lost.

Self-Care

The toddler years are amazing: You start out with a completely dependent, crawling baby in diapers, and only a few years later, you're rewarded with a walking, talking little person who can actually use the toilet, wash his hands, brush his teeth, bathe himself, dress himself and put on his own shoes and socks. (Whatever will you do with all of your spare time?)

The road to independence can sometimes be rocky, though, and it demands a lot of flexibility and patience on your part. Of course you want your child to become his own person, but your toddler's stubborn insistence on doing things *his* way, complete with folded arms and pouting lower lip, can be a challenge for any parent.

This chapter offers time-tested and parent-approved tips for self-care instruction and techniques to help increase your child's success and reduce his frustration, especially when it comes to his own dressing, grooming, and hygiene.

The Wee Walker's Wardrobe

Your toddler doesn't need a closet or chest of drawers stuffed with clothes, just a handful of mix-and-match items that are comfortable, washable, and fit well. Choose stretchy fabrics that allow for lots of movement without binding and will be easy for him to put on and take off. Avoid buying sizes that are too big, with the hope that you'll get more wear out of them—too-loose clothes can pose a choking or tripping hazard.

Here's the scoop on wardrobe:

- **Wide necks.** A toddler's head is relatively larger than the rest of his body, and he has a short neck and sloping shoulders. Go for shirts or dresses that have a snap or button neck, either on the front or on the shoulder. Avoid turtlenecks, and shirts with excessive or tiny buttons or snaps.

- **Comfortable waistbands.** Choose pants or leggings with wide, soft elastic waists. Toddlers have short legs and round little bellies, so you want pants that can go from playtime to naptime and stay on without constricting. Baby yoga pants or sweatpants will be more comfortable and work better for potty training than styles that zipper and snap.
- **Correct pants length.** Don't dress your child in pants that are too long in the hopes he will grow into them. Even if you roll up the cuffs, pants legs have a way of becoming unrolled and getting underfoot, creating a tripping hazard.
- **Complementary colors.** Bright colors and patterns are fun, but if you want your child's clothes to coordinate keep in mind that the more neutral the colors and patterns of your child's wardrobe are, the less effort it will take to put outfits together.
- **Leg covers.** Leggings or bloomers will protect the legs and bottoms of girls in dresses. Thick tights can work, too, and will spare you having to hunt down matching socks. But avoid nylon tights or hose, which bunch up, fall down, and are easily torn in the wash.

Wardrobe Check

Check your toddler's wardrobe for the following essentials:
- 7–10 pairs of pull-up pants, overalls, and/or leggings
- 7–10 T-shirts or play dresses
- Lots of socks in a matching, neutral color (pairs always get separated)
- About 40 diapers or training underpants for each week
- 1 seasonal dress-up outfit for holidays, weddings, or more special events
- 7 pajama sets
- Everyday shoes
- Rain boots, cold-weather boots, pool sandals, and dressy shoes
- 3 to 4 sweaters or front-zipping sweatshirts
- A waterproof coat that can double as a rain jacket
- Hats and mittens for cold weather

CHOOSING SHOES

Though toddlers go through shoes really quickly, the good news is that they need only a few pairs at a time: an everyday pair, possibly a spare pair, and specialized or seasonal shoes, like snow boots or water shoes for the pool.

Too-small shoes will hurt and too-big shoes will be hard to walk in. Incorrectly fitting shoes can hinder your toddler's proper foot development, so it helps to have your child's feet measured at a shoe store every couple of months. You can also buy handy home shoe sizers for about $20 (search "children's shoe sizer" on the

Web). Having a home sizer comes in handy if you plan to buy shoes online or through catalogs. You can also measure your child's foot with a ruler and refer to the chart below.

Taking off shoes is normal toddler behavior, but if your child pulls off his shoes at every opportunity or stops playing to take them off, consider that the shoes may not be fitting properly and it's time to measure his feet again.

Shoe Sizes in Inches

U.S. SHOE SIZE	FOOT LENGTH IN INCHES
4	4 ¹/₃
4 ¹/₂	4 ¹/₂
5	4 ²/₃
5 ¹/₂	4 ⁵/₆
6	5
6 ¹/₂	5 ¹/₆
7	5 ¹/₃
7 ¹/₂	5 ¹/₂
8	5 ²/₃
8 ¹/₂	5 ⁵/₆
9	6
9 ¹/₂	6 ¹/₆

Getting Dressed (and Undressed)

Just when you master diapering and dressing a squirming baby, the child takes it to a whole new level: standing up, taking off what you just put on, turning the whole getting-dressed thing into a game of naked tag. His drive is there; all that's missing is the coordination!

• **Put on a happy face.** Kids can pick up on a negative attitude instantly from your body language and tone and will mirror what you project. Even if the past few times you dressed your child were thoroughly aggravating, take a deep breath and start the process fresh, with a smile on your face and a calm and cheerful demeanor. Call it *Project Getting Dressed Is Super Fun* (even if that's not exactly what you're feeling on the inside)!

- **Start with undressing.** For toddlers, taking off clothes is easier than putting them on. As soon as your child shows signs of being able to take off shoes or jackets, at around 18 months or so, encourage his taking off his own coat each time you enter the house. Before bath time, let him take off what he can, such as his socks or his diaper. Taking off and/or putting on certain clothes will not just build fine motor skills but will also help reinforce that there are certain times when dressing or disrobing is appropriate (or not)!

- **Allow plenty of time.** There will always be days when you simply have to dress your child yourself to hurry out of the house, but try to build extra time into your daily schedule so that your child can practice his skills. Lay out clothing in advance, and put shoes and socks together in the correct positions for pulling on. Let your toddler do what he can—first putting his own arms through shirtsleeves and jacket sleeves and stepping in to pants, then progressing to pulling up pants, and finally pulling shirts or outfits over his head. It takes time to sort through the mystery of left versus right and top versus bottom. Give him an extra minute or two to figure out what should happen next, and gently offer suggestions or step in whenever he gets tangled up or frustrated. The goal is to foster independence, not to force it too early.

- **Make getting dressed fun.** Talk about each dressing step you're about to do before you do it. This helps your child prepare himself for what's going to happen next and also helps build language. Try to be lighthearted about the process: Make arm, leg, and neck holes a game of body-part peek-a-boo. ("Where are your fingers? There they are!") When your child is old enough to understand, you can ask, "Do you want to get dressed yourself, or do you want me to do it for you?"

- **Control escape routes.** When your child has outgrown being dressed on the changing table (usually when he's old enough to stand up), move your dressing operation to the floor. If your child tries to make getting dressed a game of "catch me if you can," don't play along. It will be cute the first few times but will quickly try your patience. Instead, put on your serious voice and find a smaller space to use for dressing. Limit his space: Locate your dressing spot in a corner of the room so he has to get past you to make his escape. Consider locking the door while you dress him if necessary.

- **Indulge wardrobe whims.** Even if colors clash, or he wants plaids to wear with stripes and dots, it doesn't hurt to indulge your toddler's wardrobe choices once in a while, so long as it's not inappropriate. Everyone will understand, and it might even prompt a smile. If your son is into his superhero phase, allow him to wear his cape or his gloves. He may be more inclined to dress himself if you let him choose his wardrobe.

Bathtime Fun

Most kids just love water! There's no need to invest in lots of clever bath toys to keep your toddler entertained, though there are plenty of fabulous ones out there. All you need to do is fill the tub and provide a toy or some plastic cups. Then you can relax in the bathroom until your little darling turns into a prune, entertaining yourself however you want to as long as you're within arm's reach. You could also use bath time to trim your child's fingernails—the water softens the nails, making them easier to cut.

Almost all toddlers hate having their hair shampooed. Kids' eyes are especially sensitive, and water or shampoo can really hurt. A toddler's natural reaction is to bend his head forward when water is poured on it, and that can make things worse. To rinse, a spray attachment for your tub faucet can help. Also try swim goggles or a bathing visor to keep soap out of his eyes.

Keep a towel on the side of the tub or hanging from a suctioned hook for ease of reach. Having a suction mirror on the side of the tub can help make shampooing more fun by letting him watch while you shampoo him. Silly, soapy "hairdos" are part of the fun.

Suctioned fishnet hammocks are available for holding and draining tub toys after the bath so they're out of everyone else's way.

SHOWERING SAVVY

When it comes to getting messy toddlers clean, nothing compares to a quick rinse-off in the shower. Showers save time, but the downpour of water can be scary to some kids, and the chemicals in water and shampoo can hurt their eyes.

It helps to introduce the shower experience to your toddler at a regular bath time, and not after a run-in with a skunk or a fall into a deep mud puddle.

Get in the shower first yourself, and use a hand sprayer attached to your tub faucet or shower head to gradually introduce the spraying effect, starting with your toddler's feet and working your way up, avoiding his face. Some toddlers feel safer if you hold them while you shower them.

Avoid shampooing during a first introduction to the shower. Later, when you wash his hair, keep a dry washcloth within arm's reach, just in case soap or water gets in his eyes.

BALKING AT CLEAN-UP TIME

Some toddlers go through phases when they become totally phobic about taking a bath or shower. Of course, a healthy fear of water is a good thing: You don't want your child running full-speed into it. But sometimes children develop such a fear that it becomes difficult just to keep them clean. The strong aversion may happen after a child is accidentally placed in water that's too hot, or he has had his eyes stung by water or shampoo.

And sometimes, what may at first look like a sudden and unexplained fear of water could be something else, like routine toddler limit testing just to see what will happen if he pitches a fit at bath time, or an end-of-day overtired meltdown. If he stages a meltdown when you turn on the tap, stand him in shallow water and give him a "tops and tails" (face and bottom, in that order) washing.

But if your child isn't just fussy but clearly panicked at the sight of water, don't force him into the tub or act angry or frustrated—this will only reinforce his fear. Instead, in a locked bathroom, undress him, then draw yourself a nice bath and hop in the tub with some toys, or even your toddler's big brother or sister. (Wear underwear or a bathing suit if you're weaning or not into self-exposure.)

Then play, smile, enjoy yourself, and blithely ignore your child (watching him out of the corner of your eye, of course). Eventually, his curiosity and drive to be the center of attention will get the better of him. Let him take his time. When he approaches the tub, let him play with toys in the side of the tub, placing him on your lap so he's not touching the water. Then, slowly ease him into the water as he becomes comfortable.

IMPORTANT BATHING SAFETY TIPS

Drowning and bathroom accidents are a big deal and send lots of toddlers to emergency rooms every year. Here are some important precautions to take to ensure your toddler stays safe and sound:

- **Declare taps off limits.** Lots of kids have been burned by turning hot water on themselves. Don't let your child play with the faucet, and reduce his temptation for it by seating him with his back to the faucet, or cover it with soft spout guards.
- **Stay close.** Gather all of the bathing supplies you'll need ahead of time. Never leave your toddler alone in the bathtub, even for a minute, until he's at least 5. He could slip and injure himself, and children can drown in less than an inch of water in just a few minutes. Also, if your child sees you're not there, he may try to climb out to find you and hurt himself in the process. Ignore the telephone or the doorbell, or if you must answer, wrap your child in a towel and take him with you.
- **Prevent falls.** Install slip-resistant decals or a no-slip tub mat.
- **Turn down the water temp.** The thermostat on your water heater should be set at 120°F, at most. Hot water can be dangerous: It takes only 5 seconds for a child to receive third-degree burns from faucet water set at 140°F. If you have one-tap faucets, reduce the risk of scalding by turning the cold on first and off last.
- **Don't overfill.** Keep the depth of the tub water at about your child's waist when he's in the sitting position.
- **Enforce the sit-down rule.** Don't let your child stand up in the tub unless you're rinsing him off or washing him with a washcloth and have a hand on him to catch him if he slips.
- **Avoid suctioned bathtub**

seats. They have figured in the drowning deaths of more than forty children.

- **Save soap and shampoo for last.** You don't need to soap or shampoo your toddler every time—only when he's visibly dirty or smells funny. Soaps and shampoo are drying to children's skin and can cause irritation. When you do soap or shampoo,

save it for the end of the bath so your child doesn't spend long soaking in soapy water. Don't use soap on your child's sensitive face or bottom.

- **Watch the appliances.** Keep electric appliances, including hair dryers, curling irons, radios, and other plug-ins, away from the tub. They can cause electric shock.

Dental Care

As soon as your baby's tiny tooth buds begin to emerge, it's time to make a habit of cleaning off food particles using a square of damp gauze or a finger brush and a dab of baby toothpaste.

The first appearance of little teeth also marks a good time to start looking for a dentist. Many dentist practices treat children, but you can also search for a pediatric dentist (pedodontist)—ask your own dentist or your child's pediatrician for a recommendation.

Most dentists will schedule the first exam at 1 year and the first cleaning between the ages of 2 and 3, but it's nice to have someone in your phone book before then in case you have a question or a dental emergency, such as a knocked-out or chipped tooth.

In the meantime, keep his teeth clean to prevent cavities. According to the Centers for Disease Control and Prevention, 28 percent of children 5 and under have visible cavities, and tooth decay affects one in five 3-year-olds.

In fact, tooth decay is the most common chronic disease of childhood and one out of every

two children have decay, which is caused by *Streptococcus mutans*, a bacterium that thrives inside the mouth. Not only is decay painful for your toddler, it can also affect how his permanent teeth grow in. That's because the first teeth are space holders for the adult teeth that grow in between age 5 and early adulthood. Decay can migrate into the gums and affect permanent teeth.

Drilling and filling toddler cavities is also a relatively big deal because it usually requires sedation. So as much as your toddler might dislike having his teeth brushed, it's important to do it anyway. He'll eventually, grudgingly, get used to it if you do it consistently and don't give in to squirming or fussing.

FINDING AND KEEPING A GOOD DENTIST

The AAPD recommends that a first dental checkup happen around age 1. It's great if you can find a children's dental specialist, called a pedodontist, who works solely with children. This means they'll have a child-centered office, often with lots of toys, a child-scaled dental chair, and a staff specifically chosen to work well with children.

If you don't have access to a children's dental specialist, there are still plenty of dentists in regular practices who are sensitive to children, perhaps because they are parents themselves. Other parents are a great resource for finding a good dentist who's skilled at working with young children. Signs of a not-so-good choice for children: no children's playthings in the waiting room, trying to separate child from parent "because it makes children more cooperative," using force, or chiding to have their way with an upset child.

To search the AAPD database for a pedodontist, see *www.aapd. org/finddentist/*.

Your toddler's trip to the doctor's office can be scary for him. Being touched and moved around or getting an oral injection feels like a frightful violation. You can help your older toddler to get through the ordeal by preparing him in advance, but a younger toddler won't be able to handle a dental visit longer than an hour.

Let him know on the day of the appointment that you will be getting in the car to go see the doctor. Here are a few strategies for taking the fear factor out of that first appointment:

- **Time it right.** Try to schedule appointments for the best time of day for him, when he's least likely to be hungry or tired.
- **Play while you wait.** Bring along a security object, a few small toys, a snack, or a favorite book to read in the waiting room.
- **Hold him.** If your toddler seems worried or anxious, ask the dentistry staff if it's okay for him to sit in your lap during the exam. If not, then sit or stand beside him with your hand on him to help him feel less threatened.
- **Coach the staff.** Ask the nurse or doctor to explain what they're going to do before they do it and what it's for. They can also provide the names of the things used by the doctor and explain what they're for in simple language.

HELPS FOR ORAL HEALTH

Here are some parent-tested tips for maintaining your toddler's pearly whites:

- **Ban the bottle at bedtime.** Toddlers might love having a bottle or sippy cup at bedtime, but going to sleep with a bottle of milk or juice can cause sugars to pool around your child's teeth. The end result can be "baby bottle mouth"—white, chalky decay spots on your toddler's teeth, causing them to eventually crumble and break off.
- **Beware the sticky starches.** According to the American Academy of Pediatric Dentistry (AAPD), crackers are actually worse for children's teeth than caramels! The starches in crackers are just as harmful to teeth as the sugar in candy, but caramel sugars actually dissolve more quickly. So don't let your

child snack on starchy foods such as crackers, cookies, or cheese puffs all day long.

- **Don't share mouth germs.** The group of germs that cause tooth decay can be transmitted by parents to their children through sloppy kisses and sharing eating utensils, which may make your child more prone to tooth decay. Maintain your own dental health, don't kiss your toddler on the lips, and don't share your child's utensils.
- **Encourage water drinking.** Sugars and the plaque they cause are more likely to stay in dry mouths. Giving your toddler lots of water to drink helps to wash away sugars and tooth buildup, and fluoridated water will block acid production and help to remineralize teeth.
- **Limit the juice.** Keep his intake to 4 to 6 ounces per day, and don't let him walk around with a cup of juice. If your child loves juice, stretch his daily ration by watering it down.

TOOTH BRUSHING ESSENTIALS

Most kids don't like putting anything in their mouths that isn't food or a bottle, and they're likely to clam up as soon as they see toothpaste. Still, to keep your toddler's mouth healthy, it's important to persevere and keep at it!

Pick Your Paste

For children older than 6 months, the AAPD recommends using a "smear" (about the size of a dried grain of rice) of toothpaste with fluoride, and wiping teeth off with a wet cloth afterward. Fluoride is a compound that attacks the bacteria that cause cavities, which helps prevent tooth decay.

Fluoride toothpaste for children under the age of 4 is a bit controversial, though. Swallowing fluoride can cause permanent tooth discoloration and can be toxic. Some pediatric dentists recommend using a fluoride-free paste until a child is old enough to be trusted to spit out all of the paste, or to skipping toothpaste altogether—the brushing action is the most important, they say. But, from a parent's point of view, a flavored "practice" toothpaste may motivate your child to tolerate the toothbrush in his mouth. Ask your toddler's dentist or health-care provider for a recommendation.

Select Your Scrubber

Scrubber options are a finger toothbrush, such as those by Safety 1st or Tiny Teeth, moist gauze or a damp washcloth wrapped around your fingertip, or a miniature baby toothbrush. If you choose a brush for your toddler to handle himself, select one that is small, and has a fat, easy-to-grasp handle and extra-soft, rounded bristles. There are also double-sided chewable toothbrushes, such as Brush-Baby brand, that work while your toddler chomps on them. They're not readily available, and you may need to search online or at a specialty store to find one.

There are also child-sized, battery-operated vibrating

toothbrushes. Don't spend too much on one until you know how it works, because some children are terrified of the buzzing sound. Too, the brush may be messy and will spatter when it's not inside your child's mouth. But it could be a solution for toddler jaw clamping and getting at least *some* teeth clean.

When your child begins to show improved control over his hands at about age 4 or 5, then he may be ready to try cleaning his own teeth. With a tiny dab of children's "practice" (nonfluoride) toothpaste on his finger, have your toddler practice "brushing" the front, the back, and the top of teeth in front of a mirror. He can also practice rinsing and spitting.

Pick the Place

For a younger toddler, it may be easiest and tidiest to brush his teeth while he is in the bathtub. For an older toddler, a sturdy stepstool will help him reach the sink and view himself in the mirror. It should be high enough that there's plenty of room to lean over for rinsing and spitting. Another option is to create a child-sized tooth brushing station using a low table with a mirror mounted on the wall and a nonbreakable kitchen bowl in place of a sink.

Get the Right Motion

As best you can, try to brush away from the gum line, brushing down on the top teeth and up from the bottom teeth, to flick the bacteria and plaque away from gums and off of the teeth. *Don't* go side to side, which can actually grind bacteria and plaque into the gum line and in between teeth. (Pick your battles: If he's willing to try brushing and goes side to side, allow it.)

Rinse and Spit

When it comes to rinsing and spitting, your little beginner is going to have difficulty getting water in his mouth without spilling it, drizzling it on himself, or swallowing it along with the toothpaste. With fluoride-free toothpaste (or no toothpaste) you can get away with not rinsing, but if you use fluoride toothpaste, proper rinsing is a must.

You can get the water in his mouth with a cup, water squeezed from a plastic (needleless) syringe, or a squeezable plastic water bottle with a nozzle. Convincing your child to spit water out without swallowing it is another story, though. Try showing him what to do and offer lots of praise when he gets it right.

Flossing

Flossing is an important part of daily hygiene for teeth. Your child won't be able to reliably get between all of his teeth on his own until school age. As soon as your toddler has enough teeth that they're close together and bacteria can grow between them, it's time to add flossing to your repertoire. Dental floss holders are especially helpful for getting floss into the tight spaces between molars. Flavored dental floss can make flossing more appealing.

Another option is a dental water jet (such as those made by Waterpik)—though, like electric toothbrushes, your child might be terrified of it, and water will be going everywhere. So only invest in one if you think you'll use it, too.

Stay the Course

Don't be shocked if your child clams up, tries to grab the brush, or pitches a fit when he sees the toothbrush coming toward him. Most toddlers hate tooth brushing, though some kids are more tolerant than others. The AAPD recommends "cheerful persistence." Try to stay positive and relax—don't let your body language give away that you're preparing for a battle, or you just might get one.

> **TIP**
>
> Gargling mouthwash isn't recommended for children until they reach age 6.

WHEN ALL ELSE FAILS

Tooth brushing works only if you do it consistently—at least once a day, and twice is even better. Brushing at the same time every day will also help your child get used to it. But if every brushing is becoming a battle between the two of you, here are some things to try:

- **Change it up.** Switch toothbrushes, switch to a washcloth, or try gauze instead of a brush.

- **Give him some control.** Invite your toddler to choose a new toothpaste from among a few that are appropriate for his age.
- **Get a closer view.** Use a mirror. Your toddler may be less resistant to brushing if he can watch what's happening. (Magnifying mirrors can be particularly captivating.)
- **Do a demo.** Brush your own teeth in front of him first, and later the two of you can brush teeth side by side.
- **Make it more fun.** While brushing his teeth, try singing a song, recounting everything he ate that day ("There's the beans! Let's get them out of there!"), tell a story about a lion with big teeth, count teeth one by one, or do something else playful to keep him happy and distracted.
- **Pretend on others.** Invite your toddler to pretend brushing the "teeth" of dolls and stuffed animals with a dry brush.

BREATH SAVERS

A toddler with a healthy mouth and throat shouldn't have bad breath. Cavities, tooth decay, and gum infections are primary causes of bad breath. Don't try to mask a breath problem with mouthwashes or rinses, because toddlers are likely to swallow them.

Some possible other causes for bad breath include: (1) a throat or sinus infection or other low-grade inflammation, (2) gastroesophageal reflux (GER), which allows stomach acids to travel up the throat, (3) dry mouth, trapping bacteria in the mouth instead of washing it away in saliva, possibly caused by medications, (4) mouth breathing at night, or (5) having an object stuck up his nose, such as a dried bean, raisin, or part of a toy.

Wean on Me

Just like a cherished cup of hot coffee in the morning, or your nightly serving of Ben & Jerry's, getting your toddler to wean from his beloved breast or bottle can loom as a daunting task. He may be downright addicted to his familiar way of doing things and will scream for hours in protest when he is denied his primary source of comfort. But weaning is an important part of your toddler's journey to more independence.

There is no gold standard for when and how to change your toddler's drinking habits. And no matter what doctors or your mother-in-law say, weaning your baby-turned-tot from breast or bottle is purely a personal decision on your part.

Learning to drink from an open cup or glass is an art to be mastered. Your toddler has to figure out how to prop the edge of the cup on his lower lip and to use his tongue differently while he gulps liquid slowly enough so it won't pour out the sides of his mouth and soak his clothes.

Plastic training cups with spill-resistant, snap-on lids with spouts are a great way to transition away from a bottle to beverage containers. Cups differ in how easy they are to use and how readily liquids leak when they're turned upside down—something toddlers love experimenting with.

A bottlelike nipple on the top of the cup might work best for your beginner; then again, they may protest that it's a clunky and unlovable bottle and demand the more efficient version back. Others respond well to cups, especially if they present appealing graphics and colors, such as action figures and the like.

Likely you'll need to be flexible and try out a variety of cup brands until you find the one or two versions that work best with your toddler. Choose colorful, BPA-free cups that are visually appealing. (BPA, or bisphenol A, is thought to be an unhealthy component in some plastics.)

Whichever models you choose, they need to be unbreakable, and dishwasher safe with no sharp edges at seams that could cut small hands or sensitive lips. (A cut-off fat straw stuck through the lid of a fast food beverage cup can work in a pinch.) Use art materials to put his name on "his" cups to help reinforce them as important identity objects. Encourage visits with kids who have become cup-drinking experts, or think about throwing an intimate "sippy cup" party with a few other toddlers to help to enhance his interest in this new activity.

Here are some ideas for transitioning to cups:

- **Keep the focus on comfort.** Don't try to undertake any other major habit changes, such as toilet or sleep training, at the same time. Flood your child with ample cuddling and attention, accompanied with lots of chances for rigorous play and letting off steam to heighten the need for sleep. If he's tired, he may be more willing to take a cup versus a bottle.

- **Replace the least-needed bottles first.** Some experts advise replacing a bottle with a cup at a "neutral" time of day, not at mealtime, because toddlers can get frustrated and overwhelmed if they're thirsty but can't figure out how to use the cup. When you start replacing bottle feedings with cups, try the first one in the morning, since that's when your child is the most alert, lively, and thirsty and may be willing to take a beverage however he can get it. Next try the "wake-up" bottle from naptime, followed by the "settle-down-for-naptime" one, and finally the nighttime "necessity" bottle that so many toddlers resist giving up.
- **Head off thirst.** Try instituting substitute routines for the time your child normally would be cuddling up to the bottle. If he normally needs a bottle at naptime, try offering him liquids in his sippy cup before naptime nears. It'll reduce his thirst and will introduce alternate, pleasant associations when it's sleepy time.
- **Make the bottle less interesting.** One way to diminish "bottle appeal" for an older toddler is to slowly dilute the contents of the bottle with water. Do this over the course of several weeks, starting with 75 percent milk to 25 percent water, followed by 50 percent milk and 50 percent water, then 25 percent milk to 75 percent milk.
- **Praise to the hilt.** Make a big deal out of your tot's successful use of the cup. Notice the sounds when he drinks, how he makes the milk go away, the way he holds it so tightly. Brag about his newly acquired drinking skills to others.
- **Get "authorities" to help.** Enlist the help of your child's dentist or health-care provider to help convince your child that *now* is the time to let go of bottle drinking. That will enable you to take the neutral "We're just doing what Dr. M says to do" stance.
- **Plan a "no-bottle" vacation.** Plan a family vacation with your child with bottles left at home but training cups on board so that he gets to try his wings at being bottle-free in a new setting.

SAYING BYE-BYE TO BINKY

You can probably postpone trying to break your toddler of his pacifier addiction until after the stormy and somewhat unpredictable toddler stage. Since most children give up their pacifiers voluntarily sometime between ages 2 and 4, many dentists don't get overly concerned about toddlers' pacifier habits until permanent teeth start coming in—though others feel they may contribute to ear infections.

Ultimately, because the upper jaw isn't as dense as the lower jaw, extended and intense pacifier sucking can cause the upper jaw to change from a U to a V shape. When that happens, it can cause a child's teeth to misalign with a visible opening in the front, and upper teeth may eventually protrude outward, changing how a child bites and chews foods. The misalignment can also put front teeth at risk for chipping or breaking. If your child continues to suck after his permanent teeth erupt, he may need braces.

To pull the plug on your toddler's beloved mouth stopper, you can follow some of the same strategies for weaning from bottles by getting your health-care provider(s) to give their advice and for you to mimic that advice at home, encouraging "big-kid" behaviors with ample amounts of praise for success, and starting slowly but gradually phasing out the pacifier. Be prepared for possible setbacks, but stay the course.

SIZING UP THUMB SUCKING

It's estimated that more than 3 out of 4 children suck their fingers through the first year of life, especially when they're bored, tired, or upset, and about 1 in 5 children are still doing it by age 5.

Just in case you're getting pressured by your in-laws (or elders) about your toddler's thumb sucking, here are some things to keep in mind: Most experts agree that a thumb sucker younger than 5 shouldn't be pressured to stop. The majority of children give up the habit on their own before they enter kindergarten.

Since, unlike pacifiers, fingers are permanently attached, pediatricians and dentists usually *don't* recommend that parents try to stop a finger- or thumb-sucking habit during the toddler years. It's an uphill battle, and it's likely to raise resistance or even entrench your toddler more deeply into his habit.

Thumb sucking is an appropriate and useful behavior for babies and toddlers because it helps them comfort themselves. With children entering school, the habit can lead to being rejected by peers, and it might cause an overbite and problems with pronunciations. There are other problems that prolonged thumb sucking into childhood can cause, such as calluses on the thumb, chapped skin, and sometimes fingernail infections.

For a preschooler, a chart for the kitchen with sticker rewards for days and weeks without sucking that includes a prize at the end of the week for success works pretty well, but it's not always a motivator for a toddler. Have a backup plan for slip-ups, which are bound to happen. Putting perfume or cologne chosen by your preschooler on the tip of his thumb will make it smell pleasant, but taste strange, which could serve as a gentle nighttime reminder.

Your toddler will need extra TLC while he is trying to overcome his sucking habit. That could be extra hugs, more praise and support for small victories, and offers of special outings and games to help take his mind off of the urge. And you may want to pay special attention to times when it's more likely to happen, such as sitting in front of the TV or riding in the car, and plan alternate activities for helping him get over the hump.

If these strategies don't work, there are special oral appliances that prevent sucking.

Potty Training 101

At the most basic level, potty training teaches a child how to control the two sphincter muscles that hold back elimination until it's an appropriate time to relax them. The challenge for kids is learning to recognize the sensation of needing "to go" while there's still enough time to get to the potty, get pants off, and get into the right position.

There is something called "infant potty training," which is the norm in warm rural climates, like large parts of Asia and Africa. With infant training, the baby goes bottomless or in crotchless pants starting at about 2 months of age. Caregivers (usually mom, grandma, or older siblings) stay close at hand and watch for cues that the baby is about to go. When the caregiver picks up the cue, she holds the baby in a certain position over the intended target and makes a specific noise. Using this method, by age 6 months or so, most babies become conditioned to go when they get in the position and hear the noise. This method has been adapted by some parents in the West, too.

But for most parents, potty training begins when a child recognizes the "gotta go" feeling and acts on it—at 18 months of age or older. Statistically, the average age that toddlers achieve potty-training success in the United States is 30 months (2 ½ years), with girls training a few months sooner than boys do. That average age is going up, though, and according to recent surveys 1 in 4 kids aren't trained by age 4.

It is thought this late-to-the-pot phenomenon probably has a lot to do with the wonderfully comfortable and absorbent disposable diapers in the Western world that let children reach toddlerhood without making the connection between the urge to go and the result. The convenience of disposables can also make parents less motivated than they were in cloth-diaper days when stinky diapers piled up in the diaper bucket.

> **TIP**
>
> If training becomes really stressful for either of you, consider going back to training pants and then trying it again in a few weeks or even a few months.

Quick Chart

When it comes to toileting, did you know that:
- Some children are ready for self-toileting by 2 or 2 ½ but others aren't interested in the process until much later. The average potty-training age is 34 months for girls and 37 ½ months for boys.
- On the whole, girls master self-toileting as many as 6 months earlier than boys, so avoid comparing your son's progress to that of, say, his female cousin the same age.
- Usually, but not always, having bowel movements in the toilet is achieved before gaining total urine control.
- Your toddler may be able to stay dry all day for a month or two before he stops wetting the bed at night.
- Mastery requires linking a series of smaller steps together, which usually takes time (and attention). While some rare (and usually very mature) children master self-toileting almost overnight, most take several months or even longer to become "trained," with accidents still happening occasionally, especially at night.
- "One step forward, two steps backward." Accidents and regression are more likely when there is illness, moving or traveling, a new baby's arrival, or other family stresses, such as marital discord.

Signs of Potty Readiness

When it comes to potty-training readiness, age is just a number. Rather than counting months, it's better to pay attention to developmental milestones:

YOUR READINESS	YOUR CHILD'S READINESS
You and other family members are ready to concentrate on this milestone and to be involved.	He stays dry through naps, likes to imitate parents or siblings, and talks comfortably about bodily functions.
There are no other major stresses or upcoming vacations that you know will interfere with the process.	He shows interest in using the potty and/or wearing big-kid underwear.
You're willing to take your child to the potty every single time he has to go and stay with him until he's through.	He squats, squirms, strains, or announces when he's about to go and can follow simple one-step directions.
You're willing to commit to staying positive and to resisting the urge to punish for accidents.	He has a somewhat regular stooling schedule and can pull down his pants and underwear.

GOTTA-GO GEAR

It's not unusual for toddlers (and their parents) to show some signs of readiness, but not all of them. Some kids see older siblings or parents using the potty and ask to use it too, so all that's needed is a potty chair and some encouraging words. Then again, some kids never show interest in using the potty. If your child is developmentally on track in other ways and is at least 36 months old, then you may want to consider starting the process anyway. You may discover that he needs only a little nudge—and just a few supplies—to get started.

Training Pants

Disposable training pants are convenient, but like disposable diapers, they're so absorbent and comfy they can keep kids from understanding the cause-and-effect of wetting their pants. Cotton training pants, which are like thick underwear, will help your child learn faster. One option is to use disposable Pull-Ups for a few weeks while your child is getting used to the concept, then with great fanfare make the switch to "big-boy" training pants, preferably those that have favorite characters "who don't like to get wet" emblazoned across them.

Potty Chair

It's a personal preference whether you want to use a child-sized potty chair or a toilet ring and stepstool. The advantages of potty chairs are that they're easier and safer for a child to use; toddlers going through their possessive, "It's mine!" phase will enjoy having their own private throne; and you can tote and move it to wherever is convenient. Freestanding, flushable urinals, such as Peter Potty, are also available for boy training, but they are bulky, labor-intensive to maintain, and take up a lot of bathroom space.

On the downside, all potty chairs have to be cleaned out after every use, and realistically, at some point your child will need to learn to use an actual toilet. Units that have lots of bells and whistles, like lights, toilet paper holders, and ornate add-ons, may not work as well as simple, utilitarian pots, primarily because such gadgets only signal "playtime," which may encourage your toddler to dawdle and fiddle with the gizmos rather than do his toileting "duty."

If you go the toilet-ring route, be sure to also get a stable stepstool that is the right height for your child to rest his feet on when he's seated on the toilet. (A second stepstool for hand washing at the sink will save a lot of lugging back and forth.) To prevent falls and getting fingers pinched, always "spot" him while he's climbing up and down.

The ring adaptor should fit securely to the regular toilet seat, have no pinch points or sharp edges or seams that could scratch, and be convenient to remove and store so others can use the seat, too. A front shield or mound-like guard will be useful for catching a boy's spraying accidents. Some companies, such as Potty Pal, make toilet seats that replace standard toilet versions with a hinged, child-sized ring that can be flipped into place when your child is using the toilet and flipped back up for everyone else.

For road trips, consider getting a portable, folding potty seat that you can keep in the trunk or backseat. You'll also want to bring along a hand sanitizer and tissues or wipes. Plan to give public toilet seat surfaces a quick wipedown, or use a layer of toilet paper on the seat to help protect your child's bottom from germs.

Potty-Friendly Extras

Here are a few more toileting-friendly items you can consider having on hand:

- **Clothing** that's fast and easy to pull up and down (no tights, overalls, or overly snug waistbands).
- **Support materials**, such as potty-training picture books and DVDs, such as Alona Frankel's *Once Upon a Potty*, available in both boy and girl versions (and as a DVD). Potty-training dolls come in girl and boy varieties, including Potty Scotty and Potty Patty, and there's even a Sesame Street Elmo version.
- **Flushable moist wipes** such as Huggies Clean Team Flushable Wipes.
- Washable or disposable **waterproof car seat cover** for "I can't wait any longer!" moments, such as PeeWees Disposable Seat Savers.

STEP-BY-STEP POTTY TRAINING

Before you start potty training, take a week to prepare, with the goal of getting your child and the family comfortable with pottying words and concepts. This is the week to mount an all-out media campaign by reading those potty books, watching potty DVDs, and letting your child play with a doll that sits on a toy potty and wets.

Be sure to take your child into the bathroom to model pottying behavior, but don't pressure him to use the potty himself, yet. Welcome his taking the initiative, though, since he may be more cooperative if he thinks it's *his* idea, not yours.

Revving Up the "Potty Talk"

Decide what words to use for various body parts and actions so that you can get in the habit of using the same words every time. It'll be confusing for your child if, say, you call a bowel movement "poop," your husband says "number two," and your child's caregiver uses the word "stinkies." If your child is in day care, ask what terms caregivers use and use those at home as well, for continuity.

Some people have the opinion that you should always use the "correct" terms, such as "urinate," "defecate," and so on. The important thing at this stage is for you and your child and caregivers to be consistent and use terms that everyone can understand. (For the sake of clarity in this book, we'll go with the most commonly used terms: "pee," "poop," and "potty.")

On the other hand, it's a good idea to use the proper terms for body parts, like "penis" and "vagina," because if, later on, if your child encounters a physical problem, you want him to be able to explain to you or a doctor exactly what's going on and where. Also, one person's cute word can be someone else's off-color language, and you don't want your child to use terms that might offend others.

Practice using terms that will come in handy for the act of self-toileting while you (or another family member or sibling) demonstrate and talk it through:

- I have to go potty.
- Pull down your pants.
- Sit down.
- Wipe from front to back.
- Pull up your pants.
- Stand up.

Potty-prep week is also a good time to get into the habit of giving your child positive instructions, as opposed to "don't" statements. Toddlers can get confused and may only remember what comes after the "don't."

Instead of saying this:	Try saying this:
Don't stand up yet.	Sit down (using hand gesture for "down").
Don't pull your pants up yet.	Keep your pants down (pointing finger to ankles).
Don't play with that.	Keep your hands up here (patting his thighs).
Don't use so much toilet paper.	Just this much toilet paper (showing the amount).

Choosing Your Roadmap

So you're toddler's comfortable with the potty, you've stocked up on training pants and stretchy bottoms, and you've watched *Elmo's Potty Time* and read *Everybody Poops* about a hundred times (or more). Do you really need a formal potty-training strategy?

There are a bunch of different methods out there, and pretty much anything that doesn't involve punishment or shame and employs praise for successes eventually will get the job done. Some toddlers are visual learners who respond well to books and DVDs and demonstrations by parents. Others respond best by hearing spoken directions, and still others learn best by making potty time a predictable part of a daily routine (or a combination of all of these).

Your best bet is to find a method or a combination of methods that suit your child's individual learning style. Here are a few of the most popular potty-training methods:

- **The No-Pants School.** Parents claim to have achieved accelerated potty training by devoting an entire day or weekend to having the child go bottomless around the house, and bestowing lavish praise when he uses the potty.

  This is one way to kick-start training, and it can be especially helpful for kids who show no interest or motivation to potty-train even though they're developmentally ready in every other way.

  Needless to say, you'll want to take up any antique rugs, throw a sheet over your sofa, and buy a bottle of upholstery cleaner beforehand.

This method is labor-intensive for parents, but it usually does work quickly, and if your child is ready for training, you may be able to have him largely trained within a weekend.

- **Diaper Cold Turkey.** Similar to no-pants training but slightly less messy, with diaper cold turkey you shop together for big-kid underwear or present underpants and a potty as grand gifts. Then, your toddler simply stops using diapers during the day.

  There will be accidents, and pants leak, so you'll want always to have a change of clothes, paper towels, and clean-up spray on hand. As with every method, successes are lavished with praise while accidents are treated nonchalantly: "Oh well, better luck next time!"

- **Timed Potty Breaks.** This method involves commitment to a timed schedule. You take your child to the potty at regular intervals during the day, such as 10 minutes after every meal and every half hour throughout the day. Again, success is highly praised, while accidents are minimized.

- **Any Little Doll Can Do It.** After you show your child the pottying routine, he then teaches his potty-ready dolly, or other toy or stuffed animal, how to do the same. Some specially made dolls will drink a water bottle, then pee into a doll-sized potty. Everyone claps and encourages both the toddler and the doll.

- **M&Ms for BMs.** Some parents find that material rewards like

ringing a bell, pressing a clicker, singing a special potty song, or putting stickers on a chart for hitting the mark provide that extra bit of motivation that makes a difference in pottying success.

Some parents resort to candy, O-shaped cereal, or other edibles as rewards. Unfortunately, a lot of treats for potty tricks can add up to a lot of calories until your child gets the hang of it. Plus, you might be obliged to carry the reward with you wherever you go, or give it out at inopportune times, such as before bedtime after he's brushed his teeth.

If your child is in day care or with a babysitter during the day, share ideas with his caregiver(s) to ensure that everyone stays on the same page and that any reward offered is consistent. You need to both agree on what the rewards will be and what will be rewarded—for instance, is there to be a reward for every potty trip whether it produces results or not? Will you reward only for successful results on the potty, or also for staying dry all day long? By collaborating, rewards will remain consistent.

A NOTE ABOUT CONSTIPATION

Sometimes a cold or sore throat can cause a bad stomachache in children, and more rarely, so can appendicitis, but constipation is one of the most overlooked causes of severe stomach pain. It's a common problem for infants and children and accounts for almost

3 percent of visits to pediatricians' offices.

Signs of constipation included having fewer than three bowel movements in a week, passing stools large enough to keep the toilet from flushing, leaking stool, posturing to try to hold bowel movements, and experiencing pain when trying to have a bowel movement.

Your child's doctor will be able to tell if he is constipated by pressing on his belly and by using his finger to see if there is a large stool in the colon. Significantly more girls seem to have this problem than boys.

Over time, changing your toddler's diet to high-fiber foods, such as raw and unpeeled fruits and vegetables, beans (baked, kidney, navy, pinto, and lima beans), sweet potatoes, kale and turnip greens, and raw tomatoes might help. Vegetable soups provide lots of fiber, as does fruit, and so can bran, such as bran cereals, muffins, shredded wheat, whole wheat bread, and graham crackers. More water to drink and fruit juices, such as apple, pear, and prune, may loosen stools, too.

Meanwhile, your toddler may need a laxative or a stool softener to make bowel movements more effortless and comfortable.

TIP

If your toddler is constipated, ask your child's health-care provider for suggestions about what to do.

Pointers for Boys

It's easier and far less messy if your little boy sits down to use the toilet. It won't be long before he notices how his dad and older boys stand up to pee, and he'll want to try that, too. That's the time to step in and help him perfect his aim. You (or, better yet, Dad) will need to show him how to direct his spray.

Visual cues can help, such as a sticker stuck to the back of the toilet bowl or a floating piece of cereal as a target. A sturdy stepstool pulled up to the front of the toilet will make your little shooter tall enough to hit his mark. But even with practice, expect it to take a while for him to not sprinkle the seat or the floor.

It's not unusual for little boys to develop a fascination with their body parts and both boys and girls to become quite fascinated with bodily fluids. When it comes to kids "discovering" their private parts, just like other behavior that might make you uncomfortable, it's important to remain nonchalant and matter-of-fact.

If your son figures out that playing with his penis is a way to get you all bent out of shape, the extra attention will be a bonus! Instead, take his hand away and say something like, "your penis is a private part. That's why we go to the potty in our private bathroom. So when you want to touch your penis, you need to do it in private, like in the bathroom or in your bedroom."

If your toddler isn't circumcised, it's perfectly normal for him to try to stretch back his foreskin. Babies are born with foreskin, which gradually retracts and separates as a boy gets older, usually becoming fully separated by puberty. It's common behavior for boys to want to "help out" the retraction process, but he shouldn't try to forcibly retract the foreskin—this can cause damage or infection. Just as with any other socially inappropriate touching, remove his hand and distract him or steer him to the private place where touching himself is permitted.

Q & A

Q: Our son hates wearing underwear and wants to keep wearing his diapers. When we dress him in underpants, he wets or soils them almost immediately just so we'll put his diaper back on. How can we help him accept his "big boy" pants?

A: If he likes superheroes, try to find Batman, Superman, or other themed underwear available at most department stores. Help explain that the superheroes don't like pee or poop on them, and that they are big guys who know how to use the toilet. That, plus some good parental role modeling from the same gender on the "how to" of pottying (plus lots of praise for successes) should do the trick.

Q: Our daughter seems to have an itchy, red vaginal area. She squirms a lot and often rubs herself as if she is uncomfortable. What's the matter?

A: She may have a yeast infection or a reaction to detergent, bubble bath, or scented toilet paper, but more likely it's irritation from not wiping correctly after peeing. Blotting works best. In addition, after pooping, she needs to learn to wipe from front to back to keep from spreading fecal matter to her vaginal area. Show her how to wipe after a bowel movement (flushable wipes may help) and then how to dry by patting herself using several folds of soft, unscented toilet paper. Avoid bubble baths that are irritating to tender areas, use only clear water rather than soap for cleansing, and have her wear absorbent, 100 percent cotton underpants instead of those made from synthetic materials, such as polyester, which can trap moisture inside. Apply a zinc-based diaper ointment or petroleum jelly to form a protective layer so the area can heal. If it doesn't get better right away, or if she also has a thick, bloody, or foul-smelling discharge, it's time to call your doctor.

> **TIP**
>
> Stay positive, reward successes, and ignore mistakes. You'll both get there with less stress.

Child Care and Work

In the 1960s, less than a third of families with children had two parents working full time. Today, families with two parents working outside the home are in the majority, and according to the Child Care and Development Fund, approximately 95 percent of toddlers are cared for by someone other than their parents during typical working hours.

Americans have been working more, too. In 1960, only 20 percent of mothers worked. Today, 70 percent of American children live in households where all adults are employed. Approximately one out of three mothers is single, so for most families, having child care is a practical necessity.

Finding a workable child-care arrangement is not always easy. Grandparents used to be the default day-care providers, but today live-in grandparents are rare, and relatives may not even reside in your state. Even if they do live nearby, they may be working themselves.

Day-care centers are more plentiful than ever, but quality can vary wildly. The day-care centers with better reputations usually cost more and fill up faster, so even if you can afford licensed, accredited care, it may not be available when you need it.

And some parents find themselves having to cobble together toddler care from multiple sources, such as day care for a few days, after-school care with a babysitter, and other times with a grandparent or neighbor. In this chapter, you'll find help for choosing the best care for your toddler when you can't be the caregiver.

> **TIP**
>
> By law, domestic staff who work more than 40 hours per week must receive overtime pay.

Stay at Home or Go to Work?

HOW MUCH WILL IT COST?

Some parents plan ahead, before a child is even born, to have a parent to stay at home for a certain period of time. Others plan to go back work almost immediately, but then discover that the stresses and sacrifices aren't worth the salary. Still others end up staying at home to take care of their babies and children, not out of choice, but because they've lost their jobs or aren't able to find affordable, suitable child care for their children.

Whether or not you can afford child care is an important consideration when you're thinking about whether to return to work or leave your job to be with your child. If you're not sure about finances, online calculators are available that can help you with the number crunching (search "second income calculator"); then, put together a simple spreadsheet.

In addition to child-care costs, you'll need to factor in the other costs of working and how they affect your domestic bottom line, such as:

- **Taxes.** Federal, state, and local taxes and Social Security deductions, typically amount to about one-third of take-home pay.
- **Transportation.** The IRS estimates that it costs at least 51 cents per mile to drive a car, including gas and insurance. Your costs will be higher or lower depending on your car's age and fuel efficiency and gas prices. Don't forget to factor in tolls and parking.
- **Meals.** Eating out for lunch at work, and sometimes breakfast or dinner, adds up too.
- **Clothing.** Factor in the price of your work wardrobe or uniform, plus the cost of shoes and dry cleaning, if needed.
- **Additional household expenses.** You may need to use more services, such as housecleaning, yard work, or pet sitting.

Once you have those expenses down on paper, compare them with the financial costs of a parent staying home to care for a child, including wages, benefits, and retirement contributions. Another consideration, although it's hard to quantify, is how staying at home could affect your future career prospects and long-term income, such as potential raises, commissions, or promotions, and interest on retirement contributions.

Other Things to Think About

You'll need to consider how staying at home with your toddler or going back to work could affect you emotionally. Doing well at a paid job can mean financial rewards and a feeling of accomplishment, which can be hard to come by when you're carrying the full-time load of parenting.

In spite of how important closely parenting your child may feel, it's not a job that society seems to value as much as it should. Being a stay-at-home parent is tough work, usually with no breaks or even private trips to the bathroom. Even the worst of tantruming bosses usually don't throw oatmeal or blocks at your head, or vomit on you.

On the upside, there's no doubt that being at home with your child can be immensely rewarding, fulfilling, and fun! It can also be boring, frustrating, and tedious because of the endless and repetitive nature of some of the tasks.

Studies have found that stay-at-home moms have a higher rate of depression than working ones. But working mothers sleep less and tend to have a higher level of stress, which can lead to issues like cardiovascular disease and a weakened immune system.

The biggest payoff for stay-at-home parents is being there during the formative years of your child's life—a time that only happens once. Parenting's most significant moments always happen when you least expect them, and hearing secondhand from your day-care provider that your child has learned to say "I love you" or reached some other big milestone is hardly the same thing as being there in person when it happens.

WHAT'S BEST FOR YOU AND YOUR CHILD?

The biggest question is: What's best for you? And what's best for your child?

Be honest with yourself about what is meaningful and fulfilling to you, what makes you happy. If you've always wanted to stay home with your children, but then find yourself becoming depressed and counting the minutes until naptime every day, you and your family might all be better off if you returned to work, even if you're barely making enough to cover the cost of child care.

If you cherish being home, a day-care center—even the day care of your dreams—won't compare to the meaning and joy that being with your child can deliver.

Working or not working doesn't have to be an all-or-nothing proposition, either. If you're working full time and thinking about staying home, or if you're at home and wondering if you should go back to work, weigh all your options.

Scaling back your working hours or taking time off from work may be just what you need to help you refocus. Enlightened companies are becoming increasingly more family friendly as they realize that keeping good employees is in their best interests. If you have such a working environment, you might be able to work flexible hours, part time, or as a self-employed consultant, getting paid for your skills on your own schedule.

If you returned to work after your baby was born and are now feeling regrets and wanting to return to caring for your child, remember, too, it doesn't have to mean the end of your career forever.

You can use the break from work to reassess, change your career path, start an at-home business, or go back to school. Or, you may be able to figure out a side career that will suit your skills and schedule. Here are some examples: teaching a class, freelance writing or web site design, accounting, helping out the parents in your neighborhood with child care, running errands, or event planning.

Stay-at-Home Precautions

Working from home and caring for a toddler at the same time usually doesn't work well. You'll either skimp on your work and set yourself up for failure, or you'll get the work done but at the cost of a screaming (or even unsafe) toddler at your heels. Plan on hiring a babysitter to watch your child for the hours when you'll be working.

Working from home requires uninterrupted time to focus, but toddlers demand almost continuous supervision. Even the most self-reliant toddler won't be happy playing by herself for as long as it takes for you to get anything meaningful done on a daily basis.

An ignored, bored toddler can quickly get herself into dangerous situations. So think seriously about hiring a responsible teenager or retiree or other available helping hand to come over for a few hours a day to entertain your toddler or to take her to the playground where she can let off steam.

Keeping Your Sanity Intact

If you do decide to pursue working at home, there are some important ways to keep yourself in balance:
- **Preserve your identity.** It's important to not let your sense

of identity completely revolve around being Mommy. Make time for other interests, even if it's just a few hours a week for exercise, a class, religious services, socializing with friends, or volunteering.
- **Reframe your thinking.** Don't think of staying home as giving up your career, but as moving to a new and different phase of it. Stay in touch with former co-workers and keep abreast of developments in your field.
- **Keep thinking ahead.** Keep planning for the future. Even if you're not able to pay into a 401(k) anymore, maybe you could afford investing in an IRA. And don't forget a life insurance policy—with just a modest 20- or 30-year term—in case something should happen to you.
- **Don't get trapped.** Structure your day so that you always get out of the house at least once. Having a weekly routine will be good for you and your child, too. Scout out local playgrounds, YMCA locations, gyms with child care, and coffee shops and bookstores where you can mingle with other stay-at-home parents and their kids.

STAY-AT-HOME DADS

Dads can be nurturing, attentive, and loving caregivers, and once a nursing child is weaned, a dad can do virtually everything a mom can. In 2007 the census bureau reported that about 25 percent of children with working mothers were being cared for by a stay-at-home dad, a 66 percent increase from only four years before. Those numbers are likely to increase.

Still, old stereotypes die hard. People can make unflattering assumptions about stay-at-home dads. If you're a stay-at-home dad, you may find yourself the only guy at Mother Goose story time or the Mommy and Me gym class. You might hear remarks such as, "Oh, are you watching the baby today?" and hear strangers ask your child, "Where's Mommy?"

Even more so than moms, stay-at-home dads need to work to find a community of kindred spirits. Seek out local playgroups where dads feel valued and supported. Check out the resources for stay-at-home dads at the end of this book and in the companion volume *Becoming a Dad: The First 3 Years* by John Carr. Instead of trying to be Mom, bring your own unique skills to childrearing, such as your penchant for play.

If you are the stay-at-home parent, it will likely fall to you to do the lion's share of the shopping, cooking, cleaning, and errands. If you're the working parent, you'll have to adjust your expectations and accept that taking care of a toddler is nonstop, demanding work and not every chore might be done to your standards.

Finding the Right Care for Your Toddler

CARE BY RELATIVES

During the typical workday most children are cared for by a grandparent. It's cost-effective (most grandparents don't expect to be paid, though you should offer), and the advantage of using your parents for child care is that it allows your child to be in familiar surroundings and builds an irreplaceable, multigenerational bond.

No one outside of your family will love your children more than their grandparents. And they have to be at least a little bit competent, since you or your partner managed to survive their care.

However, caring for toddlers can be physically exhausting, even for the young and spry. You may worry about a grandparent's physical ability to handle your child, to drive her around safely, or to interact for hours at a time without rest. You may worry that if disagreements arise, such as about diet or discipline, a grandparent may not accept your authority as readily as a hired babysitter would.

If you do opt for a grandparent to care for your toddler, it may be a good idea to also have a Plan B— someone who can fill in and who can be called in case of unexpected illness or injury.

It's also a good idea to discuss payment terms up front and get the matter out of the way. Some grandparents may be insulted if you offer payment, but it seems only fair that at the very least you reimburse your relative for transportation, and provide food or grocery money and a kitty of cash for expenses and activities.

NANNIES AND AU PAIRS

A nanny is someone who cares for your child in your home and may or may not live in your home with you, and an au pair is a domestic assistant, usually between the ages of 18 and 26 and possibly from another country, who lives with you. There are male nannies, too.

The term *au pair* is from the French meaning "equal to." Though au pairs are expected to perform light housework, an au pair is more like a temporary family member than a domestic employee, usually eating with the family and accompanying you on family outings and vacations.

The average nanny works 10 to 12 hours a day, and the big advantages of hiring a nanny for in-home care is that it can be the most flexible option in terms of scheduling and duties. Having your own hired person allows your child to stay in her own familiar surroundings and form a relationship with someone who will consistently stay with her. Many families form lifelong friendships with their nannies or au pairs.

On the other hand, in-home care may be the most expensive option. You can expect to pay about $450 to $1500 or more per week for a nanny, depending on benefits and a nanny's experience and education.

The average starting salary for a live-in au pair is $176 per week. Most au pairs live for nine months to two years with a host family. Typically, they help in the house for a set number of hours during the day and have two days off a week. You are expected to provide the au pair with a private room, transportation, living expenses, and cultural experiences. For an au pair on a J-1 exchange visa, families must pay at least $500 toward course work and allow time off for the au pair to complete at least 6 hours of academic credit from an accredited institution during their stay with you.

Hiring a Nanny or Au Pair

To find an au pair or nanny, you can do the legwork yourself, advertise online using a Web-based service such as *www.4nanny.com*, or *www.usaupair.com*. Or, you can use a referral agency.

Agencies typically collect a nonrefundable retainer, interview you and your family, and then advertise and recruit suitable candidates. They prescreen candidates, conduct background checks, check references, and so on.

If you decide to hire an agency-referred nanny or au pair, the agency will collect a one-time placement fee, usually a percentage of the nanny's annual salary (12 percent is standard). For international au pairs, the agency will usually handle the visa process, too.

Some Web-based referral services may post unscreened candidates and collect a fee that is not contingent upon employment.

In that case you will be responsible for performing background checks and crafting and enforcing work agreements.

Whether you're hiring an in-home caregiver from an online service or an international au pair from an agency, it's important to get a thorough briefing on how the agency screens and acquires its employees and how it matches candidates with families.

Screening In-Home Candidates

If you're hiring in-home care, then you'll need to interview candidates yourself. You'll want to discuss hours, salary, and duties, of course, and if you offer any benefits, such as sick days, holidays, or the use of a car.

If you're hiring a live-in nanny, you'll want to talk about curfew and visitor rules and accommodations. You'll need to go over any rules you may have about smoking, drinking, and other issues. Before the potential employee meets your child, give her (or him) an idea of what a typical day is like in your family and any important information about your toddler, such as any special needs, dietary restrictions, medications and health concerns, or anything unusual about your and your child's schedules.

There are important questions that you need to ask a prospective nanny. Jotting down brief notes may help you later. (Since most nannies are female, we'll use the "she" here, though male nannies are becoming more common.)

- What experience does she have with toddlers?

- What does she enjoy about working with children?
- What is her least favorite part of caring for children?
- How does she usually deal with tantrums, whining, and disobedience?
- Has she ever lost her temper with a child? What did she do?
- Has she ever hit a child? When (in her mind) would hitting be okay?
- Is there anything in particular that previous parents she's worked with have done that she liked, or didn't like?
- Does she have references? Is it all right with her if you contact them? How can they be reached?

As you listen to her answers, take stock and be attuned to body language. Does she seem honest and forthcoming? When she talks about previous employers, does she have mostly positive things to say? Does she maintain eye contact when giving an answer?

If you like a candidate, your next step is to ask her back to spend some time with your child. If they have a good rapport, your final step is to perform a basic background check online that includes criminal records, which usually costs less than $20 and is instantaneous. Some background checks also include a credit check.

If you're hiring a foreign au pair, you won't have the same opportunity to meet the candidate in person or check her background yourself in advance of her arrival. Usually a placement agency will have a whole-family interview with you. Then the agency representative will supply you with dossiers of candidates, and will set up interviews by telephone.

FAMILY CHILD CARE

Family child care is usually provided by a stay-at-home mom who cares for your child as well as her own in her own home. Home care is usually less expensive than licensed care, and in the best case, in-home care can offer your toddler a loving family atmosphere, with less staff turnover and more flexibility than commercial day-care centers.

But at-home care is also not governed by state laws and regulations as strictly as commercial day-care centers usually are. The quality of care will be as good (or bad) as the individual providing it.

Checking Out Family Child Care

Here are some things to look at when you check out in-home family child care.

Ask the same tough questions as you would a nanny (see above) and get the full name of the care provider and anyone else who will be in the house, and perform an online background check.

Ask how many other children will be cared for, and their ages. (More than six toddler-aged children per caregiver is problematic.) If there are infants in the mix, the ratio should be even smaller. Note that having a wide range of ages, such as infants with toddlers and older children, can make younger children more vulnerable to the physical aggression of the older ones.

Ask the caregiver how she disciplines children, particularly her policy on spanking.

Ask where diapers are changed and disposed of. The diapering area should be clean and dirty diapers should be kept in a sealed trash can that's well out of the reach of children. Check for the presence of gloves and/or hand sanitizer.

Check out any food storage and preparation areas to make sure they're hygienic.

Ask about the daily schedule—is there time and space for outdoor activities? Naps? Snacks? Are the kids ever allowed to watch TV?

How will she handle any medical emergencies—hers or the children's?

If you use at-home care, if possible, consider popping in unannounced on a day when you can take off early or take a long lunch. Are the children engaged in activities, or are they running around chaotically or being babysat by a television?

DAY-CARE CENTERS

So many parents wonder: What's better for kids, staying at home, or going to a group child-care center? The short answer: It depends on the center and whom you ask.

In 2003, two studies were published, one from the National Institute of Child Health and Human Development and the other from the Institute of Child Development of the University of Minnesota. Both showed that kids who spent all day in day care had higher levels of stress and more aggression than kids cared for at home.

On the other hand, other respectable studies from university and state education departments have shown that kids who have been in day care or preschool do better academically and have better social skills than those who stay home, and do better both academically and socially once they get to kindergarten.

It appears that it's the quality of care that counts, especially the amount of individual attention that children get, rather than the type of care. If a caregiver is at home but is glued to the TV or a computer and not positively interacting with a child, then a quality day-care situation might be better. If a day-care center is poorly staffed and chaotic, then stressed and aggressive toddlers might do better if they were at home.

Finding a Quality Day Care

Here are the steps you can take to find quality care for your child:

- **Start looking as soon as possible**. Even if you know you're going to stay home until your child is two or three, there's no harm in looking at programs even while you're pregnant. The sooner you start, the more options you'll have, because the best programs fill up fast. Even if you're on the fence about going back to work, it's better to lose the time and money spent on reserving space in a good center than to be without care and have to settle for a program that's not as good.
- **Ask for recommendations**. There's no better way to get the inside dirt than from parents who have dealt with a day-care center

on a daily basis. Keep in mind that the people you ask may be biased toward where they sent their own kids.
- **Call local referral agencies.** Most larger urban areas have nonprofit child-care referral agencies that keep tabs on child-care centers and home-based providers, where you may be able to get referrals.
- **Web sites**. Google the words "child care" and a zip code. State licensing agencies, major child-care organizations, and dedicated Internet sites also supply online providers' lists, such as *www. childcareaware.org*, and *www. doodledays.com*.
- **Local universities**. Universities and colleges with early-childhood-education programs usually have better-than-average quality and sometimes accept children whose parents aren't students or teachers at the university.

Evaluating a Day Care

What makes for a quality child-care center? Here are some things to look for as you tour day cares and preschool programs:
- **Low child-to-staff ratio**. The child-to-staff ratio is a good indicator that your toddler will get the attention she needs. Too few caregivers is likely to translate into more neglect and less one-on-one attention. Most states also have guidelines on teacher-to-student ratios. The National Association for the Education of Young Children (NAEYC) recommends no more than four young toddlers (age

12 to 24 months) per caregiver, with a maximum of twelve young toddlers and three caregivers per group. Further, they recommend no more than six older toddlers (age 24 to 36 months) per caregiver, and a maximum of twelve older toddlers and two caregivers per group.

- **Educated staff.** The more educated staff members are, the more likely they are to understand the subtleties of child development and to enrich your toddler's activities and curriculum. As you tour child-care centers, ask the directors about their credentials (such as if they have a college degree in early childhood education). Also ask if most staff members have college degrees, or at least have obtained high-school diplomas.
- **Low staff turnover**. Staff turnover is high in child-care centers. It's a stressful job with long hours that often doesn't pay well. As you tour centers, ask individual staff members how long they've been working there. Low turnover will mean more stability for your child and more experienced providers. Plus, it is a general sign that the center is a pleasant and low-stress place to be.
- **Hygiene and health policies**. What is the center's policy on sick children? For your child's protection, children with fevers, pinkeye, or other communicable illnesses should be sent home. There should be ample hand-washing facilities with gloves and hand sanitizer provided at diaper-changing areas. Are toys routinely wiped down or washed to prevent the spread of illnesses?
- **Activities and nutrition.** Are children of all different ages grouped together? That might mean that younger children get overrun by older ones. Children should be grouped into similar ages and offered activities that help children at each age and stage to feel creative and successful. Ask about the schedule for the day. Is there time for imaginative play? Outdoor time and physical activity? Does the center provide meals? If so, ask to see a sample menu. Are the snacks and main meals loaded with carbohydrates, or is an effort made to provide healthy, fresh foods for the children?
- **Warm interactions.** How accessible are the staff members? Do they get down on child level for interactions? Are they warm and enthusiastic, calling children by name? How does the staff deal with children who are misbehaving or upset? You should leave feeling confident that your child will be beautifully cared for and cherished as an individual, not herded around.
- **Accreditation.** Your state will have a department that oversees the licensing of child-care operations. That department will likely have a directory listing licensed child-care centers in your county or city. In addition, the NAEYC offers an accreditation program for day-care centers. There are plenty of quality programs that are not accredited, but a program with a NAEYC certification will have met certain quality standards. You can research NAEYC

accreditation and find accredited programs by visiting *www.naeyc. org*.

When Your Child Seems Unhappy

Sometimes child-care situations simply don't work, and it's hard to know how to handle that. Your toddler may appear unhappy, and you don't know if it's simply a passing phase or whether you should make a change. Consistency is important, but so is your child's comfort. You might need help assessing the situation.

It's important to build a strong, honest relationship with your toddler's caregiver. Not only should she alert you to any problems that come up for your child or the center, but you should be able to openly share what's going on at home, such as alerting her to changes in your toddler's habits or family stresses that could be affecting your toddler at child care.

You should always feel welcomed any time you want to visit the center, whether to simply observe what's going on, or to engage with your child and other children when you want to know how your child is doing and who your child's friends are. If, on the other hand, you're not invited in, that may raise questions about what's going on inside.

Your child's caregiver should be keeping a daily log that she openly shares with you. Check the log every day, and make sure it's consistent with what you observe happening with your child at home, such as how much she eats and how many diaper/training pants changes she needs.

Is your child going through a change at home? Weaning from bottle to cup, toilet training, teething, and even changing beds can all temporarily make a toddler feel unhappy or moody. Or your toddler's unhappiness could simply be a normal phase of separation anxiety. (For help in dealing with toddler separation anxiety, see Chapter 3.)

Keep tabs on the current provider-to-child ratio. It's hard to keep up when employees in child-care settings frequently come and go. Even though the ratio between caregivers and children could have seemed ideal when you signed on, when staff members leave, then fewer workers are left to care for the children. Caregivers get sick or take vacations, too. That could be stressing your child and other children in the center.

Finally, trust your intuition. You are your child's number-one advocate, and if your gut is telling you something just isn't right, then maybe it's time to start thinking about changing caregivers.

TIP

The Child and Dependent Care Tax Credit allows parents to deduct approximately one-third of child-care costs, based on income.

Q & A

Q: My son seems unhappy at his preschool. He says it's because he doesn't like another student. My son is shy and reserved, and I wonder if he is getting hurt or bullied by another child. How should I approach the day-care staff about the problem?

A: First, we'd suggest making an after- or before-school appointment to openly discuss your concerns with your son's teacher and aides. Most likely, they'll be able to share with you how your son is faring and whether he seems happy or unhappy. Your bringing up the issue might lead to some positive adult monitoring and intervention for your child. Second, consider observing in the classroom a couple of times for 30 minutes to an hour, perhaps at snack time, so you can see how your son is relating to other children, especially the child that concerns you. Hopefully you'll find that the teachers are very supportive and your son's problem is being constructively addressed. On the other hand, if you find the staff defensive and you don't get the response you should, then your options are to wait for the problem to blow over, as it likely will, or to take the problem to a higher level, or to seek another child-care setting for him.

> **TIP**
>
> The best caregivers for young children should demonstrate flexibility and kindness.

> **TIP**
>
> If your child seems genuinely unhappy with her child-care situation, follow your instincts and investigate.

11

Health, Safety, and Ability

This chapter is all about keeping your toddler well and safe, with information on how to find good health care for your child, including how to choose a care provider, identifying and treating common childhood illnesses, learning about medical procedures, and more.

You'll also find information about children's accident prevention, how to childproof your home, and instructions on family fire safety, vehicle safety, and drowning prevention. There are practical hints on how to treat minor injuries, such as removing a splinter and tending to minor cuts, and how to deal with sprains, strains, and fractures.

A special section discusses autism and finding professional and intervention services for toddlers with autism or other childhood disabilities.

Special Note

This section has been written for educational purposes only. It does not cover ALL toddler illnesses—only the most common ones (and diseases that children are vaccinated against)—as well as toddler injuries. It is not intended to serve as a substitute for medical advice from a health-care provider. Do not use this information to diagnose or treat any health problems, illnesses, or accidents your toddler has without first consulting your pediatrician or family doctor. Your toddler's health-care provider is the best person to answer any questions or concerns you may have regarding your toddler's health and safety.

Illness and Health Care

CHOOSING A HEALTH-CARE PROVIDER

If you're not happy with the health-care provider you currently have, or you're searching for a doctor during your child's toddler years, this section will help you figure out where to go to ensure that your child gets the health care he needs.

Most communities offer a variety of resources you can tap for recommendations about health-care providers. Ask your friends with children if they're happy with the care they get from their medical professionals. Your own physician may have suggestions for pediatricians.

If you have health insurance, your insurer may require that you use only those physicians who are part of its network of providers. If you can't afford health insurance, all states offer some form of medical services for children whose families have moderate or low incomes.

When choosing a health-care provider for your toddler and family, it's important to think ahead about how that arrangement will work over the years to come, and not just what's convenient right now.

Family physicians are trained to work with an entire family, parents and children alike, which can provide a welcome sense of familiarity and continuity, and they can be more convenient, too. They're a good choice if everyone in your family is generally healthy. (Should serious problems arise, you will be referred to a specialist, depending on the situation.)

Pediatricians and pediatric nurse-practitioners have specialized training in caring just for babies and children. Pediatricians are medical doctors who diagnose, treat, examine, and prevent diseases and injuries in children. A pediatrician must hold a four-year undergraduate college degree, a four-year doctor of medicine (MD) or doctor of osteopathy (DO) degree, plus at least three years of residency training. A license and board certification from the American Board of Pediatrics (ABP) are also required to practice as a pediatrician in the United States.

Nurse-practitioners (NPs) are registered nurses who have completed specific advanced nursing education, such as a master's degree, and some specialize in pediatrics. They have training in the diagnosis and management of common as well as some complex medical conditions. Depending upon the state in which they are licensed, they can perform medical exams, order tests and therapy for patients, and write prescriptions. Unlike physician's assistants, who can only practice under the license of a medical doctor, nurse-practitioners practice under their own license, and they may practice independently, or they can be affiliated with physicians' practices.

Since no two health-care

providers are the same, it makes sense to interview several providers before choosing the one that best suits your lifestyle and needs. When you meet a prospective provider, ask about nurse-practitioners, physician assistants, and other staff support, billing practices and charges, weekend and nighttime coverage, hospital affiliation, after-hours visits, home visits, and telephone consultations. Find out, too, how emergencies are handled, whether the doctor has privileges at any nearby hospitals, and how promptly you can expect a callback when there's a problem.

When you go to meet with a prospective pediatrician or other provider, pay attention not only to your comfort level with him or her, but also the way the receptionist and the rest of the staff act toward you, your child, and other patients/parents in the practice. (Once your child has been accepted as a patient, you'll probably discover that you are spending as much time interacting with the staff as you do with the doctor.)

Of course, some providers may be very popular and have very busy practices. That translates into shorter visits and less time for talking with you and answering your questions. One solution is to try to get your child's non-urgent health concerns, such as rashes, colds, cuts, and scrapes, answered by a nurse-practitioner or other professional on the staff.

To minimize long wait times in a waiting room after you've made an appointment, call ahead before you leave home to find out if the doctor is on schedule, and/or try to schedule appointments during the least busy times.

Since you're going to be relying on your doctor's support and advice for many years, pick one that not only relates well to you, but to your child, too. A child-friendly doctor will take some time to warm up to your child by smiling and talking to win his trust, rather than talking down to him. He'll take special care not to upset your toddler if possible.

If You Can't Afford Medical Care

Health departments in most cities offer well care and immunizations at low or no cost, and federal Medicaid programs administered through states provide medical care for low-income families who meet certain eligibility requirements.
• Working families who are ineligible for Medicaid could still qualify for their state's Children's Health Insurance Program (CHIP) administered by the federal Centers for Medicare and Medicaid Services.
• In some states, a family of four that earns up to about $36,200 a year may still be eligible for CHIP, but requirements vary by state. The program pays for doctor visits, immunizations, and hospitalizations.
• To apply for either Medicaid or CHIP, contact your local department of social services, often listed under the name of your county. To find out more about what programs your state offers, check out *www.insurekidsnow.gov/state/index.html* online.

MEDICAL EXAMS

Checkups for toddlers usually are at 12, 15, 18, 24, and 36 months. When your child reaches 18 months, most likely he will have received all of his immunizations until his "kindergarten shots," which are usually administered between 4 years and 6 years of age.

Before going to your first appointment, use a small notebook to write down all the questions that have been nagging you. Take the notebook and a pen along to the appointment, so that you can log all the doctor's recommendations.

Here's how a good exam is likely to go: A nurse will take your child's vital signs: temperature, heart rate (pulse), speed of breathing (respiration), weight, and height. (A child's pulse is faster than a grown-up's and is usually around 110.)

Typically blood pressure won't be measured until age 3, although doctors and health-care providers are becoming increasingly more concerned about the rising levels of chronic diseases affecting children, particularly obesity, so they are administering tests and ordering preventive care earlier than they used to.

Blood pressure is measured by inflating and deflating a small, child-size cuff around the upper arm while counting heartbeats with a stethoscope. Blood pressure (BP) measurements will show possible kidney, hormone, and circulation problems related to the heart. BP gradually increases throughout infancy and childhood, so your toddler's blood pressure may seem lower than yours is as an adult.

A practitioner skilled in treating children will be careful about how he (or she) approaches your toddler. He will wash his own hands, both to make sure they're clean and to warm them up. Then he will greet you and your child, and probably suggest that the exam take place with your toddler sitting on your lap or right beside you. A toy or doll may be used to make the procedure seem more playful. He will likely start his exam with the least-threatening body parts, your child's hands, and end it with the ears and throat.

While taking a close look at your child, he will also be conversing with you to see if you have any questions or concerns. Take your time and don't feel rushed about raising issues that are important to you, even if they could seem minor.

Even though your child's physical exam may seem cursory and fast, in fact, your child's health-care provider will be carefully evaluating a whole host of physical signs. Your toddler may stay dressed for part of the exam, but then might be asked to undress down to his diaper or underpants for the rest of the exam.

Your child's general physical appearance will be noted, as well as his activity level, how he interacts in his surroundings, and whether or not he seems to be in distress (as many toddlers are when they're in doctor's offices).

His skull shape and circumference will be noted. His skin and scalp will be examined for birthmarks, moles, or other growths and for rashes, head lice, or ringworm. The shape and position of his eyes and any abnormal eye movements or an inability to focus will be noted.

The practitioner will want to know that the inside of your toddler's nose is healthy and that his breathing passages are working well and aren't inflamed or have unusual mucus or tenderness. He'll be looking for inappropriate items in the nostrils, too.

Your care provider may ask if you suspect your toddler of having any hearing problems, will examine the shape and position of the ears, and may suggest a hearing test if your child isn't acquiring words or speaking as expected. Peering into your child's ear canal, he will be looking to see if the eardrum looks inflamed or is stiff from infection. And he'll want to make sure that there isn't something in the ear canals that shouldn't be there.

Your child will be asked to stick out his tongue, and a flat, wooden stick (tongue depressor) may be used to inspect the tongue, teeth, gums, tonsils, and palate in the back for signs of problems. Your toddler may gag, but that's on purpose so that the doctor can catch a quick glimpse deeper in his throat.

Your toddler's chest and abdomen will be examined and listened to with a stethoscope for how his heart and breathing sound.

The practitioner will also be checking his belly to see that there are no lumps or hard places. He'll want to check your toddler's muscle tone and if your child's arms and legs move okay, and that joints are not warm or swollen. He will check how responsive your child's reflexes are by gently tapping certain places on his knees, ankles, and elbows using a small rubber hammer that will make these parts of limbs automatically jump.

While some practitioners prefer to check a child's abdomen while he's lying down, others have found that a toddler might cooperate if he is sitting in your lap. While your child is cooperative, the doctor will also check the belly and other places with you helping. He will be listening for bowel sounds or unusual gurgles and growls, since the belly makes five to thirty-four sounds per minute.

A swollen or enlarged belly could mean there is a blockage, infection, or mass that's in the way.

He'll also be checking for tender spots that make your toddler wince or yelp. He will also take a quick look at your toddler's genitals by pushing the diaper to the side to ensure that everything is as expected.

IMMUNIZATIONS

Modern vaccines provide protection from major, and sometimes life-threatening, illnesses. If your toddler requires immunizations, they could be first-time vaccines or, more likely, continuations of immunizations (booster shots) that were begun in your child's first year.

Some parents have serious concerns about the safety of vaccines, and they worry about the rumors they have heard about shots causing autism. Talk frankly with your child's health-care provider about your immunization concerns and seek his or her reasoned, educated opinion about it. Also, make sure to ask about the reactions you can expect and the signs of serious side effects that could potentially result from a vaccination.

It's helpful to also do your own research about vaccines from trusted medical sources, but remember that immunizing is a hotly debated topic among parents, and they may provide highly biased views that aren't always well informed or based on research.

Some injections may cause mild side effects such as redness, swelling, and a slight fever, but serious side effects are extremely rare. Once you've got all of the information available on immunizations, you're in a better position to make an informed decision.

Getting Through Shots

Nobody likes to get shots, but they're a necessary part of preventive care. Here are a few ideas for how you can help your toddler through the process of getting injections.

- **Trust.** Have confidence that your child's health-care provider and nurse know how to administer shots quickly and correctly. Let the provider handle him. (The shot is more likely to be given in the thigh because the fat there makes it less uncomfortable than in the arm.)
- **Be calm and lighthearted.** The way you relax and act will help him to feel less anxious. Trying to prepare a toddler beforehand won't do much good.

  Make a fun little noise to distract him so he's looking at you instead of the injection shot, or place some colorful stickers on his opposite arm to peel off for a distraction.
- **Bring adhesive bandages.** Most health-care providers supply child-friendly bandages, such as those with superheroes or Elmo pictured on them, but you can also bring your own, just in case. Keep some extras at home in case he wants a fresh one later.
- **Praise.** Instead of commiserating about how "awful" the shot was, let him know how proud you are for how he acted through it. Offer a sticker or some other small reward, if desired.

Questions to Ask About Immunizations

- How serious and prevalent is the illness that this shot will help to prevent?
- How effective is this immunization?
- Will a booster be needed? How often?
- Should my child be well (fever-free and without other symptoms) to have it?
- What's the best way to prepare my toddler for the injection?
- Will there be any side effects? What are they and how should they be treated? How long do they typically last? What are the signs of a more serious side effect?
- If I am pregnant, could my toddler infect me with the vaccination virus and endanger the unborn child?

Immunization Guide

Name of Vaccine	What It Does	When It's Administered	Possible Side Effects
DTaP (Diphtheria, Tetanus, and Pertussis)	Prevents diphtheria, tetanus, and pertussis.	A series of four doses, at 2 months, 4 months, 6 months, and 15 to 18 months. Booster dose usually recommended at 4 to 6 years of age.	Rash. Allergic reactions are rare, but no deaths have been reported from allergic reactions.
Flu vaccine	Protects against most recent strains of serious seasonal influenza viruses.	Usually given each year at the beginning of flu season (September through November). Considered safe at 6 months and older.	Rarely, flulike symptoms (vaccine is made from dead viruses).
Hepatitis A	Protects against hepatitis A virus.	Two shots, at least 6 months apart between 18 months and 23 months.	Soreness at the site of the injection. Possible headache, fatigue, or loss of appetite. Severe allergic reactions are rare but could include hoarseness, wheezing, hives, paleness, dizziness, fainting, or rapid heartbeat.
Hepatitis B (HBV)	Protects against hepatitis B virus.	Three shots: at birth, between 1 month and 2 months, and between 6 and 18 months.	Soreness at the site. Possible low-grade fever. Severe allergic reactions are rare but might include hoarseness, wheezing, hives, paleness, dizziness, fainting, or rapid heartbeat.

Name of Vaccine	What It Does	When It's Administered	Possible Side Effects
MMR (Measles, Mumps, Rubella)	Protects against measles, mumps, and rubella.	Two shots: at around 12 to 15 months and at 4 to 6 years.	Fever, or mild rash 7 to 10 days after the shot.
PCV 7 (pneumococcal conjugate vaccine)	Helps protect against bacterial infections that can lead to meningitis.	One to four doses, depending on age.	Bruising at the site, mild fever.
Polio (IPV: Inactivated Polio Virus)	Prevents polio, which can paralyze muscles in arms, legs, and those used to breathe and swallow.	Four shots: at 2 months, 4 months, 6 months, and 4 years.	Fever over 102°F. Allergic reaction includes difficulty breathing or swallowing; hives; itching (especially on feet or hands); reddening of skin (especially around ears); and swelling of eyes, face, or inside nose.
PPD (Tuberculin, or Tuberculosis Skin Test)	Helps to diagnose tuberculosis (TB) exposure.	Anytime: helps to determine if a child has been exposed to TB.	Swelling and redness at the injection site signals exposure to TB. (No reaction means no exposure.)
Varicella	Helps prevent or lessen symptoms of chicken pox.	One shot at 12 to 18 months of age of those who haven't had chicken pox.	Pain, swelling, and redness at the injection site.

FEVERS AND THEIR TREATMENT

Fevers are quite common in toddlers, so it's important to have at least one type of thermometer in your first aid kit. Knowing what your toddler's temperature is can help your health-care provider decide how serious your child's fever is and how best to treat it.

Types of Thermometers

Temperature can be measured by mouth, in the ear, under the arm, or rectally. It is measured in tenths. The average temperature for children and adults is 98.6°F. If you contact your health-care provider about your toddler's temperature, you will need to tell him where it was measured—oral (mouth), aural (ear), axillary (armpit), or rectal (anus).

Type	Description	Advantages and Disadvantages
Traditional	Placed under the tongue and well back toward the molars, in the armpit, or in the rectum. Traditional "shakedown" models are now available in break-resistant plastic.	(+) Inexpensive. No batteries to buy and replace. (-) Works slowly compared to digital. Less accurate and often not suitable for small children, who are unable to hold the thermometer properly.
Electronic	Small handhelds use a disk battery; wider units use regular batteries. Some are for use in the mouth, others with cone-shaped receptors are read by ear. Newer, more costly versions use infrared technology to take temperatures from the forehead without actually touching the body. Some are embedded in a pacifier shape.	(+) Digital works rapidly, is easy to read, and signals when done. Versatile. (-) Different readings depending on placement. Some models require disposable tips that are easily exhausted or misplaced. Infrared models are costly, require remaining a specific distance from the child, and are difficult to read in the dark.
Liquid Crystal	Temperature strips (small plastic shield the size of an adhesive bandage placed on the forehead).	(+) Inexpensive, fast-acting, and disposable. (-) Inaccurate and not recommended.

Over-the-Counter Fever-Reducing Medications

When a toddler has a fever, his health-care provider may recommend an over-the-counter medication to help bring his temperature down. Your child's exact weight is important for determining how much medication to give him. Always consult your child's health-care provider first before giving any medications and follow instructions very, very precisely.

If you have ever wondered what the difference is between medications such as Motrin, Tylenol, and aspirin, here's a chart to help explain it.

Name	Uses Besides Fever Reduction	Potential Side Effects	Cautions
Acetaminophen (Tylenol and others)	Relieves pain.	Liver damage from overdosing.	Do not administer to your toddler or child unless instructed by a doctor. In excessive amounts, it can cause liver damage. Can be fatal if overdosed. Never administer it to a toddler who is dehydrated or has been vomiting.
Ibuprofen (Advil, Children's Motrin drops, Pediacare Fever, and others)	Relieves pain, reduces inflammation.	Upset stomach, heartburn. Affects blood-clotting ability.	Do not administer to toddlers and children unless instructed by your toddler's doctor. Do not give to children under 6 months of age.

Name	Uses Besides Fever Reduction	Potential Side Effects	Cautions
Aspirin (Bayer Children's and other brands)	Relieves pain, reduces inflammation.	Stomach upset, heartburn, nausea, vomiting, increased chance of bleeding. Some toddlers may be allergic. Rare serious side effects.	NOT recommended for toddlers and children unless instructed by a physician. Has been associated with Reye's syndrome, a rare but potentially life-threatening illness.

Febrile Seizures

Sometimes a rapid rise in temperature to a high fever can trigger a seizure in a toddler. These episodes can be terrifying, but they're usually harmless. They don't lead to epilepsy, nor do they cause brain damage, nervous system problems, paralysis, mental retardation, or death.

- If your toddler has a fever-related seizure, he will start to look strange, then he will stiffen, twitch, and his eyes may roll back in his head. He may be momentarily unresponsive, and have uneven breathing, and his skin may appear darker than usual. He may shake on both sides of the body, or twitching may only appear in an arm or leg on only the right or the left side of the body.
- While it's happening, quickly move your toddler away from anything he could hit if he is thrashing. Turn his head to the side so his mouth can drain, and don't try to put anything into his mouth or try to feed him until he has recovered.
- Seizures typically happen in the first few hours after the onset of fever and last less than a minute. More rarely, they may go on for up to 15 minutes. After the seizure, your toddler may be sluggish for a couple of hours but will then return to normal. It's rare that a toddler will have more than one febrile seizure in a 24-hour period. Children older than 1 year of age at the time of their first seizure have only a 30 percent chance of having a second febrile seizure.

To be on the safe side, contact your toddler's pediatrician after the seizure has ended, particularly if your child seems to be seriously ill. In rare cases, a seizure accompanied by drowsiness, a stiff neck, vomiting, or other symptoms could signal a deadly attack of meningitis that needs rapid, life-saving intervention.

Cough Medicine Warning

In 2008, the U.S. Food and Drug Administration issued a Public Health Advisory for parents and caregivers, recommending that over-the-counter (OTC) cough and cold medications not be used to treat infants and children younger than 2 years of age because of serious adverse events such as rapid heart rates, convulsions, decreased levels of consciousness, and death.

Administering Medications

Accurately measuring your toddler's medicine doses is very important. There are a variety of devices and tactics for getting medicine into your toddler. Most toddler medications come in liquid form and have a dropper inside with tiny lines for measuring doses. (Use a bright light or flashlight, if needed, to ensure you get the right amount.)

There are also medicine spoons and tiny medicine cups with dose markings. The most accurate way to measure toddler medicine and make sure it doesn't get spit out is to use a medicine syringe, which resembles a medical syringe, but without the needle. Draw the medicine up to the correct marking, and then squeeze out the medication at the back of your toddler's tongue. Many pharmacies can add appealing flavorings to children's liquid medicines. Over-the-counter flavor additives are also available, including some that are sugar-free.

Speak with your pharmacist about pill crushers that enable you to mix your child's pill with his favorite foods, such as applesauce, pudding, or soft ice cream, to make taking pills more palatable. Also ask your pharmacist about which medicines shouldn't be mixed with certain foods. Time-release medications cannot be crushed, as your child will not get the full effects of the medication.

A cold ice pop can help to numb your toddler's taste buds, making bad-tasting medicine easier to take, and if swallowing a pill is required, a product called Swallow Aid is a gel that can be placed on a spoon to coat the pill, making it go down easier.

Sniffing a strong aroma, such as lemon zest or peppermint flavoring, while taking medication can help reduce your toddler's awareness of bad-smelling liquids.

There are also suppository medications for fever or vomiting that you painlessly insert into your toddler's anus.

A Note About Antibiotics

Antibiotics are used to fight bacterial infections, such as those that affect the ears, the throat, and the lungs, including tonsillitis (swollen inflamed glands in the throat) and bronchitis (infection in your toddler's lungs).

More than sixty antibiotics are approved for use in pediatrics, and if your toddler has an infection you may well walk out of the hospital or doctor's office with a prescription for something you've never heard of.

Antibiotics for toddlers are usually in liquid form, so make sure you have a good, easy-to-clean medicine dropper. Amoxicillin is the oldest and most prescribed for ear infections or strep throat, and is commonly used to treat acute middle-ear infections, but there are also other names and brands.

Whatever the prescription, it's important to limit the use of antibiotics only to a diagnosed bacterial infection, because antibiotics can increase your toddler's risk of developing asthma. Excessive antibiotic use can also contribute to the rise of antibiotic-resistant strains of bacteria. But, if your toddler does have a serious bacterial infection, antibiotics can be a (literal) lifesaver. It's important that you follow your health-care provider's instructions to a tee.

> **TIP**
>
> Never give your toddler any drug without your doctor's prior approval and directions, including those available in drugstores or labeled "for children."

> **TIP**
>
> The National Poison Center has poison experts (including for accidental medication overdose) on call 24 hours a day: 800-222-1212.

> **TIP**
>
> Antibiotics fight only bacteria, not viruses.

TYPICAL TODDLER ILLNESSES

Having your child come down with an illness can be distressing. Often toddlers are cranky and out of sorts before the symptoms of an illness actually show up. Your child may refuse to eat, or he may look different, too, perhaps more pale or red-faced, or with dark circles under his eyes, and he may be more whiney than usual.

As luck would have it, most parents don't discover that their kids are really sick until the middle of the night, the day before a critical meeting or job interview, or on weekends when doctors (and babysitters) are hard to find.

There's no need to panic or fear for the worst, though. Most children run a whole gamut of garden-variety illnesses before their immune systems become strong enough to help them ward off encroaching bacteria and viruses. Once their bodies get used to handling the bugs, most toddlers sail through weeks and even months without coming down with something.

Below is a quick-reference guide to common toddler illnesses and physical problems you may encounter. The chart lists symptoms and gives you page numbers for where to find more detailed descriptions in this section or in other parts of the book.

ILLNESS	BODY PART AFFECTED	SYMPTOMS
Allergies (see page 223)	Respiratory system, digestive system, and skin	Clear nasal discharge, breathing problems, headache, fever, diarrhea, stomach pain, vomiting, and rashes.
Anemia (see page 224)	Circulatory system	Blood test results and/or fatigue and sluggishness, and pale appearance with discoloration under the eyes.
Appendicitis (see page 225)	Appendix, a small pouch in the lower right side of the large intestines	Begins with a mild fever and pain around the belly button. May be accompanied by vomiting, diarrhea, or constipation. The stomach pain usually becomes more severe and focuses on the lower right side of the belly. Jumping off the bed or a stair step may suddenly increase the pain.
Asthma (see page 225)	Respiratory system	Fast, labored breathing, gasping sounds, chest sucks inward around the rib cage, wheezing (whistling sounds) with breathing.
Boils (see page 227)	Skin, especially the diaper area	Raised, red, tender bumps on the skin that may have blisters containing pus on the top.
Bronchiolitis (see page 227)	Lungs	Starts with cold symptoms then can progress to severe breathing problems, including sunken ribcage and flared nostrils. (Also see: Respiratory Syncytial Virus.)
Bronchitis (see page 227)	Lungs	Cold symptoms (see "Colds and Coughs," below), low fever, harsh cough that worsens at night, rapid breathing, paleness, and sluggishness.
Chicken Pox (see page 227)	Skin	Fever, a rash resembling insect bites that often start on the trunk and spread to other parts of the body. The bumps form blisters that turn into itchy sores and scabs.

ILLNESS	BODY PART AFFECTED	SYMPTOMS
Cold Sores (see page 228)	Mouth	One or more sores on the lip or inside the mouth, gum inflammation, possibly fever, swollen lymph nodes in the neck, and a sore throat. Also known as Herpes Simplex One (HSV 1).
Colds and Coughs (see page 228)	Sinuses, nose, throat	Watery nasal discharge that thickens and later turns yellowish. Sneezing that may later lead to coughing, fever, listlessness, and breathing problems while eating.
Conjunctivitis (see page 229)	Eyes	Infected, bloodshot-looking, teary eye(s) with reddened, swollen eyelid(s). Also known as pinkeye.
Constipation (see page 190)	Bowel	Infrequent bowel movements and hard, pelletlike stools.
Croup (see page 230)	Throat, lungs	A deep, hacking cough that sounds like a dog's bark, and a squeaking noise upon inhalation.
Cryptosporidiosis (see page 230)	Bowel	Watery diarrhea and stomachache. May include nausea and vomiting, malaise, fever, and sometimes blood in the stool.
Diaper Rash (see page 230)	Diaper area	A number of types: red marks from diaper chafing; redness around the anus; bright red rash in diaper area folds and creases; and boil-like eruptions. Also known as atopic dermatitis.
Diarrhea (see page 231)	Bowel	Watery, unformed stools occurring more than three times in one day.

ILLNESS	BODY PART AFFECTED	SYMPTOMS
Ear Infection (see page 232)	Inner ear	Cold symptoms, including thick nasal mucus. Could also include eye and ear drainage, pulling at ears. Often accompanied by crying or screaming.
Eczema (see page 233)	Skin	Itchy skin breakouts often starting on the face, the crooks of the arms, or on the backs of the legs and knees.
Fifth Disease (see page 233)	Skin	"Slapped face" appearance of a red rash on the toddler's cheeks and/or a lacelike red rash on trunk, legs, and arms, and, rarely, a slight fever and painful joints.
Hand, Foot, and Mouth (HFM) Disease (see page 233)	Throat, gums, hard palate or inside the cheeks. Sometimes feet, palms, or buttocks	Small, red, painful, fluid-filled blisters in the throat, tongue, gums, hard palate, or inside the cheeks. Soles of feet and palms, or a pink rash may be seen on other parts of the body, such as the buttocks and thighs. Child may complain of a sore throat, and find eating or drinking painful, drooling because it hurts to swallow. Also, there may be a fever, muscle aches, or other flu like symptoms.
Heart Murmur (see page 234)	Heart	Abnormal heart sounds detected by a stethoscope.
Heatstroke (see page 234)	Body	Hot, dry (or sometimes moist) skin, extremely high fever, possible convulsions, and loss of consciousness.
Hepatitis A (see page 235)	Liver	Nausea and vomiting, dark urine, tenderness over the liver (below the right ribcage).

ILLNESS	BODY PART AFFECTED	SYMPTOMS
Hepatitis B (see page 235)	Liver	Nausea and vomiting, dark urine, tenderness over the liver (below the right ribcage).
Hernia (see page 235)	Navel or scrotum (testicle pouch)	Umbilical hernia–bulging around the belly button when the toddler cries, coughs, or strains. Inguinal hernia: swollen scrotum, accompanied by tenderness and redness.
Impetigo (see page 235)	Face or buttocks	Small red spots that turn into tiny blisters that rupture and become patches below the nose or on the buttocks that produce an oozing, sticky, honey-colored crust.
Influenza (see page 236)	Body	Fever and clear, runny nose, possible vomiting, cough, and diarrhea.
Measles (see page 236)	Body	Coldlike symptoms followed by fever, cough, bloodshot eyes, and, around fourth day, a deep red rash that starts on face and joins together as it spreads over the rest of the body. (See also Rubeola.)
Meningitis (see page 236)	Head and neck	Begins like a cold, flu, or an ear infection, but with increasing sluggishness, drowsiness, vomiting, stiff neck, or stiffening when the legs are raised for diapering. The soft spot on the skull might bulge.
Mononucleosis (see page 237)	Lymph nodes (glands in neck and other body areas) and throat	Unusual tiredness, possibly sore throat or mild fever.
Mumps (see page 237)	Skin, lymph nodes	Starts like the flu and an upset stomach followed 2-3 days later by tender, swollen glands beneath the earlobes or swollen jaws. Possible low fever.

ILLNESS	BODY PART AFFECTED	SYMPTOMS
Pneumonia (see page 237)	Lungs	Bacterial pneumonia: high fever, chills, shallow rapid breathing, fast heart rate, a wet cough, abdominal pain, and vomiting with the toddler becoming sicker over time. Viral pneumonia: low fever, no chills, a lingering cough with symptoms that linger for 3-4 weeks.
Ringworm (see page 238)	Skin	Itchy irritation, sometimes blisters, caused by a fungus. Easily treated with topical antifungal creams. Disappears in several weeks.
Roseola (see page 238)	Skin	Sudden onset of a high fever (may lead to febrile convulsions, see page 215) that breaks about the third day followed by a faint, pink rash (not red as with measles) on the trunk and extremities lasting about 1 day.
Respiratory Syncytial Virus (RSV) (see page 239)	Nose, throat, and lungs	Begins with cold like symptoms: runny nose, nasal congestion, a low-grade fever, decreased appetite, and general irritability and proceeds to a cough. Although serious for young infants, usually mild for young toddlers.
Rotavirus (see page 238)	Stomach and digestive tract	Mild to moderate fever, vomiting, and diarrhea. Highly contagious. Dehydration is common, and severe cases may require hospitalization.
Rubella (see page 239)	Skin	Low-grade fever, slight cold or other flu like symptoms followed by a pinkish-red, spotted rash that develops first on the face then spreads rapidly to the trunk and disappears after the third day. The toddler will look unwell and may have swollen glands behind the ears or nape of the neck. (See also Measles.)

ILLNESS	BODY PART AFFECTED	SYMPTOMS
Shigellosis (see page 240)	Stomach and digestive tract	Diarrhea, fever, stomach cramps. Chance of seizures. Easily spread. Some strains resistant to antibiotics.
Strep Throat (see page 240)	Throat and tonsils	Runny nose, rising and falling fevers, irritability, loss of appetite, pale appearance, and possible sore throat. (Uncommon in toddlers under 2 years of age.)
Thrush (see page 241)	Tongue and mouth, diaper area	Yeast infection affecting the toddler's tongue and cheeks with white, milky-colored patches that can't be wiped off. Diaper area may also have a bright, cherry-red rash caused by the yeast.
Urinary Tract Infection (UTI) (see page 241)	Bladder and urine	Painful urination; scant, strong-smelling, or reddish urine; possibly one-sided flank pain.
Whooping Cough (see page 242)	Breathing passages	Common cold, followed by spastic, deep-sounding coughing spells that follow in 1 to 2 weeks. Also known as pertussis.

TIP

Place a humidifier far enough away from the crib and other furniture to prevent moisture damage to wood surfaces.

TODDLER ILLNESSES A TO Z

Allergies

Sometimes the toddler's body reacts to contact with substances and the immune system releases histamines and other chemicals to fight what the body believes to be an invader.

Symptoms of an allergic reaction may include any of these: a stuffy or runny nose (usually with clear discharge); sneezing or wheezing; red, itchy skin or rashes; and red, watery eyes. While some allergic reactions happen almost immediately, others may take days to happen, making it harder to find the cause.

Your toddler will be more likely to have allergic reactions if he is exposed to cigarette smoke, if you have a family history of allergies, including rashes, sneezing, asthma, or eczema, or if your toddler has been given antibiotics.

Sometimes toddlers will have allergic reactions to plant pollens and animal fur, foods, medications, or plastics found in disposable diapers.

Allergic rhinitis is the swelling and inflammation of the lining of the nose that lingers, rather than disappearing in a week to 10 days as a cold would. In addition to displaying some of the symptoms listed above, toddlers may have dark circles under their eyes, called "allergic shiners," and a puffy-looking face.

Your doctor may recommend tests to help determine the cause of your toddler's reaction, and a special elimination diet may be recommended to test for food reactivity. Medications may also be suggested.

A pediatric allergist/immunologist may be needed to help ferret out the cause of your toddler's reactions. This is a medical doctor trained to treat babies and children who have allergies.

TIP

A severe allergic reaction may be indicated by anaphylactic shock (red, itchy whelps [hives], difficulty breathing). Call 911; every second counts.

TIP

Ana-Kit and EpiPen are brand names of epinephrine emergency kits designed to help reduce the effects of severe, life-threatening body reactions (anaphylactic shock).

Anemia

Iron is important in your child's diet, particularly during the toddler years of rapid brain growth. The body uses iron to carry oxygen through the blood to the tissues. Iron deficiency can cause serious damage during these formative years.

Anemia is very common during toddlerhood due to toddlers' dietary changes, such as switching from breastmilk or iron-fortified formula to regular cow's milk or changing from iron-fortified baby cereals to regular cereals, appetite changes, or drinking juices that don't supply iron.

Several studies have shown that being iron deficient can also increase a toddler's vulnerability to lead poisoning, which can cause serious neurological damage.

If your toddler looks pale and

seems tired a lot, anemia could be the cause. Other symptoms include a rapid heartbeat, irritability, loss of appetite, brittle nails, and a sore or swollen tongue.

Ask your toddler's health-care provider about iron supplementation. Typically, 10 milligrams of elemental iron from iron-fortified drops are suitable for children ages 1 to 6.

Appendicitis

Appendicitis is one of the most common causes for having an operation in childhood. It happens to about 4 out of every 1,000 children. It is an infection in a small, fingerlike pouch in the lower right-hand side of the large bowel.

The most common symptom is pain starting around the belly button that migrates to the lower right side of his abdomen, a tenderness that he doesn't want touched, and sometimes nausea and vomiting. Your toddler may have trouble eating, or seem unusually sleepy, and in young children, diarrhea may be an early symptom. If your child has appendicitis and is horrified at having his belly touched, you can help your doctor examine him by offering to push on your child's belly as directed or by putting your child over your shoulder so he's facing away from the doctor and having the doctor slip his hand between you and your child to feel his abdomen.

Stomach pain is a familiar complaint of toddlers, and that makes it hard to tell if appendicitis or something else is the problem. Only about 3 percent of the time is

appendicitis the source of stomach pain. For example, constipation is a much more common cause of severe stomach pain.

If your doctor suspects appendicitis and has your child hospitalized, the chances are 82 percent that he's right. Perforation is when the swollen appendix balloons and becomes so large that it bursts, sending infectious material into the abdomen, which can be life threatening. The perforation rates for appendicitis are much higher for children than adults (about 30 to 65 percent of the time).

The cure for appendicitis is abdominal surgery, called an appendectomy, to remove it, hopefully before it can rupture, which could lead to lead to a life-threatening inflammation of the abdomen and other organs.

An open appendectomy involves making an incision over the appendix to remove it. A laparoscopic appendectomy uses a special tubular instrument inserted into a tiny incision that allows the surgeon both to view the appendix and to remove it.

Asthma

Asthma is a recurrent inflammatory condition of the bronchial airways. In layman's terms, it's difficulty breathing, but it's also known as *bronchial asthma, asthmatic bronchitis, reactive airway disease, bronchitis*, and *wheezy bronchitis*. It affects nearly five million children in the United States.

It has become so widespread that it is now considered one

of the most common childhood illnesses. Toddlers and children are more likely to develop asthma if they have allergies or a family history of allergies and asthma, were exposed to tobacco smoke in utero or after birth, were born with low birthweight, or have frequent respiratory infections.

A baby's or toddler's first asthma attack can be triggered by a number of things: a chest cold, cold air, exercise, some types of viral infections, changes in air quality (such as cigarette smoke in the air), and allergens such as dust mites, mold, pollen, or animal dander.

During an attack, the lining of your toddler's lungs will become inflamed, and his airways will spasm and produce mucus. Symptoms will include: coughing, tightness in the chest, shortness of breath, and an unusual wheezing or whistling sound when your toddler exhales.

There are many different kinds of asthma. Your child's health-care provider is the best person to help you decide if your child has asthma and what treatments should be used. Your child may be prescribed an inhaler (bronchodilator) with a breathing mask for use during attacks without the need for daily medications. If your child develops moderate, persistent asthma, then an inhaled anti-inflammatory steroid and a long-acting bronchodilator may be recommended.

A 2002 study published in the *American Journal of Respiratory and Critical Care Medicine* found that wheezing or coughing in babies and toddlers 2 years or younger was not necessarily a sign of developing lifelong asthma.

But, after age 2, these symptoms could signal that the child might be vulnerable to asthma later. The largest majority of children who developed chronic asthma were found to have a history of asthma in the family. But, the study showed, even with a strong family history of asthma, more than 60 percent of children in asthma-vulnerable families did not go on to have lifelong asthma.

Reducing Asthma Attacks

Take these steps to help to reduce the severity of your toddler's asthma attacks:

- **Eliminate triggers.** Keep your home as free as possible of dust and animal hair and dander, eliminate carpeting, and vacuum the floor and stuffed furniture frequently using a vacuum with powerful filters. Change linens frequently, and use allergen-proof casings on all bedding.
- **Clean the air.** Stop smoking and don't allow others to smoke in your home. (Even if you smoke outdoors, your lungs will exhale smoke for days, and smoke will also cling to your hair, skin, and clothing when you are indoors.) Constantly run a fan-style air cleaner that contains high-density filtration layers in your child's bedroom.
- **Lower exposure.** If pollen is a trigger, you may need to reduce outdoor activities in spring and fall, and be vigilant during sudden or extremely cold temperatures in winter.

Boils

Boils are raised, red bumps on the skin that may develop into infected white-topped blisters. They can erupt anywhere on the skin, but for toddlers who are still in diapers, they most often appear in the diaper area. It's best to let a boil heal on its own.

Don't try to pick or squeeze the bumps, as this could cause the infection to spread and could also lead to scarring. If the bump seems seriously infected, your toddler's doctor may decide to open the boil, and may recommend antibiotic ointment to help with healing.

Bronchiolitis

Bronchiolitis is a viral infection of the tiny bronchioles deep in the lungs of babies and toddlers who are usually less than 2 years of age. In many cases RSV (Respiratory Syncytial Virus) is the culprit. The illness begins with typical cold symptoms, including nasal congestion, a fever of 100 degrees or higher, and mild coughing. It then can progress to become more severe and life-threatening when the lungs' smallest air passages become inflamed. Signs of severe bronchiolitis include: sucking in of the skin around the ribs and the base of the throat when the child tries to breathe (retractions), flaring nostrils, and grunting. A baby or young child can become exhausted from the effort required to breathe, and in some cases breathing may completely stop. In those cases, emergency care is required. (See also Respiratory Syncytial Virus).

Bronchitis

When the large breathing airways become swollen, bronchitis results. There are two types: *acute* and *chronic*. Symptoms of acute bronchitis include fever; a painful cough; a sore throat; thick, yellow mucus; and shortness of breath.

Acute bronchitis is usually the result of a cold or flu, and while this kind of bronchitis is not dangerous in itself, it may lead to pneumonia. If your toddler shows any signs of breathing problems accompanied by a fever, you should call your health-care provider right away. In children, bronchitis is nearly always caused by a virus.

Your doctor will recommend a cough suppressant and/or other methods of treating the individual symptoms. The best ways to prevent bronchitis are to keep your child away from people who are ill, and away from pollution and secondhand smoke.

Chronic bronchitis is bronchitis that lasts for three months or longer. Pollutants, such as second-hand smoke or dust, can make it worse.

Chicken Pox

Chicken pox is a highly contagious childhood disease caused by the varicella zoster virus (VZV), a member of the herpes family. It can be very serious for young toddlers. If you are an adult and haven't had chicken pox, you may catch it, too. Your toddler may be contagious 1 to 2 days before symptoms show.

Chicken pox is spread by other children, so keep your toddler away from children who have been exposed to chicken pox at school or from siblings. The varicella vaccine is available, and is recommended between 12 to 18 months of age. (And it is also recommended for you if you're not pregnant and for your toddler's siblings if any of you have not had the disease.)

The symptoms of chicken pox are sluggishness, frequent crying, and loss of appetite. Several days after exposure, a rash of flat, red, splotchy dots will erupt. It usually starts on the chest or stomach and back, then spreads to the face and scalp a day or so later. The red dots of the rash then join together to form clusters of tiny pimples, which then progress to small, delicate, clear blisters with new rash areas developing each day. The blisters form into extremely itchy scabs. Recovery can take as long as two weeks.

Oatmeal baths can be very soothing to dry, itchy skin. Tie a handful of raw oatmeal in a washcloth and swish it around in your child's bathwater. Your toddler's health-care provider may prescribe creams to put on the itchy spots, or over-the-counter lotions, such as calamine lotion, to help relieve the intense itching.

Cold Sores

Cold sores, also known as fever blisters, are small, fluid-filled blisters that crop up on or near the lips, and are very common during childhood. They can appear individually or in clusters. Despite their name, they have nothing to do with colds, but are caused by the herpes simplex virus type 1 (not herpes simplex virus type 2

that causes genital herpes, though either can cause sores in the facial or genital area).

Your toddler can catch the virus by sharing a cup, utensil, or slobbery toy with another person who has the infection or carried in his saliva through mouth-to-mouth kissing. During the first bout, called primary herpes, there may be mouth soreness, gum inflammation, possibly fever, swollen lymph nodes in the neck, and a sore throat, but symptoms could be very mild.

Recovery is in about 7 to 10 days, but the virus will stay in his body for life. For some children, the virus lies dormant; for others, it will periodically show up again. These flare-ups are called secondary herpes and can erupt from stress, fever, and sun exposure. Secondary flare-ups may be milder without swelling of his gums or lymph nodes or a fever or sore throat, but he will have the telltale blistering on or near his lips.

If your toddler develops a sore on his eyelid or the surface of his eye, call your health-care provider right away. Your child may need antiviral drugs to keep the infection from scarring his cornea. (In rare cases, ocular herpes can weaken vision and even cause blindness.)

Most treatments reduce the pain of the sore, but the virus has to run its course.

Colds and Coughs

It's likely that your toddler will have more colds and other upper respiratory infections than any other illnesses throughout his childhood. On average, children catch nine colds during their first 2 years. Your toddler will be more vulnerable to these infections with more public contact, because viruses and bacteria are spread by contact and his body hasn't yet learned how to fight them.

If your toddler has a cold, it will usually begin with clear fluid running from the nose, sneezing, and possibly a low fever. Though exposing your toddler to cold air doesn't cause a cold, exposure to cold weather changes the way our bodies fight off viruses. The protective mucus and cilia in the respiratory tract do not function as efficiently, so if you get exposed to a virus in those conditions, you're more likely to catch it.

If your toddler has a difficult time blowing his nose, treat his nasal congestion by using a ball-shaped, rubber suction bulb. Squeeze the bulb part of the syringe first, carefully place the tip into one nostril, and then gently release the bulb to create suction. Only a slight suction is needed. If secretions are particularly thick, your pediatrician may recommend mild saline nose drops. Using a dropper that has been cleaned with soap and water and rinsed well with plain water, place two drops in each nostril, and then immediately suction with the bulb. However, don't suction too often as this can cause irritation. You might also try placing saline in the nose several times during the day.

When your child has a cold or an upper respiratory infection, place a cool-mist humidifier in his room to keep the air moist and make him more comfortable, being sure to clean and dry the humidifier thoroughly each day to prevent bacterial or mold contamination. (Hot-water vaporizers are not recommended because they can cause serious scalds or burns at their spouts.)

> **TIP**
>
> Nose drops that contain medication may be harmful to toddlers.

Conjunctivitis

Sometimes toddlers' eyes get swollen or crusty, either because one or both tear ducts are plugged, or due to an infection, such as conjunctivitis (pinkeye). One or both eyes will appear red and swollen, crusty, or sticky with mucus. The infection can be caused by bacteria, a virus, or plugged tear ducts.

The home remedy is to dip a clean, soft washcloth or cotton ball in mildly warm water, squeeze out the excess moisture, and then gently massage the affected area every 2 to 4 hours. If symptoms persist after a day of lukewarm compresses, call your toddler's health-care provider. Special eye drops or an ointment are likely to be prescribed. Most cases clear up in 3 to 5 days.

The viral and bacterial forms of pinkeye are highly contagious and can be spread very easily from one person to another, usually through hand-to-eye contact. Make sure everyone in the family keeps their hands clean when there's an outbreak, and don't allow anyone to share washcloths or towels.

Constipation

(See Chapter 9.)

Croup

Croup is not a single problem, but a symptom that occurs when a child's upper airway swells and becomes narrowed by an illness or an allergic reaction. It causes a cough that sounds like a dog's bark, and a squeaking noise when the child inhales. Croup is most common in babies and children between 3 months and 5 years.

Croup is usually not serious and can be helped with a cool-mist humidifier or by holding your toddler in the bathroom while a hot shower fills the room with steam. However, if your child shows signs of having difficulty breathing and/or swallowing or is breathing rapidly, or the skin between his ribs pulls in with each breath, and/or he has a fever, call your pediatrician immediately.

In some toddlers and children, croup is a recurring problem, and those who are vulnerable to it may have three to four bouts of croup per flu season. Usually, croup doesn't present a serious problem, but you should always seek your doctor's advice. In most cases, children outgrow croup when their air passages mature and increase in size.

Cryptosporidiosis

Cryptosporidiosis, called crypto for short, is an infectious diarrheal disease caused by the *Cryptosporidium* parasite. It's common among children in child-care settings, but it can also be transmitted at swimming pools, especially kiddie pools.

Cryptosporidiosis is spread through fecal-oral transmission by feces of an infected person or an object that has been contaminated with the infected person's feces. Infection can also occur if contaminated food or water is ingested. Outbreaks in child-care settings are most common in August and September.

Symptoms can take a week to develop and usually include watery diarrhea and stomachache, but can also include nausea and vomiting, general ill feeling, and fever, and sometimes there may be blood in the stool. The most severe part lasts from 4 to 7 days, but symptoms may come and go for up to 30 days.

The spread of cryptosporidiosis is highest among children who are not toilet-trained, and higher among toddlers than infants, because of their increased movement and interaction with other children. Child-care providers can get it from diaper changing.

The parasite is hard to detect, as few laboratories run tests for it, and there is no effective treatment for it. It simply runs its course.

Diaper Rash

Diaper rash is a red, sore patch of skin on your child's bottom, genital area, or between the creases inside his thighs. It's common for diaper users between 5 and 15 months of age. There are a variety of causes, but usually the red patches last for only a few days and then disappear.

Skin infections break out in the diaper area when moisture has broken down the skin's naturally protective, oily barrier. Sometimes the breakdown is worsened by harsh chemicals produced when urine and feces mix together in the diaper and stay there for a while. That's why it's important to change your toddler's diaper frequently and to keep the area rinsed off with clear water after a bowel movement.

Frequent airing out of the diaper area, preferably with some sunlight, can also help to improve the rash by letting the skin dry out. Baby powder and cornstarch don't help diaper rash; in fact, they can make it worse, as can alcohol-based wipes. A thick layer of a zinc-based diaper cream can help to protect the skin long enough so that the rash can heal.

A cherry-red, oozing diaper rash may signal a yeast infection that may need special treatment. Your toddler's health-care provider may recommend an anti-fungal cream, ointment, or a mild topical steroid. But don't apply any over-the-counter products yourself unless they've gotten your health-care provider's approval.

Contact your health-care provider if the rash doesn't go away, or if it worsens, such as spreading to other body parts, there's a fever involved, or it turns into pimples, blisters, ulcers, acne-like bumps or pus-filled sores.

Diarrhea

Diarrhea is loose, watery stools occurring more than three times per day. It is not the occasional loose stool or the frequent passing of barely formed stools. There are many possible causes of diarrhea in toddlers, such as bacterial infections, viruses, and parasites, and sometimes it can be caused by medical conditions, or allergic reactions to foods or milk products. One of the most common causes of toddler diarrhea is a stomach flu (*viral gastroenteritis*). Although many different viruses can cause stomach flu in toddlers, the most common one is called *rotavirus*.

Toddlers with diarrhea are a special concern because of their small body size, which puts them at greater risk for dehydration, particularly if the diarrhea is accompanied by vomiting. Your health-care provider will want to treat against dehydration by replacing lost fluid and electrolytes (sodium and potassium).

Giving special fluids by mouth (oral rehydration therapy) may be recommended using rehydration drinks such as Pedialyte, which can be found in bottles or as a powder to be added to water in most pharmacies and supermarkets and purchased without a prescription. (Note: Rehydration fluids have a brief shelf life. Once a bottle has been opened or a mix prepared, it must be used or thrown out within 24 hours. Bacteria rapidly grow in the solution, and a toddler could easily drink three or four bottles of the fluid during an illness.)

Do not try to treat diarrhea without first consulting with your toddler's health-care provider. For home treatment, allow your toddler's system to settle for a few hours after a diarrhea attack before encouraging him to eat again. If vomiting is involved, offer him small sips of water, or clear liquids, such as chicken or beef broth, or let him suck on ice chips. After several hours, gradually reintroduce food, starting with bland, easy-to-digest foods, such as applesauce, strained bananas, strained carrots, rice, or mashed potatoes.

Intestines that have been damaged by severe diarrhea may have trouble digesting whole cow's milk, and your toddler's health-care provider can suggest alternative liquids.

Diarrhea can cause your toddler's diaper area to become red and sore. Use a thick layer of zinc-based diaper cream, to provide a shield for the skin. Change diapers frequently, rinsing his bottom with water and air-drying it, and cut down on the use of baby wipes, which can be irritating to toddlers' irritated skin.

Ear Infection

Next to colds, middle-ear infection (*otitis media*) is the most common cause for trips to the pediatrician. As many as three out of four children have some form of ear infections by age 3.

There are two different kinds of infections: otitis media with effusion (OME), which means there is fluid in the middle ear, and acute otitis media (AOM), which refers to fluid in the middle ear that also comes with pain, redness, and a bulging eardrum.

Children with OME will seem completely fine, and you won't know anything is wrong unless your pediatrician discovers the infection during a well-toddler visit. But toddlers with AOM will be fussy, especially at night, and may have a fever and other coldlike symptoms.

After a case of AOM, your toddler will probably have a case of OME for several weeks afterward. Typically, an acute infection will set in a few days after a cold has started. You can't see that the toddler has the infection, but your health-care provider will be able to detect it by looking for swelling in your toddler's ear with an otoscope and by blowing air on the eardrum to see if it's swollen (the toddler will hate this, so be prepared for screaming).

If your toddler has an ear infection, a painkiller such as acetaminophen may be recommended along with a course of antibiotics that will usually come in liquid form. (If your toddler rejects the liquid, try mixing it in applesauce or yogurt.) In the meantime, your toddler may be more comfortable upright than lying down. Applying a warm, moist towel to your toddler's cheek near the ears could help soothe the pain.

Usually ear infections get better after several days of treatment. If ear infections are recurrent (more than three episodes in 6 months), and your pediatrician believes the infections interfere with your toddler's hearing and language development, minor surgery may be recommended that involves placing tiny tubes in the ear for draining fluid.

Eczema

Eczema (or *atopic dermatitis*) produces thickened, red, dry, flaky skin patches that itch. Sometimes the patches can become infected and look weepy with crusts, especially if your toddler scratches them. While eczema usually shows up on babies' faces, toddlers get the rash around their knees, elbows, and ankles.

Eczema is thought to run in families who have other allergies, too, such as asthma and hay fever. It is not a direct allergic reaction itself, but certain things can trigger it, such as something your toddler eats or comes in contact with, such as wool or chemicals in detergents, soaps, lotions, and fabric softeners. Too much sun can also set off an attack.

Practical treatments can help to soothe the skin during an attack. Daily baths in lukewarm (not hot) water using bath oil and a soap substitute can help, but be careful to not rub the skin when drying off. Moisturizers are soothing. They may need to be applied repeatedly throughout the day, and sometimes moist wraps also can help to soothe the skin. Sunscreen can help to protect the skin from burning. Keeping fingernails trimmed and clean will help to reduce inflammation. (Mittens or socks over your toddler's hands may help keep him from scratching himself during the night).

A recent study found that soaking a child for 5 to 10 minutes twice a week in a highly diluted bleach bath was five times more effective in treating eczema than plain water. The researchers' treatment instructions were to stir a scant 2 teaspoons of bleach per gallon into bathwater (or ½ cup per full tub) before your child enters the tub with the caution that your child not be allowed to drink the water. Ask your health-care provider first before trying it.

Fifth Disease

A fine, lacy pink rash starts on the cheeks, giving the toddler a "slapped cheek" look, and it may then move to the backs of the arms and legs. It may show up and disappear over the process of 1 to 2 weeks, especially in response to a toddler bath or irritation. Rarely, the rash is accompanied by a slight fever and achy joints. The rash on the face will usually disappear within 4 days after it shows up, while the rash on the rest of the body will take 3 to 7 days to go away. Usually, the only symptom is the rash, and it will disappear on its own.

German Measles

(See *Rubella*.)

Hand, Foot, and Mouth Disease

Hand, Foot, and Mouth Disease (HFMD) (*coxsackie virus*) is common among toddlers, especially children in child care. It is caused by a highly contagious virus, which is mostly spread through coughing and sneezing. The incubation stage is about 3 to 6 days, and, unfortunately, a child is most contagious before he shows any symptoms.

When they do appear, the symptoms include a blistery rash on the hands, feet, and mouth. There may also be an accompanying sore throat, fever, and a general sense of feeling unwell.

If a toddler refuses to eat or drink because his mouth and throat are too sore, it can lead to dehydration, a serious condition that can be detected by decreased urination. If his fever rises above 103°F, see his health-care provider.

Like most viruses, HFMD has no cure, and it simply has to run its course, which takes about 7 to 10 days.

Heart Murmur

Heart murmurs are common in children, and they're often harmless. "Innocent" or "harmless" heart murmurs, as health-care providers call them, are simply the sound the blood makes as it moves through the chambers of the heart. They may get louder when a child's heart beats faster, and softer when he's calm.

More serious murmurs are caused by something wrong with a child's heart, such as a hole in it, or a leaky or narrow heart valve. If your health-care provider is concerned about what is being heard with the stethoscope, your child may be refered to a pediatric cardiologist (children's heart doctor). Your child will have an exam, and he may be given tests, such as a chest X-ray, an electrocardiogram (EKG, or ECG), or an echocardiogram ("echo") to find out what is making the unusual sound. Depending upon the severity

of the heart problem, medication or surgery may be options.

Heatstroke

Heat stroke occurs in toddlers when their bodies are unable to cool themselves down because of high temperatures, humidity or becoming dehydrated from insufficient fluids. Young children's bodies don't adapt as quickly to heat changes as adults' do. They don't sweat very well and can overdo their activities without realizing that they are too hot or thirsty. Fevers and medications can also make toddlers more susceptible to overheating, as can wrapping them up during a cold or flu in an attempt to cure it. (Never, *ever* leave your toddler in a hot car!)

Heat stroke at this age can be deadly and result in serious organ damage. If your toddler is in trouble, he may spike a high temperature (103°F and above), he may appear red-faced and feel hot and dry, he will have dark urine or none at all, and he may either not sweat at all or have profuse sweating. If he is dehydrated, his mouth will appear dry and parched, his eyes may appear sunken, and his hands and feet may feel cold or look splotchy. He may act sluggish, dizzy, or confused, see things that aren't there, or even lose consciousness.

If you suspect heat stroke, notify 9-1-1 immediately, and meanwhile, get your child into the shade or inside a cool building. Offer him tepid water to drink. Apply cool or tepid water to the skin and seek out a vent or fan his wet body to help cool him down. Ice packs wrapped in towels and placed under the arms or at his crotch may help. Your child will likely be given fluids containing electrolytes to drink or through a vein.

Hepatitis

There are many types of hepatitis. All are infections of the liver. Some may be silent and hard to detect, while others may result in jaundice—a yellowing of the skin and whites of the eyes—combined with nausea and weakness. Other symptoms could seem similar to the flu, such as loss of appetite, nausea, vomiting, diarrhea, and itchiness. Most children recover from hepatitis, but some go on to have chronic liver problems.

Hepatitis A is a liver inflammation. The virus can be passed through contaminated food, water, or contact with small amounts of an infected person's bowel movements. It is usually short lived and may not lead to the serious consequences of hepatitis B.

Hepatitis B is a serious infection of the liver transmitted by exposure to an infected person's blood. It can be transmitted from mother to baby during delivery. Hepatitis B infects more than 200,000 people each year in the United States and 4,000 to 5,000 die as a result of chronic problems relating to it. Since 1991, the Centers for Disease Control and Prevention have recommended that toddlers be vaccinated against hepatitis B through a series of shots given during the first 6 months after birth.

Hernia

A hernia is the protrusion of an organ through the structure that normally surrounds or contains it. With an umbilical hernia, a bit of intestine or fatty tissue near the navel breaks through the muscular wall of the abdomen. The hernia will bulge out around the belly button when the toddler cries, coughs, or strains.

Umbilical hernias are much more common in African-American toddlers than other races, and they usually resolve on their own by age 4. (Note: Having a permanent "innie" or "outie" belly button is *not* a hernia).

An inguinal hernia occurs when a small portion of the toddler's intestine becomes captured in the scrotal sac (that holds his testicles) and causes swelling, tenderness, and redness. It may first happen after a bout of vigorous crying. Since it may cause severe problems with blockage in the intestine, medical intervention may be necessary.

Impetigo

Impetigo is a bacterial skin infection caused by a staph or strep bacterium. It begins as tiny blisters. The blisters burst and leave brown or red wet patches of skin that may weep fluid that forms a yellowish, honeycomb-like crust, usually around the nose and mouth or the buttocks, and sometimes the hands and forearms.

Your toddler's health-care provider may recommend applying an over-the-counter antibiotic ointment or prescribe an oral antibiotic to prevent its spreading.

Also be sure to cut your toddler's nails short to prevent scratching and a spread of the infection.

If applying antibiotic ointment doesn't make the rash noticeably better in a few days, contact your pediatrician. In rare cases, impetigo may lead to a kidney problem known as *glomerulonephritis*, which causes the urine to turn dark (cola) brown. In most cases, impetigo is short lived and usually heals completely in children.

Influenza

Typically, flu starts with a fever, fatigue, and chills, followed by a runny nose with clear mucus and a cough. Your toddler may also be irritable and have swollen glands, arch his back with abdominal pain, have smelly, explosive diarrhea, and projectile vomiting.

In other words, if your toddler gets the flu, it's going to be a long, long night. Your health-care provider may want to examine your toddler to be sure that there are no other causes, and she might tell you that the most you can do is keep the toddler fed and hydrated, and be on the lookout for a high fever or signs of dehydration (sunken eyes and decreased urination).

Your health-care provider may prescribe an antiviral medication that can lessen the symptoms and shorten the length of the flu by a day or two. The trick is in making the diagnosis as soon as possible, because the medication must be given in the first 48 hours. Once that 48-hour window closes, the antiviral medications are no longer effective.

Also, you may be able to prevent your toddler from catching the flu in the first place by asking your health-care provider to give your toddler a flu shot at the beginning of flu season (usually in late fall).

Measles

Measles is a highly contagious viral illness characterized by coldlike symptoms, fever, cough, conjunctivitis (pinkeye), and a deep red rash that starts on the face. Around the fourth day, the toddler will seem more ill as the rash spreads over the rest of the body.

Over the last few decades, measles cases have decimated in the United States and Canada because of widespread immunization. Before widespread immunization, measles was so common during childhood that the majority of the population had been infected by age 20. Rarely, measles can develop into pneumonia, encephalitis (brain swelling), and ear infections. (See also *Rubella*, below.)

Meningitis

Meningitis is a rare but sometimes deadly infection of the tissues that cover the brain, and it can be deadly within a matter of hours. The beginning signs of meningitis are subtle and not very different from coming down with a bad cold. There may be fever, vomiting, and a general feeling of unwell. Your child may complain that his head or neck area hurts and he seems to dislike bright lights.

As meningitis progresses, your toddler may have seizures or become extremely sluggish, sleepy, and difficult to wake, which calls for racing to the emergency room. Sometimes a rash may be involved (be sure to tell your child's health-care provider about that).

A blood test to check for a bacterial infection may be called for, and possibly a spinal tap to see if the spinal fluid is infected. If meningitis is treated aggressively and quickly with antibiotics, the crippling and long-lasting effects of the disease can be minimized.

Mononucleosis

Mononucleosis ("mono," or glandular fever) is caused by *Epstein-Barr virus* (EBV). Although it is more common among teenagers, it can also affect young children. In younger children there may be only a mild fever, and the child may not appear ill, but other symptoms may include being more tired than usual and having swollen lymph nodes (small, round infection-fighting lymph glands in different places on the body), and a mild fever.

A specific blood test for mono is available. It is transmitted by fluids from the nose and throat and sharing of utensils or cups. There is no current treatment for mono except plenty of rest. Once a child gets over the active phase, it will remain active in his body throughout his life and it may occasionally reactivate.

Mumps

Mumps is a highly contagious viral infection that spreads from child to child through saliva. It can be caught by sharing eating utensils

or drinks, or even breathing the air immediately after someone has sneezed or coughed.

The first symptoms are usually mild: a fever and loss of appetite. Then, within a week, the area in front of your toddler's ears, the parotid glands, will noticeably swell, giving your child a chipmunk appearance. Other symptoms could also include a stiff neck (see also *meningitis*), sluggishness and weakness, and painful chewing and swallowing. Sometimes mumps will affect the salivary glands under the tongue or chin or in the chest area.

Since it is caused by a virus, antibiotics don't help, but having your child innoculated with the MMR vaccine before he is exposed to it can help to protect him from it. Generally, having mumps conveys lifelong immunity to catching it again. (See immunization table on page 211.)

Pneumonia

Pneumonia is an inflammation or infection of the lungs, when the air sacs fill with pus, mucus, and other liquid that interferes with their functioning. There are multiple causes and types of pneumonia. The symptoms of bacterial pneumonia are a fever, chills, rapid breathing, fast heart rate, a wet cough, abdominal pain, and vomiting, with the toddler becoming sicker over time.

Viral pneumonia is marked by a low fever, no chills, and a lingering cough, but with the toddler seeming almost normal and with symptoms persisting for 3 to 4 weeks. Lobar pneumonia refers to pneumonia in a section (lobe) of a lung, while bronchial pneumonia (or bronchopneumonia) refers to pneumonia that affects patches throughout both lungs.

In serious cases of pneumonia oxygen can't reach the blood, and when there is insufficient oxygen in the blood, body cells can't function properly and may die. Prompt treatment with antibiotics and oxygen almost always cures bacterial pneumonia, but treating it aggressively and early is important.

Ringworm

Ringworm is a harmless and sometimes itchy skin inflammation that often appears as a round ring of tiny blisters with a sharp border between the skin and the dime- to quarter-sized lesions, often with clear skin inside the ring. It is not caused by a worm, but by one or two types of fungus, *Trichophyton* and *Microsporum*, and it often shows up on the face, trunk, or limbs.

It is easily treated by topical, over-the-counter antifungal creams that contain clotrimazole (brand name Lotrimin or Mycelex) and are applied twice a day to the reddened area and surrounding skin. Your health-care provider will be able to recommend the most effective treatment.

The fungi in the rash are contagious by direct contact with the rash or from the hands of an infected person who has been scratching the rash. Your child can also catch it from infected pets, especially dogs and cats.

It will disappear with treatment after several weeks.

Roseola

Roseola infantum is a very common viral illness found in children all over the world. In the United States, about one in three children have some kind of roseola, and 86 percent of children have acquired the virus' antibodies by 1 year of age.

Your toddler could be a carrier for the virus and neither show symptoms nor appear ill, or he could suddenly develop a fever between 102°F and 104°F that lasts for 3 to 5 days. In some cases, the sudden rise in the fever may lead to febrile seizures (see page 215).

Your toddler will have decreased appetite, mild diarrhea, a slight cough, and a runny nose, and seem more irritable and sleepy than usual. His eyelids may seem swollen and droopy.

The fever will likely break on about the third day and be followed by a faint, pink rash (not red as with measles) on the toddler's trunk, arms, and legs that will last about a day. After the fever subsides, a faint, pink rash develops on the body, spreads to the upper arms and neck, and then disappears in a day or so. Your toddler's health-care provider may prescribe medications to increase comfort.

Rotavirus

Rotavirus is responsible for approximately 5 to 10 percent of all cases of diarrhea among children under 5 years of age. It accounts for more than 500,000 physician visits and approximately 55,000 to 70,000 hospitalizations each year among children under 5 years of age, and, sadly, an estimated 1 in 200,000 toddlers worldwide with rotavirus diarrhea die from the complications of the infection.

Symptoms can be mild to severe. It begins with few or no symptoms, or a mild to moderate fever followed by severe vomiting followed by diarrhea. The incubation period is about 2 days before symptoms appear, starting with vomiting followed by 4 to 8 days of profuse diarrhea. It is highly contagious and usually spread when children touch or place in their mouths small, usually invisible amounts of fecal matter found on surfaces such as toys, books, and clothing, or on the hands of caregivers. It can also be transmitted through contaminated water or food, and possibly by respiratory droplets in a sneeze, cough, or exhalation.

Dehydration is the most dangerous side effect of the virus. Your health-care provider will guide you in how to provide hydration, such as electrolyte solutions (Pedialyte), to keep your toddler well hydrated. Severe cases may require hospitalization with intravenous fluids.

Rotavirus can be prevented with a vaccination that usually is administered in 2 doses during infancy. Once a child has it, later infections are apt to be less severe as his immune system may provide some protection.

RSV

RSV stands for respiratory syncytial (pronounced "sin-SHISH-al") virus. It infects most children sooner or later (usually by the age of 2), but during toddlerhood, it is rarely more troublesome for a child than the common cold. (It is more serious in babies and can cause serious respiratory infections such as bronchiolitis and pneumonia.)

RSV begins with coldlike symptoms, such as a runny or stuffy nose, a minor cough, and fever, with the cough becoming more pronounced after a few days. In severe cases, your toddler may have labored breathing (faster than 40 breaths per minute), flared nostrils, rib cage expanding more than usual, wheezing or grunting when breathing, bluish lips or fingernails, and a fever that rises to over 103°F—all of which are signs to contact your health-care provider.

Because RSV is a virus, antibiotics and other medications aren't effective. Milder symptoms usually last 5 to 7 days and go away on their own, but the cough may linger for weeks longer. Severe forms may call for hospitalization for oxygen treatments, intravenous fluids, and drugs to help open your toddler's airways.

A vaccination is available called Synagis, but the protection is only temporary and monthly shots may need to be given during RSV season, between October and April.

Rubella

Sometimes called "3-day measles" or German measles, this virus starts with mild symptoms of illness, such as a low-grade fever, a slight cold, or flulike indications. Then, a pinkish red, spotted rash develops, first on the toddler's face and rapidly spreads to the trunk. It disappears after the third day. The toddler will look unwell and may have swollen glands behind the ears or nape of the neck but will recover within a few days. Contact your toddler's health-care provider, although no medical treatment is usually needed.

More rarely, rubella can lead to brain swelling or a problem with bleeding. It is the most dangerous when mothers without immunity catch it and transmit it to their babies in utero during certain months of pregnancy. It can cause a fetus to be stillborn, or to be born blind or deaf or with learning disabilities. Rubella immunization is part of MMR shots (see immunization chart on page 211).

Shigellosis

Shigellosis is an infectious disease caused by a group of bacteria called *Shigella*. Toddlers who are infected with *Shigella* develop diarrhea, fever, and stomach cramps 1 or 2 days after being exposed to the bacterium, and diarrhea is often bloody.

The bacteria are present in the diarrheal stools of infected person while they are sick and for a week or two afterward, and it can be passed by soiled fingers from one person to another by mouth, particularly between children who are still wearing diapers. It also can be caught by swimming in contaminated water or eating vegetables that have been grown in fields contaminated by sewage.

It is more common during the summer months and in toddlers from 2 to 4 years of age. In some young children, the diarrhea can be so severe and the risks of dehydration so severe that hospitalization may be recommended. A high fever may also be associated with seizures in children younger than 2 years of age. Some persons who are infected may have no symptoms at all, but may still pass the *Shigella* bacteria to others.

Children with mild infections will usually recover quickly without antibiotic treatment, but it may take several months until their bowel habits return to normal. Some forms can later lead to Reiter's syndrome, which causes joint pain, eye irritation, and painful urination that can last for months or years, and possibly lead to chronic arthritis.

Effective treatment depends on which germ is causing the diarrhea. Usually it is treated with antibiotics to kill it and shorten the illness. Unfortunately, some *Shigella* bacteria have become resistant to antibiotics and using antibiotics to treat shigellosis can actually make the germs more resistant in the future.

> **TIP**
>
> Avoid antidiarrheal medicines to treat shigellosis, as they are likely to make the illness worse.

Strep Throat

Officially called *streptococcal pharyngitis*, strep throat is caused by streptococcal bacteria. In children, the infection can cause red, swollen tonsils covered in a white, smelly material, red patches on the roof of the mouth, a white tongue, a high fever, swollen glands, abdominal pain, vomiting, and trouble swallowing. Neck glands may also be swollen.

In toddlers the symptoms are usually milder, and include a runny nose, rising and falling fevers, irritability, loss of appetite, and a pale appearance. The infection usually lasts about a week, but some toddlers can have chronic strep infections that last longer.

Your health-care provider will collect a culture from your toddler's nose or throat to confirm that the infection is strep. Then it will be decided whether antibiotics will be needed to prevent more serious complications such as ear and sinus infections, or involvement of other organs such as the lungs, brain, or kidneys, or rheumatic fever. (Note: Strep throat is very rare in children under 2 years of age.)

Thrush

If your toddler's tongue and cheeks stay coated in white patches that won't wipe away, he may have thrush, a fungal problem. This yeast infection grows in moist places on the inside and on the skin, and it may also appear as red, irritated patches in the folds of your toddler's skin, such as the neck, the armpits, and the thighs. Sometimes a cherry red diaper rash that doesn't clear up easily can also be caused by yeast. Your health-care provider will suggest medication to treat it.

Urinary Tract Infection (UTI)

A urinary tract infection causes irritation of the lining of the bladder, urethra, ureters, or kidneys, just like the inside of the nose or the throat becomes irritated with a cold. The signs of a UTI may not be clear, since a toddler may not be able to describe how he is feeling. Sometimes symptoms include a high fever, irritability, and loss of appetite. And some children have a low-grade fever, nausea, and vomiting.

Urine may have an unusual smell, and your toddler may urinate more than usual. If he has a high temperature and appears sick for more than a day without signs of a runny nose or other obvious cause for discomfort, he or she may need to be checked for a bladder infection. If the kidney is infected, a child may complain of pain under the side of the rib cage, called the flank, or low back pain.

Crying or complaining that it hurts to urinate and producing only a few drops of urine at a time are other signs of urinary tract infection, or a child may have difficulty controlling the urine and may leak urine into clothing or bed sheets, and it could smell unusual or look cloudy or red.

If a urinary tract infection is suspected, your child's urine will be collected. Toddlers who are not yet toilet trained may be fitted with a plastic collection bag over the genital area that is sealed with an adhesive strip. An older child may be asked to urinate into a container, or a small tube may be directly fed into the urethra to directly drain into a container, or a needle may be placed directly into the bladder through the skin of the lower abdomen.

Urinary tract infections are treated with antibiotics.

Whooping Cough (Pertussis)

Also known as pertussis, whooping cough is a highly contagious respiratory illness that used to kill thousands of people every year. But now, thanks to the DTaP vaccine, there are only a handful of deaths from the disease every year. Still, cases of pertussis seem to be on the rise, particularly among infants younger than 6 months who are not yet protected by immunizations, and in young adults whose childhood vaccines have begun to wear off.

If your toddler develops a spastic, honking cough, and possibly vomits after coughing, contact his health-care provider, who will probably prescribe antibiotics. Your toddler will be contagious until the course of the medication has been completed, which is about 5 days.

Safety

ACCIDENT-PROOFING YOUR TODDLER

Protecting your exploring toddler from his own curiosity is a full-time job! Your ever-moving child is driven by a powerful, innate urge to explore the world: to see, taste, and experience everything that attracts him.

Unfortunately, a toddler isn't very discerning. He'll try to open the bleach bottle, perch

---

Emergency Medical Restraint

If your child has been injured and needs treatment but isn't able to cooperate, you may need to help medical personnel in restraining him so he can be examined or treated. Here's how to hold your tot with your body to keep him still so he can be helped:

- **Get into a sitting position.** Sit in a chair or on the floor with your back against a wall.
- **Place your child in your lap.** Sit your child on your lap with his back to you.
- **Hold his legs between yours.** Cross your legs so that his legs are held still in between yours.
- **Use one hand on his forehead.** Gently press your child's head toward your chest so you can talk softly to him in his ear.
- **Hold him across his chest.** Cross his chest with your other arm so that both of his arms are held in place.
- **Unwind.** Once your child has calmed down or the procedure has ended, start by slowly letting his legs go, followed by his arms and then his head.

When Your Toddler Should Stay Home from Child Care

Most child-care centers have their own rules about when kids have to stay home and when they can come back after illnesses, but here's a quick reference guide to help you make the decision.

- **Fever.** Your toddler has a temperature according to the definition given by your toddler's child-care provider.
- **Breathing problems.** Difficulty breathing, wheezing, or coughing.
- **Diarrhea.** Blood in stools not explainable by dietary change or medication.
- **Vomiting.** Two or more episodes in the previous 24 hours.
- **Persistent abdominal pain.** Complains of unusual belly pain that continues for more than 2 hours.
- **Mouth sores.** Outbreak on the lips, inside the mouth, or in the throat.
- **Rash.** Combined with a fever or overall sense of illness.
- **Eye infection.** Purulent conjunctivitis ("pinkeye") with thick discharge from the eye, until after treatment has started.

precariously on a second-story window ledge, and race unknowingly into traffic. He'll pull any dog's tail, drag down kitchen pots, and tug on electrical cords.

Many toddlers are raced to emergency rooms every year with serious injuries sustained from accidents in and around their homes and even from playgrounds designed for children. Most often, these accidents arise from toddlers just acting like toddlers.

What seems like simple exploration and play can turn tragic in only a matter of minutes when an adult is momentarily distracted by something else.

Hazards Inside Your Home

If you have a toddler, you've probably already discovered that all the decorative touches in the home, like figurines, ceramics, and glass objects, need to be put out of reach.

Pathways need to be as safe as possible to help reduce tripping. Electrical cords, throw rugs, and other "loose" things that could trip your toddler should be kept out of the way.

The truth is, during the toddler years, the most innocuous things can be potential dangers for a fearless and curious toddler. Low shelves can be climbed, appliance or floor-lamp cords could be pulled, and coffee tables can become stages of disaster.

Here's a list of some potential hazards around the home and some easy solutions:

- **Bureaus and shelves.** Simple chests with drawers and open shelves don't look dangerous, but when tots try to use them as steps for getting to the top, they can be downright deadly. Drawers can also drop out, crashing on small heads, hands, or feet. Too often television sets tumble from the tops of dressers, too.

  Prevention: Fasten the chest and

Protecting Your Toddler from Accidents

- **Burns.** Set the water heater's temperature control to 120°F or less, and always check the water temperature carefully before allowing your toddler near the bath.
- **Choking.** Don't let your toddler play with small objects, particularly coins, buttons, latex balloons, and marbles—anything with a diameter of less than an inch and a half. Avoid hot dogs, nuts, cheese cubes, and grapes— that could get caught in his throat.
- **Drowning.** Never leave your toddler alone near the bathtub, a bucket of water, a child's wading pool, a swimming pool, or an open body of water, even for a short time. Never use a suctioned toddler bath seat.
- **Falls.** Use safety gates on all stairs. Keep your toddler from climbing on tables, sinks, and other high surfaces.
- **Fires and Suffocation.** Install smoke detectors, and test them periodi- cally. Install a carbon monoxide detector if you have a flame-burning furnace, fireplace, or woodstove.
- **Heatstroke.** Protect your toddler from getting overheated in unshaded places and never leave him unattended in a car. Don't bundle him up to help him "sweat out" a fever.
- **Strangulation.** Tie up cords from curtains, wall hangings, and blinds to keep them out of your toddler's reach. Never suspend toys from a string tied across a crib or playpen. Use fitted sheets and tuck blankets below your toddler's underarms.
- **Vehicle accidents.** Install and use an approved car seat appropriate for your toddler's weight.

shelves in your child's room to the wall using a special safety strap, or an L-shaped bracket found in hardware stores. Install stops at the backs of drawers so they can't be pulled out. Move the television off the dresser and out of reach.

- **Cribs and bunk beds.** More babies and toddlers die from crib- and bunk bed–related accidents than from any other children's product-related accidents. Hand-me-down cribs can be lethal when their slats are too wide and capture children's heads and necks. Children fall from bunk beds or their heads get captured in bunk bed ladders or side railings. **Prevention:** Don't accept an old crib; instead, purchase a new,

certified model. (You'll spot the sticker on the frame.) Don't buy a bunk bed, but if your children are already using one, keep your toddler on the bottom bed, carefully inspect for capturing gaps in head and foot boards and ladders, and don't allow your kids to play on the beds.

- **Detergents and cleaners.** Toddlers aren't discerning about what's safe to put in their mouths and what's not. Bleach, cleaners, and detergents—the types of bottles and boxes you store under your sink are dangerous! Dishwashing detergents can cause severe, disfiguring mouth and throat burns—most often when a tot scoops some out of the cup on the dishwasher door before the door is closed.

Prevention: Store toxic detergents and chemicals high out of toddler's reach. Don't have the dishwasher door open when your tot's in the kitchen. Wipe down detergent spills and residues with paper towels and discard them immediately.

- **Fires.** Children from birth to 4 years old account for 65 percent of deaths in house fires. Things ignite on the stove, and faulty electrical wiring and appliances start fires. More commonly, smokers fall asleep with cigarettes in their hands, or children start fires when they play with lighters and matches.

Prevention: Install smoke alarms on all floors of your home. Have a fire evacuation plan in place, and rehearse it regularly, including teaching your young children how to call 911. Store a fold-up window ladder in your children's closets, and mark your children's rooms using stickers on their bedroom windows (ask your fire department). Make sure your address is easy to see from the street.

- **Stairs.** Crawling and newly walking toddlers are fascinated by staircases.

Prevention: Protect your toddler from falling by installing safety gates, which are usually constructed of wood, metal, molded plastic, or combinations of these materials. There are three basic types: those that attach to the wall with screws (hardware-mounted gates), those that cling to the wall using the suction of rubber gaskets (pressure-mounted gates), and expandable corrals. Hardware-mounted gates are

considered the safest. Specialty gates help shield wide and unusual openings in homes, such as dining room entries or open stairs with iron railings on the side. Taller-than-normal gates are also available for pets that may work for toddlers who are climbers.

- **Toys and toy chests.** Toys send thousands of kids to emergency rooms every year. Most of the injured children are under 2 years old. Toy chests have figured in numerous deaths when they've fallen on children's necks, cutting off their air supply.

Prevention: Buy quality age-appropriate toys and inspect them for sturdiness. Make sure there are no sharp corners and edges that could hurt if your child falls on them and check for pinch points. Look for small parts that could come loose, choke, or be swallowed, particularly for children under age 3.

Safety Gate Checklist

Here's what to look for when you shop for a safety gate:
- Latches that are impossible for toddlers to work, but easy for older children and adults
- No finger-pinching hardware.
- Slats or narrow plastic mesh to make it hard for your toddler to get a foothold for climbing.
- Easy opening and closing that can be done with one hand.
- No tripping hazards, such as bars that go across the floor.

Once you get your safety gate installed, don't allow anyone to step over it instead of opening and closing it properly.

• **Vitamins and medications.** "Childproof caps" on medicines aren't childPROOF! They simply serve to slow children down several minutes before they get inside. Children can overdose on chewable vitamin pills if they manage to get into them. Ingesting too much iron is particularly dangerous. Acetaminophen (Tylenol, for example) can cause organ damage if a child accidentally eats the pills. Heart medicines, antidepressants—the types of medications that a child can easily access in purses and bedside tables—can be harmful and possibly fatal.
Prevention: Put medications and vitamin products in a box somewhere out of reach. (Store toothbrushing supplies—toothpaste, mouthwash—similarly.) If you keep medicines in your purse, store it out of reach. Measure liquid medications with extreme care under a bright light, and administer them only under your physician's advice. And keep the national poison control center's number handy (800-222-1222).

• **Hair dryers, radios, and other electronics.** People can be electrocuted, especially in older homes without circuit breakers, when hair dryers and radios fall into sinks and bathtubs. Kids love experimenting with electrical outlets because they're usually at child's-eye level. They get their small, damp fingers wedged between a plug and the outlet, or they stick pins, keys, or other metal objects in the outlet and get shocked.

Prevention: Unplug and store hair dryers and radios out of reach until you're ready to use them. Install circuit breakers for bathroom outlets. Cover electrical outlets in the rest of the house with screw-on cases that snap shut to protect plugs from small hands. Find these at hardware and retail stores.

> **TIP**
>
> Small, plastic plug covers can be pried loose by a child and can choke.

Garage Hazards

The garage or basement may be a domain best forbidden to toddlers. Consider the following hazards, though, if your child follows you into the garage:

• **Garage door.** Children have been killed when they were captured and crushed after automatic garage doors slammed down on them.
Prevention: Test your automatic garage door to make certain it springs back open when it encounters any resistance, such as a brick or a carton. If your garage door doesn't stop immediately and reverse, have the safety reverse repaired or replace the door.

• **Paint thinners, gasoline, antifreeze, and other chemicals.** Tots will play with caustic chemicals and even drink them.
Prevention: Keep chemicals in a locked cabinet and store them in their original containers (so you know accurately what is in each container). Post the number of

the nearest poison control center near the kitchen phone. If your child does ingest a toxic chemical, don't try to make him vomit unless you're instructed to do so.

- **Garage ladders and shelves.** Toddlers love to climb and don't understand that shelves and ladders will fall forward if they pull on them.
  Prevention: Hang ladders up on hooks and bolt shelves to the wall.

- **Tools.** Toddlers like to imitate what their moms and dads do. They will pull down and handle drills, saws, and other dangerous tools, and may even succeed in turning them on.
  Prevention: Put a safety gate on the door to your work area. Shorten electrical cords so they are out of reach, and unplug tools and store them safely out of reach when not in use. Keep tots away or restrained while you're working.

Outdoor Hazards

- **Vehicles.** Children are at risk of being rolled over by vehicles backing out of the garage or driveway.
  Prevention: Always check around your car before backing out, and have an alert installed in your car that sounds when the car is in reverse. Create a secure, fenced-in area for your child to play, rather than using the garage or driveway as a play area.

- **Pools, tubs, and buckets.** Small children can drown in only a couple of inches of water within a few minutes. Toddlers drown in bathtubs, wading pools, and water buckets.
  Prevention: Protect an outdoor

pool of any size with a fence and a gate that locks, preferably one that locks automatically. Drain all containers and store them upside down. If there's an unprotected pool or body of water nearby, teach your tot about the dangers of water and have him wear a life vest outdoors.

- **Lawnmowers.** Toddlers have been horribly injured from falls and being run over by mowers, or hurt when the mowers threw up sticks and rocks. Curious tots have lost fingers and hands from reaching under the mower deck while it was idling and a parent's back was turned.
  Prevention: Remember that lawnmowers are not big, friendly ride-on toys. Keep your toddler safely inside while the lawn is being mowed.

- **Dogs**. More than 800,000 people visit emergency rooms each year for dog bites. Most victims are children, and the children usually know the dog that bites them.
  Prevention: Teach your child proper "animal manners," even with familiar animals, and warn him not to approach unfamiliar animals or to try to corner them. Get rid of a pet that snaps at your child, and insist that local fence and leash laws are enforced in your neighborhood.

- **Plants.** Many household plants and blossoming spring flowers can be toxic. Though most are not fatal if swallowed, they can burn the mouth as well as cause stomach pain.
  Prevention: For an extensive list of poisonous plants, the Children's Safety Association of Canada (*www.safekid.org/*

plants.htm) offers a list of common plant dangers.

- **Playgrounds.** Although they appear to be great for meeting children's play needs, most playgrounds have serious hazards, too. For example, children have sustained severe head injuries from falling from playground equipment onto non-cushioned, hard surfaces, such as asphalt and compacted earth. Even a headfirst fall from just 2 feet can cause a serious head injury. Children's monkey bars and climbers result in falls and broken bones. Sliding boards strangle children when the hood strings from coats entangle in hardware. Toddlers are routinely struck by swings. Sandboxes are breeding grounds for parasites thriving in animal feces.

Prevention: Always supervise your kids at play. If the surface beneath climbing structures isn't adequately cushioned, don't allow your children to use the equipment. Avoid public sandboxes, and keep home sandboxes covered when not in use.

- **Walkers and ride-on toys.** Often parents make the mistake of buying a ride-on toy, tricycle, or beginner's bicycle that's too large in hopes that their child will grow into it. Toddlers' ride-on toys don't have brakes. They fall over when the front wheel is turned too far to one side, which only makes them more difficult to control. Children sustain injuries when bikes fall over or go out into the street.

Prevention: Before you buy a wheeled toy, make sure you have access to a safe riding place that isn't near a driveway or road. Postpone buying a ride-on toy or trike until your toddler is at least 3 years old, and then be sure to teach him how to steer and stop. Always stay right with your child when he's on a ride-on vehicle.

The Toddler-Safe Home

One study of childproofing products found that they were far from fail-safe. Cunning toddlers could figure out safety locks and other devices within a few minutes. Those findings underscore the fact that nothing can protect your toddler better than your own constant supervision.

Here's a checklist of toddlerproofing items to consider:
- **Safety gates** (at top and bottom of staircases)
- **Electrical outlet covers** (on all electrical outlets)
- **Stove knob covers** (on front of stove)
- **Fireplace guard** (in front of fireplace)
- **Corner guards** (on coffee or end table corners)
- **Double-sided rug tape** (on throw rug)
- **Cord shorteners** (on kitchen appliances and drapery cords)
- **Skid-proof tub mat** (in bathtub)
- **Lid lock** (on toilet seat)
- **Medicine cabinet lock** (on medicine cabinet)
- **Drawer and cabinet locks** (on kitchen drawers, and on TV stand doors)
- **Lowered mattress support** (on crib)
- **Shelf fasteners** (L-shaped bracket on back of shelf)

TREATING COMMON TODDLER INJURIES

It's almost inevitable that, at some point during your child's toddler years, you'll have a moment of total terror when he chokes, swallows or stuffs an object in his ear or nose, or falls and gets a nosebleed, cut, or worse.

Accidents, including falls and poisonings, are really common. Nearly one-fourth of all children suffer an injury severe enough to require medical attention. In fact, accidents are the leading cause of death of all people ages 1 to 21. And no matter how watchful and careful you are, your toddler can get hurt before you can intervene—even if you're only a few feet away.

Abrasions

Prevention: Restrict unstable toddlers from playing on concrete, asphalt, or hard dirt surfaces.
Treatment: Rinse the area to remove all dirt, gravel, or sand; wash with soap and running water without rubbing. Dry thoroughly and apply an antibiotic ointment. Cover with an adhesive bandage or gauze pad on elbows and knees. Change dressing frequently until the wound begins to heal.
Get Help: If the wound covers a large surface, such as the back or abdomen, or if it is on the face, especially near the eye. When it's embedded with dirt, stones, or gravel that are not easily removed (they may cause scarring). When there are signs of infection, such as warmth, redness, swelling, or puslike drainage.

Airway Obstruction

Prevention: Keep your toddler safe from ingesting small objects such as small toys (deflated balloons) or chunks of food (carrot coins, cheese chunks, hot dogs, meat sticks), and getting entangled in window treatment cords or hood ties. Have every adult in the family learn CPR.
Treatment: Try to clear the obstruction. Perform CPR (see *www.heart.org)* while someone calls 911.
Get Help: Call 911 and/or go to the emergency room for any kind of breathing problem.

Animal Bites

Prevention: Keep your curious toddler away from animals, and especially guard him when he is in others' homes and yards.
Treatment: If the skin is broken, wash thoroughly with soap and running water and dab hydrogen peroxide in the wound. Cover the wound with sterile gauze or a bandage. Infection is a danger. Try to have the animal confined for rabies testing. A rabies vaccination may be needed.
Get Help: Any child with a bite wound should have medical treatment.

Cuts or Scrapes

Prevention: Remove square-cornered coffee tables and other sharp-edged or glass-topped tables from your living area. Don't allow a newly walking toddler to play on gravel or asphalt surfaces.
Treatment: Wash your hands with

soap and water, and then gently wash the toddler's wound. Pat the area dry with a sterile gauze pad, using pressure to help stop the bleeding, if needed. Apply antibacterial ointment. Wash your hands again to get the grease from the ointment off your fingers, then cover the wound with a bandage. Newer, waterproof bandages work best. Change the bandage daily, inspecting for redness or pus, signs of infection.

Get Help: If your toddler's wound is jagged, deep, or longer than 1 inch, or if it keeps bleeding for longer than 5 minutes. If your toddler has been bitten by an animal (or human); if the sore is contaminated with gravel or dirt; or if it's a puncture wound from a nail or other rusty object, such as barbed wire.

Head Injuries or Concussion

Prevention: Don't let your toddler climb on furniture. Use screw-mounted safety gates at the tops of staircases. Never leave your toddler to nap or allow rough play in an adult bed. Pad concrete surfaces at the bottom of staircases. Exercise caution with children's climbing equipment, especially if the surface underneath isn't well padded.

Treatment: Soothe the toddler, examine the injury for cuts. Monitor for signs of concussion (loss of consciousness, headache, dizziness, confusion, nausea, or vomiting).

Get Help: If the toddler loses consciousness at any time, has more than one bout of vomiting, or is unusually sluggish.

Insect Bites and Stings

Prevention: Avoid areas where bees, wasps, hornets, or yellow jackets congregate, or when you are doing yardwork or digging in the earth. (Don't count on insect repellants, which can be toxic to toddlers and young children. Read the label.)

Treatment: Try to identify the insect. Most bite reactions are temporary and heal on their own. Remove the stinger from a bee with a scrape of your fingernail or a charge card. Aloe vera gel from the plant can be soothing for minor bites.

Get Help: Seek immediate medical attention if your child develops breathing problems or shows signs of anaphylactic shock (see page 224).

Mild Burns

Prevention: Set your water heater to 120°F or cooler. Don't drink hot beverages near your toddler. Keep cups and bowls containing hot liquids and pots and appliances (irons, hair wands, coffee makers) and cords away from counter and table edges. When there is a hot oven, keep toddler out of the kitchen with a gate or play yard. Shield heaters, wood stoves, and fireplace openings.

Treatment: Run cool water over the burn as quickly as possible to cool down the area. Apply aloe vera gel or cream, but don't put butter, ice, or other home remedies on the burn. They can actually make it worse. Your toddler's health-care provider may recommend an antibiotic ointment applied several times a day to keep mild burns from becoming infected.

Get Help: For all serious burns, such as an electrical burn, a large burn over his body, or if he stops breathing after being burned. If the burn begins to blister, looks chalky, covers a large area of skin, or is on the toddler's face, hands, feet, or genitals.

Snake Bites

Prevention: Keep your toddler away from wood and mulch piles, rocks or boulders, tall grasses, the edges of streams, and other areas where snakes have been reported.

Treatment: Try to identify the snake, but do not pursue it or try to capture it. Your child's reaction, whether mild or severe, depends upon the snake and the amount of venom. Symptoms may include swelling at the wound site, shortness of breath, and shock. Don't try to suck the venom, apply a tourniquet, or cut the wound, which may only cause more tissue damage or introduce infection.

Get Help: Always seek immediate medical attention for snake bites.

Splinters and Embedded Shards

Prevention: Keep shoes on your toddler's feet if he is walking on rough wooden flooring or is outdoors. Don't let him climb on woodpiles; keep wood furniture and windowsills sanded and stained. Clean up all glass splinters and safely dispose in a thick paper bag. Keep cacti well out of reach.

Treatment: Wash your hands and the splinter area with warm, soapy water. Use tweezers and pull out the splinter at the same angle it went in. Apply antibiotic ointment and bandage the area.

Get Help: If your child is in pain; you're having trouble removing the splinter; for a deep puncture from a needle or toothpick; if the injury was caused by rusty metal, such as a nail or a fish hook with a barb; if it's a pellet from a BB gun; if it's clear plastic or glass that's hard to remove; or if it's an imbedded pencil lead that could cause a permanent mark under the skin. (Note: pencil lead is graphite, not lead, so it's not toxic.)

Sunburn

Prevention: Stay out of the sun from midmorning until midafternoon, when the sun's rays are the strongest. Stay in the shade or use an umbrella at the beach and swimming pool. Apply toddler-safe sunscreens (30 SPF and above) on exposed skin when you're going to be outdoors for more than a few minutes.

Treatment: Apply aloe vera and/or cool compresses of water and baking soda. Give plenty of fluids.

Get Help: Call your pediatrician if your toddler has a fever and/or blistered skin.

Ticks

Prevention: Inspect pets that go outdoors daily for ticks, and give them tick-repellent medications. Look for ticks on your child after walks, and dress him in long pants tucked into socks to help prevent ticks from jumping on his skin.

Treatment: Ticks usually burrow

next to the scalp or in other warm places. Do *not* try to pull the tick off with your fingers. Grasp as close to the head as possible with a pair of tweezers. Pull slowly and firmly. Once the tick is removed, wash the wound with soap and water, then wipe it down with rubbing alcohol or hydrogen peroxide to disinfect it. Apply an antibiotic ointment and cover with an adhesive bandage.

Get Help: If the bite site becomes infected or develops a rash or red ring around it, which could signal Lyme disease.

EMERGENCY PLANNING

Tens of thousands of children are rushed to emergency rooms in the United States each year as the result of accidents and severe illnesses. Emergency rooms can be chaotic, crowded, and sometimes unhealthy places. They can also be downright frightening to vulnerable, highly emotional toddlers.

Here are some strategies for anticipating the unexpected:

• **Research hospital options in advance.** Investigate local hospitals and walk-in centers to weigh your options before your toddler ever needs emergency care. First, find out which hospitals are covered by your insurance and where your toddler's doctor has admitting privileges, since that hospital will have the quickest access to your toddler's medical records, which could expedite his care. Also ask your doctor for the

names of preferred emergency rooms. (Some emergency rooms are better equipped than others for handing pediatric emergencies, such as burns, falls, and fractures.)

Contact the hospitals to ask questions about the emergency services offered and how admissions work. (When emergency rooms are crowded, toddlers who show the symptoms of the flu or who are deemed to have less-than-life-threatening injuries may be diverted to a different treatment area in the hospital to make room for more serious cases.) Consider checking on your hospital's score from the Joint Commission on Accreditation of Healthcare Organizations (*www. jcaho.org*).

• **Keep a "loaded" cell phone in the car.** Keep a cell phone and car charger in the car at all times so you will always have a device for summoning help. Load the phone with your pediatrician's number, the numbers of key relatives, customer service for your health insurance, and the hospital's emergency number so you'll have rapid access to whomever you need. Phone your toddler's pediatrician, who can give the hospital the heads up that you're on the way and any details about your toddler's condition, and possibly meet you there. Knowing that your doctor is on the way may improve the efficiency of your care and your state of mind.

• **Notarize a "consent to treat" form.** Make sure that whoever has responsibility for your child's care has a signed form from you that allows your toddler to be treated in an emergency. You can find a printable version for treating children by doing an Internet search for a "consent to treat form for minors."

- **Create an emergency information packet.** Each person in your family should have a packet. Your toddler's packet should includes his full name, sex, a photocopy of the front and back of his health insurance card, a recent picture, address, telephone number, date of birth, weight, height, blood type, doctor name and contact info, a short list of relatives to contact, a list of any medications he is taking (including vitamins), and a detailed description of any preexisting conditions he has.

  Fold the information into a self-sealing, transparent sandwich bag, mark it with "IN CASE OF EMERGENCY" and the child's name, and duct tape it onto the inside of your refrigerator door where you (or emergency personnel) can grab it in a hurry. That will save you having to divert your attention from your toddler when rescue squad members require critical information before they transport your toddler to the hospital.

- **Plan backup support.** Rehearse with your partner, your next of kin, and your neighbor(s) about what you will do if you have a family emergency and you need someone to be with you at the hospital, or someone to care for your child(ren) should something unexpected happen.

- **Get insurance pre-approval.** If there's time, contact your health insurance company on the way to the hospital or shortly after you arrive, or ask one of your support people to do that for you. Health insurance companies may require notification when a patient is receiving emergency medical care. Informing them may help to smooth out problems with billing and paperwork later.

- **Expect to call 911.** When your toddler's emergency is serious, call for help rather than trying to drive your toddler to the hospital yourself. He will have professional care and attention all the way to the hospital, and he will also get a more rapid response once he arrives there. Ambulance services are expensive, but the few minutes that it takes the rescue squad to arrive may make a huge difference in the speed and quality of intervention your toddler receives.

- **Be assertive.** You are your toddler's primary source for security, safety, and protection, so it's important to be firm and insistent when it comes to going along with your toddler, rather than allowing the emergency staff to whisk him away without you. Explain that you will remain quiet, but as your toddler's guardian, you must insist that you stay with him.

- **Maintain records.** Keep a record of the staff members who treat your child in the emergency room in case your insurer needs further proof that your toddler's visit was warranted. Calling the insurer may help to reverse denied coverage.

When your toddler is discharged, ask for a copy of his X-rays and lab results. It's much easier to take them at the time than it is to ask the hospital for them weeks later. Having them in hand will help when you go for a follow-up appointment with your toddler's doctor.

> **TIP**
>
> If any toy can fit through a cardboard toilet paper tube, it can pose a choking hazard.

> **TIP**
>
> Among children of all ages, balloons are the most common cause of toy-related choking death.

Life-Threatening Emergencies

These are the leading causes of children's deaths from trauma (in order of frequency):
• Motor-vehicle accidents
• Drowning
• Fires/burns
• Suffocation and choking
• Firearms
• Falls
• Poisonings

An emergency is termed "life-threatening" when a toddler's critical body functions, such as breathing or circulation, start to fail. When this happens, your toddler might be in danger of dying, which requires an immediate response, even before you summon help. Some life-threatening accidents include: poisoning, drowning, electric shock, an obstructed airway, serious burns, and heavy bleeding from a wound.

An accident is "life-endangering" when a toddler is unconscious and his body is going into shock. The term *shock* refers to the way a body reacts when the blood supply to vital organs, including the brain, heart, liver, and kidneys, has been threatened. It can be caused by significant loss of blood or bodily fluids, but it can also be the result of an allergic reaction to drugs or insect bites.

A toddler in shock will have rapidly falling blood pressure, and will seem to get progressively worse. Hypovolemic shock occurs when there is a rapid loss of blood or other body fluids. It can happen after any serious injury, and a burn, or result from a bleeding wound. It can also be caused by severe dehydration when a toddler isn't getting enough fluids or is ill and vomits a lot, has prolonged diarrhea, or is suffering from heat exhaustion.

If your toddler is going into shock, he will appear pale, have cold and clammy skin, a rapid but weak pulse, and shallow breathing, and will seem extremely irritable and uncomfortable. Alternatively, he could be extremely sluggish and hard to wake up. Your toddler may also have nausea and vomiting and appear extremely thirsty.

Emergency CPR

Basic life support is designed to keep your child alive and breathing until help comes. It is very rare for a toddler to need emergency resuscitation, but it's important to take a course in life support or CPR (cardiopulmonary resuscitation) through your local American Red Cross chapter or the American Heart Association.

In the meantime, here are some basic instructions to rehearse:

1. Ascertain whether your toddler is breathing or moving. Mucus, blood, vomit, a solid piece of food or candy, or the tongue can easily obstruct a toddler's small airways, causing him to become unconscious.
2. Shout for help.
3. Have a second person call 911.
4. If there's been an accident, try to see how seriously your toddler is injured and whether he is unconscious. He might not respond to gentle motions or to tapping his feet.
5. If you suspect that your toddler has a head or neck injury, take special care not to move his body, which could make the spinal cord vulnerable.
6. Look, listen, and feel your toddler's chest. If there is no one to help you, and your toddler is obviously not breathing or turning blue, perform CPR (see *www.heart.org*) for 1 minute before calling for help. Remember, a toddler's lungs are tiny, and so are his air passages.

Severe Bleeding

A 25-pound toddler's body holds only about a quart of blood. In a serious bleeding situation, your toddler's body and brain can be seriously compromised unless immediate action is taken.

Here are the steps to take if your toddler has been seriously injured and is bleeding:

- **Enlist help.** Get someone else to make the emergency call while you stay with your toddler. If emergency help is delayed, have someone else drive you to the ER while you stay close to the toddler.
- **Stop the bleeding.** Use a piece of cloth or a shirt to apply steady pressure to the wound to stop the flow of blood. Put more cloth over the old pad when it becomes soaked, rather than changing dressings, since that might dislodge early clotting.
- **Raise the wounded limb.** If you're sure that your toddler's spine has not been injured, raise the arm or leg above the heart to help slow down the loss of blood. (Your toddler's limbs may be limp and numb if there has been a spinal injury.)
- **Await instruction.** Once your child arrives at the hospital, he may require stitches (sutures) or surgery to repair the wound. You will be given instructions about what to do for your child once the bleeding has been stemmed and the wound dressed.

Product Recalls

Federal agencies have the power to recall toddler products that pose dangers, and literally millions of toddler products have been banned, pulled off shelves, or undergone "corrective actions" that retrofit the unsafe parts of a product.

• In spite of federal actions, product-related accidents and injuries continue to happen, killing hundreds of babies and toddlers every year, and rushing over 10,000 children to emergency rooms for treatment. New products introduce new dangers into the marketplace; old and worn out products fail; and greedy importers ignore federal regulations by selling shoddy goods that fail federal standards.

• Keep on top of recalls and report toddler product problems by frequently accessing these federal sites:

U.S. Consumer Product Safety Commission (CPSC)
Bethesda, MD 20814
800-638-2772
www.cpsc.gov
Regulates the safety of most children's products, clothing, bedding, and toys. (Car seat recalls generally come from the National Highway Traffic Safety Commission.)

National Highway Traffic Safety Administration (NHTSA)
Washington, DC 20590
888-327-4236
www.nhtsa.dot.gov
Regulates and recalls children's car seats and rates their installation instructions.

Food and Drug Administration (FDA)
Silver Spring, MD 20993
888-INFO-FDA (888-463-6332)
www.fda.gov
Regulates formula and baby food, medicines, and cosmetics, such as bathing products and diaper rash creams.

TIP

Safety gates send thousands of children and adults to emergency rooms when they fall in attempts to step over closed gates.

SPECIAL SECTION: Autism and Other Disabilities

A lot of parents of toddlers are concerned about autism, and rightfully so. According to the Centers for Disease Control, autism rates have spiked in recent years, with 1 out of every 150 children currently being diagnosed with it, with numbers expected to continue rising. As yet, no one knows for sure yet why so many more toddlers and children are being diagnosed with it, but there are suggestions that it might be genetic.

Autism is sometimes called Pervasive Developmental Disorder (PDD), which is an umbrella term used when a more specific diagnosis is unknown, such as Asperger's syndrome, Childhood Disintegrative Disorder, or Rett syndrome. How autism presents itself in a child is as unique as every child is, although some tendencies are more common than others, such as having difficulties with communication and social interaction, and the appearance of repetitive behaviors.

It is now believed that some children have a strong genetic predisposition to autism that may be set off by something that happens in their environment, but researchers don't know yet what the triggers are. One early warning signal for autism that is now being studied is an unusual head growth pattern.

Researchers have observed that babies who were later diagnosed as having autism may be born with smaller-than-average head circumferences, but the great majority of those children experienced a period of unusually rapid head growth between ages 1 and 14 months. It's important to note, though, that this head growth pattern was also found in 6 percent of normally developing children. It is thought that identifying these growth patterns early in life could be useful in getting an earlier diagnosis, when interventions can have the most impact.

What causes autism in children simply isn't clear yet. There are a number of theories for its causes, from mercury (thimerosal) exposure in vaccines or exposure to other environmental toxins, genetic mutations, or an interaction between inborn vulnerability and environmental factors.

In 1998, British researchers raised a furor with a controversial report suggesting a link between the rising number of children being diagnosed with autism and preservatives in the measles, mumps, and rubella (MMR) vaccine. But early in 2004, ten of the thirteen original authors of the study retracted the statements in the paper, saying that their data was not strong enough to support that conclusion. Before-and-after studies have compared the rates of autism and appear to refute the idea that thimerosal is implicated in autism. Not only did cases of autism *not* go down after the removal of this preservative from vaccines, but they actually rose substantially.[1]

Meanwhile geneticists are getting closer to pinning down certain gene anomalies that may be associated with autism. Late in 2009, Dutch geneticists have reported specific genetic anomalies that appeared to be connected to a set of physical characteristics associated with autism. Autistic children with the genetic disorder were found to have prominent foreheads, large ears, a smooth philtrum (between the nose and lips), a pointed chin, wide mouth, different degrees of mental impairment, and brain structure abnormalities.[2]

Since 2004, the National Institutes of Health has been helping underwrite the Autism Cohort Study in Denmark. The study is closely following 110,000 children from pregnancy onward in an attempt to identify factors related to autism, such as diet, vaccinations, birth weight, and head circumference, and exposure to toxins, including mercury.

Meanwhile, developmental experts are working hard to identify signs of autism earlier to help improve children's long-term outcomes. Since 2007, the American Academy of Pediatrics has recommended that all patients between the ages of 18 months and 24 months be screened for autism.

SOME EARLY SYMPTOMS OF AUTISM

No two children with autism are alike. One child may have no language but be very affectionate. Another with Asperger's syndrome, a high-functioning autism spectrum disorder, might have a large vocabulary but not be able to use it appropriately. He may be able to label a flamingo, but not be able to answer simple questions, such as, "What did you eat for breakfast?"

Child development experts are beginning to develop a clearer understanding of the early signs of autism spectrum disorders that appear during the first year of life. Most normally developing babies enjoy sharing an object or event with another person by glancing back and forth between the two. An older baby will use gestures and speech to try to engage another person as he learns about the enjoyment of sharing experiences. He will smile in recognition and give other responses to the smiles and voices of his parents or other familiar caregivers.

At about 8 months of age, a neurotypical baby will follow his parent's gaze and look in the same direction, but a baby with autism may fail to engage in that way. Between 10 months and 12 months of age, babies showing symptoms of autism may fail to follow a parent's finger, no matter how hard the parent tries to engage his attention.

By 12 months to 14 months, a non-autistic child will begin pointing at things himself, first to ask for something he wants that's out of his reach, and later to draw his parents' attention to something he sees that he wants to share. Pointing may be accompanied by expressive sounds, such as "uh" or actual words. A child with autism may try rudimentary pointing by opening and closing his hand while raising it to request an object, or try to lead his parent to the object, but without the back-and-forth glancing that's part of nonverbal communication.

A child with autism may hear well but could appear to have selective hearing. He may be acutely aware of certain sounds but be unresponsive to human voices. He may also obsess on small details, and he may repetitively rock himself, or mouth, twirl, bang, and manipulate objects in unusual or ritualistic ways. Some toddlers may also have mild speech delays and an inability to articulate themselves. Others might not exhibit these behaviors.

Approximately 25 percent to 30 percent of children with autism have age-appropriate language skills but then stop speaking, usually between the ages of 15 months and 24 months, or they gain other skills only to lose them. They may suddenly or gradually stop gesturing, waving, pointing, seeking eye contact, or responding to praise, and they may show unusual development patterns or an unusually intense interest in objects or other nonsocial things.

Not all mainstream doctors and health-care professionals know how to properly diagnose early signs of autism. If you believe your child may have early signs of autism, First Signs

(*www.firstsigns.org*) has a large collection of videos comparing neurotypical toddlers with those who have autism that can help you figure out where your tot stands. If you see warning signs, it's important to seek diagnosis and intervention while his behavior patterns can still be helped.

Startling Autism Facts

- At some point in their lives, 1 in 63 U.S. children (160 per 10,000) will receive an autism-related diagnosis.
- Out of every 160 children diagnosed with autism, 60 of them (37.5 percent) will somehow go on to lose that diagnosis.
- With boys, 34.6 percent originally diagnosed with an autism spectrum disorder may not continue to have the diagnosis later, while 44.5 percent of girls lose their diagnosis.[3]

HELP FOR TODDLERS

"Disability" is a big umbrella term covering anything that keeps your child from being able to interact with the world in the same ways most kids of the same age do. When it comes to intervening with toddlers who have problems, sooner is a lot better than later. And getting an accurate diagnosis of a problem early on will help you get hooked up with programs and resources that can help.

Having an accurate diagnosis will also help to protect your toddler from being labeled with negative and wrong pseudo-diagnoses for problems, such as being "aggressive," "difficult," "lazy," "clumsy," "poorly socialized," "a behavior problem," "zoned out," or "not really trying" by misinformed child-care workers and teachers. Those hurtful labels tend to stick from year to year and may delay your child getting the skilled and productive interventions he deserves (and is legally entitled to) to help him live to his full potential.

Federal Early Intervention

The federal Individuals with Disabilities Education Act of 2004 (IDEA) is a law that requires that children under the age of 6 who have or are at risk of developing school-related problems be screened for potential disabilities. Part C of IDEA provides a federal mandate for services for young children from birth through age 3 who are at risk of developmental delays or disabilities. (Part B of IDEA provides the federal mandate for students with special needs, age 3 years to 21 years.)

Early Intervention (EI) is a term used to describe specific agencies, programs, services, and resources provided for children birth to 5 and their families. Each state provides its own Early Intervention system of services under IDEA, usually run by the state Department of Education or the state Department of Health. A baby, toddler, or child can be referred for screening by his parents, physicians, educators, or others who are concerned about the child.

The National Early Childhood Technical Assistance Center (NECTAC) can help you navigate the maze of Early Intervention services. The National Dissemination Center for Children with Disabilities (*www.nichcy. org/states.htm*) offers state-by-state directories for the agencies offering services to children (and adults), and the Centers for Disease Control and Prevention has links to information for families for children with disabilities (*www. cdc.gov/actearly*).

The EI program for babies and toddlers provides access to therapeutic services designed to help each unique child reach his full potential. Getting your toddler evaluated is free of charge to you, and in most states, rather easy to arrange. Everything usually gets started with a simple telephone call.

Each state has different rules and regulations about which children qualify for special services. The National Dissemination Center for Children with Disabilities (*www.nichcy. org*) is a good place to start your information search for IDEA, since it can help you find the lead agency in charge of Early Intervention in your particular state.

How Early Intervention Works

State services are typically offered by county, and your journey may differ, depending upon what state you live in. It usually begins with a telephone intake interview with your state's Early Intervention office. An Initial Service Coordinator (ISC) will talk with you about your family history, your child's milestones, and your concerns about your toddler. You will be asked about your toddler's typical behaviors and will have a chance to fully air your concerns.

Your toddler's assessments and other appointments are likely to be carried out in your own home. Team members will bring along props, including age-appropriate toys, that will help the team assess how your child navigates his home, how he responds to others, and how he responds to new situations. You will also be informally interviewed about his behavior.

Even though the EI representatives assigned to work with you and your child are not doctors and cannot make official medical diagnoses, they are well trained in evaluating babies and toddlers, having worked with hundreds of them. What they *can* do is tell you if your child's challenges qualify him for special services.

The goal of each EI agency is to pull together a "dream team" for your child to ensure that he receives the services that he needs to reach his maximum potential to function in the world and at school.

If you are only concerned about a speech delay, then a speech evaluation will be set up for you. If you have concerns about multiple areas of your child's functioning, such as social abilities, communication, and physical development, then the evaluation will be with a physical therapist, occupational therapist, and/or a special education therapist.

Once your EI team has a clearer idea of your child's situation and needs, an Individualized Family Service Plan (IFSP) will be created.

Your input will be included in the plan tailored to your toddler's unique needs. The team may also offer you feedback about your family dynamics as it affects your toddler, and team members work with you to set up realistic goals for your child over time.

Formal Disability Definitions

If your toddler has been diagnosed with autism or another disability, he may be eligible for special education and related services under IDEA if he meets very specific criteria that show his educational performance could be adversely affected due to his disability. There are fourteen specific terms used to define a child with a disability, which will determine whether a child can receive special care at no charge.

Here are the formal definitions of disabilities that will open the gate for your toddler getting special intervention:

Autism. A developmental disability significantly affecting verbal and nonverbal communication and social interaction, generally evident before age 3 that adversely affects a child's educational performance. Other characteristics often associated with autism are engaging in repetitive activities and stereotyped movements, resistance to environmental change or change in daily routines, and unusual responses to sensory experiences. (The term *autism* does not apply if the child's educational performance is adversely affected primarily because the child has an emotional disturbance.)

Deaf-Blindness. A child has both hearing and visual impairments together that cause such severe communication and other developmental and educational needs that he cannot be accommodated in special education programs solely for children with deafness or children with blindness.

Deafness. A hearing impairment so severe that a child is impaired in processing linguistic information through hearing, with or without amplification, that adversely affects a child's educational performance.

Developmental Delay. Children from birth to age 3 (under IDEA Part C) and children from ages 3 through 9 (under IDEA Part B), as defined by each state, means a delay in one or more of the following areas: physical development; cognitive development; communication; social or emotional development; or adaptive (behavioral) development.

Emotional Disturbance. Children who exhibit one or more of the following characteristics over a long period of time and to a marked degree that adversely affects a child's educational performance: (a) An inability to learn that cannot be explained by intellectual, sensory, or health factors. (b) An inability to build or maintain satisfactory interpersonal relationships with peers and teachers. (c) Inappropriate types of behavior or feelings under normal circumstances. (d) A general pervasive mood of unhappiness or depression. (e) A tendency to develop physical symptoms or fears associated with personal or school problems.

The term includes schizophrenia. The term does not apply to children who are socially maladjusted, unless it is determined that they have an emotional disturbance.

Hearing Impairment. An impairment in hearing, whether permanent or fluctuating, that adversely affects a child's educational performance but is not included under the definition of deafness.

Mental Retardation (Intellectual Disability). Significantly below average general intellectual functioning, existing at the same time with deficits in adaptive behavior and manifested during the developmental period, that adversely affects a child's educational performance.

Multiple Disabilities. Combined, multiple impairments (such as mental retardation–blindness, mental retardation–orthopedic impairment, etc.), which cause such severe educational needs that they cannot be accommodated in a special education program solely for one of the impairments. (Does not include deaf-blindness, which is in a different category.)

Orthopedic Impairment. A severe orthopedic impairment that adversely affects a child's educational performance. The term includes impairments caused by a congenital anomaly, those caused by disease (e.g., poliomyelitis, bone tuberculosis), and those from other causes (e.g., cerebral palsy, amputations, and fractures or burns that cause contractures).

Other Health Impairment. Having limited strength, vitality, or alertness, including a heightened alertness to environmental stimuli, that affects the educational environment, which: (a) is due to chronic or acute health problems such as asthma, attention deficit disorder or attention deficit hyperactivity disorder, diabetes, epilepsy, a heart condition, hemophilia, lead poisoning, leukemia, nephritis, rheumatic fever, sickle cell anemia, or Tourette's syndrome; and (b) adversely affects a child's educational performance.

Specific Learning Disability. A disorder in one or more of the basic psychological processes involved in understanding or in using language, spoken or written, that may manifest itself in the imperfect ability to listen, think, speak, read, write, spell, or to do mathematical calculations. The term includes such conditions as perceptual disabilities, brain injury, minimal brain dysfunction, dyslexia, and developmental aphasia. The term does not include learning problems that are primarily the result of visual, hearing, or motor disabilities; of mental retardation; of emotional disturbance; or of environmental, cultural, or economic disadvantage.

Speech or Language Impairment. A communication disorder such as stuttering, impaired articulation, a language impairment, or a voice impairment that adversely affects a child's educational performance.

Traumatic Brain Injury. An acquired injury to the brain caused by an external physical force, resulting in total or partial functional disability or psychosocial impairment, or both, that adversely affects a child's educational performance. The term applies to open or closed head injuries resulting in impairments in one or more areas, such as cognition; language; memory; attention; reasoning; abstract thinking; judgment; problem-solving; sensory, perceptual, and motor abilities; psychosocial behavior; physical functions; information processing; and speech. (The term does not apply to brain injuries that are congenital or degenerative, or to brain injuries induced by birth trauma.)

Visual Impairment Including Blindness. An impairment in vision that, even with correction, adversely affects a child's educational performance. The term includes both partial sight and blindness.

Medicaid Disability Waiver Program

The Medicaid Disability Waiver program is another federal program that provides services to children with intellectual and developmental disabilities. It is designed to provide services in homes and neighborhoods of children who might otherwise require care in a Medicaid-funded facility. It may also supply respite for caregivers of these children. Other state programs may help to provide comprehensive health care for families who make too much to be eligible for Medicaid, but not enough to afford health insurance. Programs may provide for physician or clinic services, surgery, drugs, dental care, occupational and physical therapy, and additional services for children with mental or physical conditions.

Gaining access to these services is not a quick process by any means, but once you are in, you can be eligible for respite care, which enables you to have a qualified and trained person come to your house and watch your child to give you time off, or you may be eligible to receive respite reimbursement, which means you can get reimbursed for part of what you pay your babysitter or qualified person to help you with your child.

NEXT STEPS

You will be given guidance about a variety of activities you can pursue with your child; you may also receive parenting resources that you can access in your community.

EI specialists will guide you about what to do next. If your child's problems are thought to be serious enough to warrant formal interventions, it will likely be recommended that you make an appointment for more evaluation by a developmental specialist, such as developmental pediatrician, a pediatric neurologist, or other specialist (see pages 266-267 for descriptions of these professions). Of course, your toddler's pediatrician is another health-care provider who can supply you with formal referrals to experts.

As you begin your services, you will be assigned a Family Service Coordinator who will help guide you through EI and help

you address any issues that may surface. You will get the green light for services for 6 months, and then another meeting will be held to see how your toddler is doing and what services should be continued or discontinued.

Ask your EI Family Service Coordinator about special preschool groups or developmental play groups in your area. These groups can include toddlers who are on the autism spectrum or have other special needs, and benefit from being in a specialized toddler class where more aides are available to provide one-on-one assistance in encouraging peer interaction (circle time, play time, snack time). Whether the class is a "mommy and me" type class or not, you are sure to meet other moms and dads who are going through what you are going through.

Getting the Diagnosis Confirmed

Some parents feel that EI doesn't afford them the amount of hours of professional help that their toddlers need. For example, if your toddler is a preemie with a speech delay, but shows no other signs of a speech disorder or any symptoms for autism, he may not qualify for speech therapy, or he may qualify for only an hour of speech therapy per week. To you, an hour per week barely touches the surface, while 5 hours per week would be phenomenal and make definite changes in your child's maladaptive speech patterns.

It's in your child's benefit to get a second opinion from a

developmental pediatrician or pediatric neurologist, both of whom are experts in children's development. The findings may help your child access a higher level of services than in the original plan.

The American Academy of Pediatrics has information on developmental pediatricians, pediatric neurologists, and dozens of other subspecialties. Visit *www. aap.org* and click on the "Find a Pediatrician" link on the homepage for the Pediatric Referral Service.

Your pediatrician can give you a referral, but you may have to pay for the appointment out of your own pocket. Fortunately, many health insurance policies will cover a visit to a specialist if your child's pediatrician deems it necessary. Since these specialists are rare and in high demand, it may take months to get the first appointment. If you're not covered by insurance, your Family Service Coordinator may be able to offer suggestions on which specialist to choose.

We suggest making the appointment almost as soon as you receive your child's first diagnosis and that you ask to be called if there is a cancellation when a family can't make an appointment. If you have the opportunity to get in, give a spontaneous "Yes!"

Meeting Your Team

The speed with which you receive EI services varies from state to state, but typically programs start at least 30 days after your initial EI evaluation. If your services have started by the time you meet a specialist, your toddler could benefit from additional hours after receiving an official diagnosis.

If you are able stay home with your toddler or schedule home lessons around your work schedule, it will take both you and your toddler time to get used to the routine of having visitors come. After the first month, your family and your child will get accustomed to it, and you'll look forward to seeing your child's progress and breakthroughs, and you won't even worry if your house isn't "visitor ready." Don't worry about how clean your floor is or if your child is still wearing his pajamas when they knock on your door at 11 a.m.

Your toddler's therapists, his therapist task force, will always arrive equipped with a bagful of preferred toys.

Depending on how your toddler responds to therapy, you may sit in on lessons or step away or out of the room if your presence is distracting to him. Over time, your child's therapists may start to feel like family.

If you feel that your toddler's service provider is falling short of your expectations, you have the right to request a different therapist in your area. Keep an open dialogue with your Family Service Coordinator about your likes and dislikes.

Experts and Their Specialties

If you can afford it, you may want to consider hiring your own specialists and therapists in addition to what EI can offer. Specialists often can work together to apply their expertise to deciding what your toddler needs. Here is a brief description of what different service providers do:

Profession	Specialization
Pediatrician	Diagnoses physical and developmental problems, diseases, structural defects, refers to specialists.
Family Physician	Diagnoses physical and developmental problems, diseases, structural defects, refers to specialists.
Psychiatrist	Diagnoses psychological problems, chemical imbalances, attention deficit disorder (ADD) or attention deficit hyperactivity disorder (ADHD), autism, pervasive developmental disorders. Performs intelligence assessments.
Pediatric Neurologist	Deals with seizure activity, abnormal brain activity, brain injury.
Optometrist/ Opthalmologist	Diagnoses vision problems, cross eyes, nearsightedness, farsightedness, astigmatism, binocular, and other vision problems.
Audiologist	Assesses hearing loss, auditory processing, receptive language problems.
Speech Language Pathologist (SLP) or Speech Therapist (ST)	Assesses and treats speaking problems, language delay, and swallowing problems.
Pediatric Occupational Therapist (OT)	Assesses and treats sensory processing disorders, problems with spatial relationships, visual discrimination, coordination, and social skills.
Pediatric Physical Therapist (PT)	Assesses and rehabilitates children with fine and gross motor impairments due to developmental delays or physical problems, such as cerebral palsy, spina bifida, and torticollis.

Profession	Specialization
Developmental Psychologist	Assesses and provides therapy for children with emotional and behavioral disorders. Evaluates the extent of developmental disabilities, such as language delays.
Developmental Pediatrician	A board-certified pediatrician with special training in diagnosing and treating of children with developmental and behavioral disorders, such as autism spectrum disorders. Provides recommendations and referrals to other treatment options.
Special Education Instructor	Provides one-on-one play therapy and learning experiences to enhance children's cognitive skills.

Your Toddler's First Appointment

Your toddler's appointment with a specialist, such as one of those described above, is likely to run anywhere from 1 to 3 hours. Typically, the specialist will want to observe your toddler being his natural self. He will carefully observe how your toddler plays with toys, how he interacts with and responds to others, and how your toddler reacts to being in a strange setting.

You will also be given time to discuss your concerns and to solicit the pediatrician's opinion about what kind of therapies would work best for your toddler. Typical questions that parents ask have to do with what comes next, such as: "Which schools/programs in our area would be the right fit for our child?" "What are your opinions on specific treatments?"

The specialist will prepare a formal report, and may even scribble his findings and his proposal about what to next on a prescription pad and hand them over to you. With this tiny piece of paper you'll have proof to give your EI official or school district that shows that your child needs help *now*, and that he needs to be assigned a slot for a special education class or other toddler programs available in your area.

You wouldn't be human or a real parent if your heart didn't ache or grieve if your worst fears are confirmed. But the good news is that a child who has an "official" diagnosis for developmental delays has an opportunity to receive Early Intervention therapies, which are key to helping your toddler reach his full potential.

STRATEGIES FOR PARENTS OF DISABLED TODDLERS

If your toddler is diagnosed with any of these impairments, and you would like to seek special intervention to help him, here's how to proceed:

- **Research.** Learn all you can about your child's condition and what kinds of doctors, therapists, medicine, support, and supplies he's likely to need.
- **Keep a journal with dates.** Write down the names and contact information for all referrals, appointment dates, notes on what you've been told, immunizations and questions after appointments to research or ask the next time around. Don't forget to also jot down your feelings and reactions. That will help you keep perspective and may be useful for helping other parents who seek your advice.
- **Find another "go-to" parent.** Raising a toddler with special needs can be a roller-coaster ride on some days. One way to make it through is by having a go-to mom to share advice, to give you the inside scoop on a doctor, or just to share a good laugh.
- **Make parent-to-parent connections.** Nonprofit organizations, informal parenting groups, societies, associations, or even online parenting groups can provide much needed social and comic relief. Contact charities in your area that support your toddler's disability for volunteer opportunities or that sponsor charity walks you can participate in.
- **Scope out good places.** Get to know which restaurants and other public places are the most accommodating to your toddler's needs, and which inspire

meltdowns. Get to know your toddler's preferences: Maybe he is more comfortable at fast-food joints or he seems calmer in rowdy sports-themed restaurants or diners, and go with what works for the two of you.

Emotional Effects of Your Child's Diagnosis

Even though you may have waited for months for that fateful appointment with a specialist, finally being given your toddler's diagnosis can come as a relief (now you know what's wrong), but also a devastation, and perhaps information overload, which can lead to panic or depression.

Keep in mind that no matter how expert or prominent a specialist is, he or she doesn't have a crystal ball. No human can truly predict what a child will be doing when he is 16, or when he grows into an adult, especially considering all the new research and treatments that are still emerging and could make a big difference down the road.

Once you find the best interventions for your child, things will start to feel less threatening and more balanced. You will be able to access support from specialists, your family, other parents, or your faith, and eventually you will come to realize that your love for your child hasn't changed.

Sharing "the News" with Others

There's no need to feel pressured to let your inner circle know the official news until you've had a chance to get used to it yourself.

True friends will understand that you have a lot on your mind, and they will accept your promise to reconnect again once you've had time to wrap your mind around everything that's going on.

Once you decide to break "the news" to loved ones, you're likely to be bombarded with lots of questions. People will want to know what all that means and what you're doing about it. There will always be people—even friends and family—who say the wrong things to try to cheer you up, or who try to offer their own suggestions, things you have already tried or wouldn't want to try.

Sometimes people are prompted to share their war stories about their own children or others they've heard about. Then again, they may also deliver stories that bring a glint of hope: "My friend's son was diagnosed with autism as a toddler, and now he is doing great!" or "They said our daughter would have motor problems, but now she dances and plays tennis!" Probably, both super downs and super ups delivered by others need to be taken with a big grain of salt.

It can be a lonely feeling to realize that most advice givers can't fully grasp what it's like to be in your shoes or to shoulder the responsibility you do for caring for your toddler, unless they have gone through that experience themselves. It bears repeating that the people who love you and your child the most will still be there for you, no matter what, and their feelings won't change simply because your child has a diagnosis.

If you get sincere offers of support from family and friends, by all means accept their help. If they truly want to be helpful, hand them a to-do list. Here are some examples: Check out books from the library; do research on the Internet; take a sibling out for play date; babysit. Don't think you're selfish to ask family and friends to give you some time off simply to rest and restore yourself after the all the stress you've been through. Your toddler will survive, and you'll return better able to cope with everything on your platter.

The Importance of Keeping Records

There will be lots of paper trails to keep up with when it comes to having your child diagnosed and treated. To begin with, keep photocopies of all applications for services.

You have a legal right to all of your child's medical records, including doctors' and therapists' notes and findings. Sometimes you have to press for these, but insist that all lab and evaluators' written reports be sent in duplicate to you and your child's primary care physician.

Sometimes offices are hesitant or negligent about releasing them, and they will probably require you to sign a formal release form with the names and addresses where records are to be sent. Then, it may require more than one telephone call or by direct visit to get all of the paperwork in hand.

This documentation will be invaluable for your research into your child's problems, for seeking second opinions, and for asking advice from your child's physician. Create a file (or a designate a file drawer or special box) to store all of your child's records, including immunizations and treatments, brochures and information sheets, and printouts from your Internet searches and other research you've uncovered that could apply to your child's diagnosis.

Helping Siblings Understand

It may be natural for siblings to wonder out loud about their baby sibling. Teach them that he'll be able to love them and share in the family fun no matter what his capabilities and skills. Many times, older siblings will enjoy taking part in Early Intervention lessons, and take pride in being the assistant teacher.

Look into extracurricular programs at special needs schools in your area, or connect with a society. Sometimes schools will have special groups set up where other siblings of children with special needs can socialize and discuss things they are going through. There may be things they may feel more comfortable talking about with other kids.

Siblings can become little brother or sister's best advocate, but they can also secretly or not-so-secretly want more attention. They may also start asking you questions about their sibling with special needs. "Will Johnny ever get married?" "Why can't he walk yet like I can?" "Why can't he speak to me?" "Why does he act like that?" "Why can't we go to the circus just because Johnny doesn't want to go?" These are familiar questions from older siblings. It's important to talk with siblings about how life is different right now for their brother or sister, and it's also important to keep reassuring them of your equal love for them.

By communicating honestly and openly with siblings, you may find yourself becoming more open to discussing your child's diagnosis with others and sharing with them what you are learning as you go along.

Resources

If you're looking for more information in a particular topic area, no matter the subject, you'll be able to find words about it on the Internet. The big problem with online information, though, is that it's not always easy to tell right away which sites are based on solid research from reliable sources, which might actually just be somebody's ill-informed opinion, and which have an agenda to push. Some sites will also use scare tactics or inflammatory content just to get readers to return, which boosts page views and advertising revenue.

The following is a selection of sites that are reliable and generally offer balanced information (and, if they are trying to sell you something, are transparent about it). If we've missed any of your favorite sites, please write us in care of our publisher and we will try to include your resource in our next edition.

CHILD CARE

Aupair.com
www.aupair.com
A Germany-based online database of au pairs

Care.com
www.care.com
An online service that lets users search and post reviews for babysitters, nannies, tutors, and other in-home care providers

Child Care Aware
www.childcareaware.org
A service of the National Association of Child Care Resource & Referral Agencies that helps parents find child care in their area. Also has a budgeting calculator to help families decide if child care is cost-effective

Doodle Days
www.doodledays.com
List of child-care providers

4 Everything Nanny
www.4nanny.com
Nanny referral service

HomeWork Solutions, Inc.
www.4nannytaxes.com
A national nanny payroll and tax-compliance service

InsureKidsNow.gov
www.insurekidsnow.gov/state/index.html
National database of pediatricians and dentists

KindyList
www.kindylist.com
A national database of child-care centers

The Nanny Authority
www.nannyauthority.com
A New York–based national nanny screening and placement service

The Nanny Network
www.nannynetwork.com
A comprehensive directory of nanny placement and referral agencies

National Association for the Education of Young Children (NAEYC)
www.naeyc.org/families/search
Local accredited programs by city or zip code

US Au Pair
www.usaupair.com
Au pair referral service that prescreens and offers J-1 exchange visitor visas

U.S. Department of Health and Human Services Administration for Children & Families
www.acf.hhs.gov/programs/ccb/general/index.htm
The Child Care Bureau supports low-income working families through child-care financial assistance. Web site provides links to state child-care agencies

US Search
www.ussearch.com/consumer/background-check/
Background checks of potential babysitters or caregivers

HEALTH AND WELL-BEING

American Academy of Pediatric Dentistry (AAPD)
www.aapd.org/finddentist/
Database for finding a pediatric dentist

American Academy of Pediatrics
www.aap.org
Pediatricians and information on child health, safety, and development

American Heart Association
www.americanheart.org
Information on dietary recommendations and infant/child CPR

American Medical Association
www.ama-assn.org
America's largest professional association for physicians, with a specialist locator

Childhelp National Child Abuse Hotline
www.childhelp.org
Twenty-four-hour support and local referrals by trained professional counselors

FindCounseling.com
www.findcounseling.com
Search for therapists in a limited number of states

Joint Commission (formerly Joint Commission on Accreditation of Healthcare Organizations)
www.jointcommission.org
Information on hospital admissions and health-care accreditation

Mayo Clinic
www.mayoclinic.com

Health information, including searchable guides to symptoms, drugs, supplements, and healthy recipes

Medline Plus
www.nlm.nih.gov/medlineplus/infantandtoddlerhealth.html
A service of the U.S. National Library of Medicine and the National Institutes of Health that lets visitors search a variety of medical information sources

Google Scholar
http://scholar.google.com
Internet search engine for scholarly literature, including theses, books, abstracts, and articles

Children's Safety Association of Canada
http://www.safekid.org/plants.htm
Canadian list of poisonous houseplants and outdoor plants

NUTRITION

Little Stomaks
www.littlestomaks.com
A blog of evidence-based toddler nutrition

The International Food Information Council Foundation
www.foodinsight.org
Food safety, nutrition, and healthful eating information for consumers

PARENTING STYLES

Attachment Parenting International
www.attachmentparenting.org
Nonprofit devoted to "heightening global awareness of the profound significance of secure attachment"

Rebel Dad
www.rebeldad.com

News, statistics, and links for and about at-home fathers

AtHomeDad
www.athomedad.org
Resources, information connection, and community for at-home and involved dads

Mothers of Preschoolers
www.mops.org
Christian nonprofit that organizes mothers' groups nationwide

Kodak
www.kodak.com
Library-quality bound photo books

Shutterfly
www.shutterfly.com
Photo books available in a huge array of colors, patterns, sizes, and formats

PRODUCT SAFETY

Centers for Disease Control and Prevention (CDC)
www.cdc.gov/actearly
Information for families on disabilities

Consumer Product Safety Commission
www.cpsc.gov
Product recalls and product safety standards

Consumer Reports
www.consumerreports.org/cro/babies-kids/index.htm
Independent, nonprofit testing and information for consumers

Dr. Toy
www.drtoy.com
Annual rating of best toys for babies and children

Food and Drug Administration (FDA)
www.fda.gov
Regulates baby formula and food,

medicines, and cosmetics such as diaper rash creams

National Dissemination Center for Children with Disabilities
www.nicihcy.org
Information on Early Intervention by state

National Early Childhood Technical Assistance Center (NECTAC)
www.nichcy.org/states.htm
State-by-state directory of services for children and adults

National Highway Traffic Safety Administration (NHTSA)
www.nhtsa.dot.gov
Regulates and recalls children's car seats and rates their installation instructions

SPECIAL NEEDS

American Academy for Cerebral Palsy and Developmental Medicine (AACPDM)
www.aacpdm.org
Education, research, and understanding of cerebral palsy and other developmental disabilities

Autism Speaks
www.autismspeaks.org
Science and advocacy organization for autism

Council for Exceptional Children (CEC)
www.cec.sped.org
Professional organization dedicated to improving the educational success of individuals with disabilities and/or gifts and talents

First Signs
www.firstsigns.org
Autism diagnosing advice and videos

TOYS, CLOTHES, AND GEAR

Beyond Play
www.beyondplay.com
Products for toddlers and young children with special needs

One Step Ahead / Leaps and Bounds
www.onestepahead.com; www.leapsandbounds.com
Pretested baby and toddler products, specializing in educational toys. One Step Ahead is for babies 0 to 3; Leaps and Bounds is for preschoolers 3 and older.

TWINS AND MULTIPLES

Mothers of Supertwins
www.mostonline.org
National nonprofit provider of support, education, and research on higher-order multiples

National Organization of Mothers of Twins
www.nomotc.org
Resources for mothers of multiples, including a searchable database of local parents-of-multiples clubs

Endnotes

1 Your Unique Toddler

1. M. Prior, D. Smart, et al., "Does Shy-Inhibited Temperament in Childhood Lead to Anxiety in Adolescence?" *Journal of the American Academy of Child and Adolescent Psychiatry* 39, no. 4 (April 2000): 461–468.
2. J. Kagan, J. S. Reznick, et al., "Behavioral Inhibition to the Unfamiliar." *Child Development* 55 (1984): 2212–2225.
3. A. Sanson, and M. K. Rothbart, "Child Temperament and Parenting," in *Parenting*, M. Bornstein, ed. (Hillsdale, N.J.: Lawrence Erlbaum, 1995).
4. H. J. Eysenck, "Genetic and Environmental Contributions to Individual Differences: The Three Major Dimensions of Personality," *Journal of Personality* 58 (1990): 245–261.
5. D. Reiss, "Mechanisms Linking Genetic and Social Influences in Adolescent Development: Beginning a Collaborative Search," *Current Directions in Psychological Science* 6 (1997): 100–105.
6. D. Daniels and R. Plomin, "Origins of Individual Differences in Infant Shyness," *Developmental Psychology* 21 (1985): 118–121.
7. L. H. Cyphers, K. Phillips, et al., "Twin Temperament during the Transition from Infancy to Early Childhood," *Journal of the American Academy of Child and Adolescent Psychiatry* 29 (1990): 392–397; H. H. Goldsmith, K. A. Buss, et al., "Toddler and Childhood Temperament: Expanded Content, Stronger Genetic Evidence, New Evidence for the Importance of Environment," *Developmental Psychology* 33 (1997): 891–905; K. J. Saudino and S. S. Cherny, "Parent Ratings of Temperament in Twins," in *The Transition from Infancy to Early Childhood: Genetic and*

Environmental Influences in The Macarthur Longitudinal Twin Study, R. N. Emde and J. K. Hewitt, eds. (New York: Oxford University Press, 2001), 73–88; and J. Stevenson and J. Fielding, "Ratings of Temperament in Families of Young Twins," *British Journal of Developmental Psychology* 3 (1985): 143–152.

8. S. C. Messer and D. C. Beidel, "Psychosocial Correlates of Childhood Anxiety Disorders," *Journal of the American Academy of Child and Adolescent Psychiatry* 33, no. 7 (1994): 975–983.

9. S. P. Putnam, A. V. Sanson, et al., "Child Temperament and Parenting," in *Children and Parenting*, M. Bornstein, ed. (Mahwah, N.J.: Lawrence Erlbaum, 2002), 255–277.

10. S. Crockenberg and E. Leerkes, "Infant Social and Emotional Development in Family Context" in *Handbook of Infant Mental Health*, 2nd ed., C. H. Zeanah Jr., ed. (New York: Guilford Press, 2000), 60–90.

2 Physical Skills

1. K. E. Adolph, et al., "What Changes in Infant Walking and Why," *Child Development* 74 (2003): 475–497.

2. B. Jacobs and D. Eastwood, "Orthopedic Problems in Toddlers," *Pulse* (April 9, 2008): 45.

3. M. Annett, "Hand Preference Observed in Large Healthy Samples: Classification, Norms and Interpretations of Increased Non-Right-Handedness by the Right Shift Theory," *British Journal of Psychology* 95 (2004): 339–353.

3 Emotions

1. J. Huttenlocher, O. N. Newcombe, et al., "The Coding of Spatial Location in Young Children," *Cognitive Psychology* 27 (1994): 115–147.

2. I. Bretherton, S. McNew, et al., "Early Person Knowledge as Expressed in Gestural and Verbal Communication: When Do Infants Acquire a 'Theory of Mind'?" in *Infant Social Cognition*, M. Lamb and L. Sherrod, eds. (Hillsdale, N.J.: Erlbaum Associates, 1981), 333–373.

3. M. Lewis and L. Michalson, *Children's Emotions and Moods: Developmental Theory and Measurement* (New York: Plenum, 1983).

4. P. Smiley and J. Huttenlocher, "Young Children's Acquisition of Emotional Concepts," in *Children's Understanding of Emotion*, S. Saarni and T. Trabasso, eds. (Cambridge: Cambridge University Press, 1989).

5. T. M. Parrott and V. L. Bengtson, "The Effects of Earlier Intergenerational Affection, Normative Expectations and Family Conflict on Contemporary Exchanges of Help and Support," *Research and Aging* 21, no. 1 (1999): 73–105.

6. L. R. Brody and J. A. Hall, "Gender and Emotion," in *Handbook of Emotions*, M.

Lewis and J. M. Haviland, eds. (New York: Guilford Press, 1993), 447–460.

7. J. Condry and S. Condry, "Sex Differences: A Study of the Eye of the Beholder," *Child Development* 47 (1976): 812–819.

8. E. A. Lemerise and K. A. Dodge, "The Development of Anger and Hostile Interactions," in *Handbook of Emotions*, M. Lewis and J. M. Haviland, eds. (New York: Guilford Press, 1993), 537–546.

9. A. Sanson and M. K. Rothbart, "Child Temperament and Parenting," in *Parenting*, vol. 4, M. Bornstein, ed. (Hillsdale, N.J.: Lawrence Erlbaum, 1995), 299–321.

10. D. Fuchs and M. H. Thelen, "Children's Expected Interpersonal Consequences of Communicating Their Affective State and Reported Likelihood of Expression," *Child Development* 59 (1988): 1314–1322.

11. R. A. Thompson and R. Goodwin, "Taming the Tempest in the Teapot: Emotional Regulation in Toddlers," in *Socioemotional Development in the Toddler Years: Transitions and Transformations*, C. A. Brownell and C. B. Kopp, eds. (New York: Guilford Press, 2007), 323–334.

12. P. Wingert and W. Brant, "Reading Your Baby's Mind: New Research on Infants Finally Begins to Answer the Question: What's Going On in There?" *Newsweek*, August 15, 2005, p. 35.

13. R. A. Thompson, "Empathy and Emotional Understanding: The Early Development of Empathy," in *Empathy and Its Development*, N. Eisenberg and J. Strayer, eds. (Cambridge: Cambridge University Press, 1987), 129.

14. C. Zahn-Waxler, M. Radkey-Yarrow, et al., "The Impact of the Affective Environment on Young Children," paper presented at the meeting of the Society for Research in Child Development, New Orleans, La, 1977. Cited by R. A. Thompson, "Empathy and Emotional Understanding: The Early Development of Empathy," in *Empathy and Its Development*, N. Eisenberg and J. Strayer, eds. (Cambridge: Cambridge University Press, 1987).

15. A. Bergman and A. Wilson, "Thoughts About Stages on the Way to Empathy and the Capacity for Concern," in *Empathy II*, J. Lichtenberg et al., eds. (Hillsdale, N.J.: Lawrence Erlbaum Associates, 1984).

16. N. Eisenberg, C. L. Shea, et al., "Empathy-Related Responding and Cognition: 'A Chicken and the Egg' Dilemma," in W. M. Kurtines and J. L. Gerwitz, *Handbook of Moral Behavior and Development*, vol. 2. (Hillsdale, N.J.: Lawrence Erbaum, 1991), and D. Bischof-Köhler, "The Development of Empathy in Infants," in *Infant Development: Perspectives from German Speaking Countries*, M. E. Lamb and H. Keller, eds. (Hillsdale, N.J.: 1991), 245–273.

17. S. A. Denham, *Emotional Development in Young Children* (New York: Guilford Press, 1998), 34.
18. J. B. Shonkoff, "The Science of Early Childhood Development: Closing the Gap Between What We Know and What We Do," presentation at the National Council on the Developing Child: Early Childhood Partners Meeting, Washington, D.C., January 18, 2007.
19. For a good discussion on the long-term benefits of waiting skills, see J. Lehrer, "Don't: The Secret of Self-Control," *New Yorker*, May 18, 2009, www.newyorker.com/reporting/2009/05/18/090518fa_fact_lehrer?currentPage=1.
20. A. S. Masten and J. D. Coatsworth, "The Development of Competence in Favorable and Unfavorable Environments: Lessons from Research on Successful Children," *American Psychologist* 53 (1998): 205–220, and E. E. Werner, "Protective Factors and Individual Resilience," in *Handbook of Early Intervention*, 2nd ed., J. P. Shonkoff and S. J. Meisels, eds. (Cambridge: Cambridge University Press, 2000), 115–132.
21. K. A. Gordon Rouse, "Infant and Toddler Resilience," *Early Childhood Education Journal* 26 (1998).

4 Behavior

1. L. Rowell Huesmann and Nancy Guerra, "Children's Normative Beliefs About Aggression and Aggressive Behavior," *Journal of Personality and Social Psychology* 72, no. 2 (1997): 408–419.
2. A. Furnham, "Attitudes to Spanking Children," *Personality and Individual Differences* 19, no. 3 (September 1995): 397–398.
3. E. E. Maccoby and J. A. Martin, "Socialization in the Context of the Family: Parent-Child Interaction," in *Handbook of Child Psychology*, vol. 3, P. H. Mussen and E. M. Hetherington, eds. (New York: Wiley, 1983), 1–101, and W. D. Donovan et al., "Maternal Illusory Control Predicts Socialization Strategies and Toddler Compliance," *Developmental Psychology* 36 (2000): 402–411.

5 Language

1. E. Galinsky, *Mind in the Making: The Seven Essential Life Skills Every Child Needs* (New York: HarperCollins, 2010).
2. D. F. Hay, "Yours and Mine: Toddlers' Talk About Possessions with Familiar Peers," *British Journal of Developmental Psychology* 24 (2006): 39–52.
3. L. P. Acredolo, et al., "The Signs and Sounds of Early Language Development," in *Child Psychology: A Handbook of Contemporary Issues*, L. Balter and C. Tamis-LeMonda, eds. (New York: Psychology Press, 1999), 116–139, and S. Goodwyn, et al., "Impact

of Symbolic Gesturing on
Early Language Development,
Journal of Nonverbal Behavior
24 (2000): 81–103.

6 Play

1. V. J. Rideout, et al., *Kaiser Foundation Report: Zero to Six: Electronic Media in the Lives of Infants, Toddlers and Preschoolers* (Menlo Park, Calif.: Henry J. Kaiser Foundation, 2003).
2. American Academy of Pediatrics Committee on Public Education, "Policy Statement: Children, Adolescents and Television," *Pediatrics* 107, no. 2 (February 2001): 423–426, updated in *Pediatrics* 124, no. 5 (November 2009).
3. V. C. Strasburger, "First Do No Harm: Why Have Parents and Pediatricians Missed the Boat on Children and Media?" *Pediatrics* 151, no. 4 (2007): 334–336.
4. M. Krcmar, et al., "Can Toddlers Learn Vocabulary from Television? An Experimental Approach," *Media Psychology* 10, no. 1 (2007): 41–63.
5. L. S. Pagani, et al., "Prospective Associations Between Early Childhood Television Exposure and Academic, Psychosocial, and Physical Well-Being by Middle Childhood," *Archives of Pediatrics and Adolescent Medicine* 164, no. 5 (2010): 425.
6. Report from an interview with Anderson by Ellen Galinsky in her book *Mind in the Making* (HarperCollins, 2010), cited earlier.
7. S. Wimbarti, "Indonesian Children's Play with Their Mothers and Older Siblings," *Child Development* 66 (1995): 1493–1503.
8. Ibid.
9. B. H. Fiese, "Playful Relationships: A Contextual Analysis of Mother-Toddler Interaction and Symbolic Play," *Child Development* 61, no. 5 (1990): 648–656, and L. M. Youngblade and J. Dunn, "Individual Differences in Young Children's Pretend Play with Mother and Sibling: Links to Relationships and Understanding of Other People's Feelings and Beliefs," *Child Development* 66 (1995): 1472–1492.
10. D. F. Hay, "Yours and Mine: Toddlers' Talk About Possessions with Familiar Peers," *British Journal of Developmental Psychology* 24 (2006): 39–52.
11. L. G. Fasig, "Toddlers' Understanding of Ownership: Implications for Self-Concept Development," *Social Development* 9 (2000): 370–382.
12. C. S. Tamis-LeMonda and M. H. Bornstein, "Individual Variation, Correspondence, Stability, and Change in Mother and Toddler Play," *Infant Behavior and Development* 14 (1991): 143–162.

8 Nutrition

1. Material adapted from S. S. Golding, et al., "Dietary Recommendations for Children and Adolescents: A Guide for

Practitioners," Pediatrics 117 (2006): 544-559. Accessed May 10, 2011, from the American Heart Association, http://www.heart.org/HEARTORG/GettingHealthy/Dietary-Recommendations-for-Healthy-Children_UCM_303886_Article.jsp

2. C. L. Wagner, et al., "Prevention of Rickets and Vitamin D Deficiency in Infants, Children, and Adolescents," Pediatrics 122, no. 5 (November 2008): 1142–1152.

3. B. L. Specker, et al., "Sunshine Exposure and Serum 25-Hydroxyvitamin D Concentrations in Exclusively Breastfed Infants," Journal of Pediatrics 107 (1985): 372–376.

4. T. L. Clemens, et al., "Increased Skin Pigment Reduces the Capacity of Skin to Synthesise Vitamin D3," Lancet 1 (1982): 74–76.

5. B. A. Dennison, et al., "Excess Fruit Juice Consumption by Preschool Aged Children Is Associated with Short Stature and Obesity," Pediatrics 99 (January 1997): 15–22.

6. www.consumerlab.com/news/Multivitamin_Multimineral_Contamination_Problems_Comparison/1_19_2007 (accessed 05/24/10).

7. See "Position of the American Dietetic Association: Vegetarian Diets," Journal of the American Dietetic Association (July 2009), and nutrition information on VRG's Web site, www.vrg.org.

11 Health, Safety, and Ability

1. P. Stehr-Green, et al., "Autism and Thimerosal-Containing Vaccines: Lack of Consistent Evidence for an Association," American Journal of Preventive Medicine 2, no. 25 (2003): 101–106.

2. M. H. Willemsen, B. A. Fernandez, et al., "Identification of ANKRD11 and ZNF778 as Candidate Genes for Autism and Variable Cognitive Impairment in the Novel 16q24.3 Microdeletion Syndrome," European Journal of Human Genetics (November 2009).

3. http://www.huffingtonpost.com/david-kirby/autism-rate-now-at-one-pe_b_256141.html

Index